ROUSSEAU'S CRITIQUE

Rousseau's *Discourse on the Origin of Inequality among Men*, published in 1755, is a vastly influential study of the foundations of human society, including the economic inequalities it tends to create. To date, however, there has been little philosophical analysis of the *Discourse* in the literature. In this book, Frederick Neuhouser offers a rich and incisive philosophical examination of the work. He clarifies Rousseau's arguments as to why social inequalities are so prevalent in human society and why they pose fundamental dangers to human well-being, including unhappiness, loss of freedom, immorality, conflict, and alienation. He also reconstructs Rousseau's four criteria for assessing when inequalities are or are not legitimate, and why. His reconstruction and evaluation of Rousseau's arguments are accessible to both scholars and students, and will be of interest to a broad range of readers including philosophers, political theorists, cultural historians, sociologists, and economists.

FREDERICK NEUHOUSER is Professor of Philosophy at Barnard College, Columbia University. He is the author of *Rousseau's Theodicy of Self-Love: Evil, Rationality, and the Drive for Recognition* (2008), *Actualizing Freedom: The Foundations of Hegel's Social Theory* (2000), and *Fichte's Theory of Subjectivity* (Cambridge, 1990).

ROUSSEAU'S CRITIQUE OF INEQUALITY

Reconstructing the Second Discourse

FREDERICK NEUHOUSER

CAMBRIDGE
UNIVERSITY PRESS

University Printing House, Cambridge CB2 8BS, United Kingdom

Cambridge University Press is part of the University of Cambridge.

It furthers the University's mission by disseminating knowledge in the pursuit of education, learning and research at the highest international levels of excellence.

www.cambridge.org
Information on this title: www.cambridge.org/9781107644663

First published 2014
First paperback edition 2015

A catalogue record for this publication is available from the British Library

Library of Congress Cataloguing in Publication data
Neuhouser, Frederick.
Rousseau's critique of inequality : reconstructing the second
discourse / Frederick Neuhouser.
pages cm
ISBN 978-1-107-06474-4 (hardback)
1. Rousseau, Jean-Jacques, 1712–1778. Discours sur l'origine et les fondements
de l'inégalité parmi les hommes. 2. Equality. 3. Natural law.
4. Political science. 5. Social justice. I. Title.
JC179.R9N48 2014
320.0101–dc23
2014004725

ISBN 978-1-107-06474-4 Hardback
ISBN 978-1-107-64466-3 Paperback

For Connie, who taught me to read

Contents

Acknowledgments

Many people have contributed to the development of the ideas I present here. In addition to Akeel Bilgrami, Christopher Brooke, Robin Celikates, Joshua Cohen, Maeve Cooke, Jeremy Forster, Andrew Franklin-Hall, Michael Friedman, Rafeeq Hasan, David Hills, Axel Honneth, Rahel Jaeggi, David James, Timo Jütten, Patricia Kitcher, Philip Kitcher, Felix Koch, Niko Kolodny, Tyler Krupp, Michael Nance, Andreja Novakovic, Dirk Quadflieg, Jeppe von Platz, Dasha Polzik, Jon Rick, Carol Rovane, John Scott, Herman Siemens, Daniel Viehoff, David Wiggins, and Allen Wood, I would also like to thank the unnamed members of audiences of talks I have given at a variety of North American universities – Berkeley, Binghamton, Chicago, Columbia, Harvard, Hunter College, New York University, the New School, North Carolina, Penn, Princeton, Stanford, and Toronto – as well as at a number of institutions abroad: University College Dublin, Humboldt University in Berlin, and the universities of Basle, Giessen, Frankfurt, Halle, Leiden, Oslo, and Sussex. In addition, Hilary Gaskin provided invaluable advice as to how the first draft of the manuscript could be improved. My greatest intellectual debt, however, is to the many students who have listened to, challenged, and helped me refine my interpretation of Rousseau over a period of many years and at a variety of institutions. Jason Hill played a substantial intellectual and personal role in the writing of this book, especially in the first years of the project, and I remain deeply appreciative of all that he contributed to it and to me. Joachim Bergström's friendship was particularly important to me during the year in which I completed the manuscript. A very special thanks goes to István Hont whose untimely death I heard of while working on the book's final revisions. It's both sad and strangely consoling to realize how much so many of us will miss him.

Some of the material of this book is based on previously published papers: "Rousseau and the Human Drive for Recognition," in Hans-Christoph Schmidt am Busch and Christopher F. Zurn, eds., *The Philosophy of Recognition* (Rowman & Littlefield, 2010), 21–46; "Die normative Bedeutung von 'Natur' im moralischen und politischen Denken Rousseaus," in Rainer Forst, Martin Hartmann, Rahel Jaeggi, and Martin Saar, eds., *Sozialphilosophie und Kritik* (Suhrkamp, 2009), 109–33; "Jean-Jacques Rousseau and the Origins of Autonomy," *Inquiry* 54 (2011), 478–93; "The Critical Function of Genealogy in the Thought of J.-J. Rousseau," *Review of Politics* 74 (2012), 371–87; "Rousseau und die Idee einer 'pathologischen' Gesellschaft," *Politische Vierteljahresschrift* 53 (2012), 628–45; "Rousseau und Hegel: Zwei Begriffe der Anerkennung," in Stefan Lang and Lars-Thade Ulrichs, eds., *Subjektivität und Autonomie* (de Gruyter, 2013); and "Rousseau's Critique of Inequality," *Philosophy and Public Affairs* 41 (2013), 193–225. I am grateful to the publishers of these papers for permission to include some of that material here.

Abbreviations

OC	*Oeuvres Complètes*, ed. Bernard Gagnebin and Marcel Raymond (Paris: Gallimard, Bibliothèque de la Pléiade, 1959–69), 4 vols. ("*OC* III" refers to vol. III).
OL	*Essay on the Origin of Languages*, in *The Discourses and Other Early Political Writings*, trans. Victor Gourevitch (Cambridge University Press, 1997), 247–99.
PE	*Discourse on Political Economy*, in *The Social Contract and Other Later Political Writings*, trans. Victor Gourevitch (Cambridge University Press, 1997), 3–38.
RJJ	*Rousseau, Judge of Jean-Jacques: Dialogues*, trans. Judith R. Bush, Christopher Kelly, and Roger D. Masters, in *The Collected Writings of Rousseau* (Hanover, NH: University Press of New England, 2001), vol. I.
RSW	*The Reveries of the Solitary Walker*, trans. Charles E. Butterworth, in *The Collected Writings of Rousseau* (Hanover, NH: University Press of New England, 2001), vol. VIII, 1–90.

REFERENCES TO WORKS OF JOHN RAWLS

JF	*Justice as Fairness* (Cambridge, Mass.: Harvard University Press, 2001).
LHPP	*Lectures on the History of Political Philosophy*, ed. Samuel Freeman (Cambridge, Mass.: Harvard University Press, 2007).
PL	*Political Liberalism* (New York: Columbia University Press, 1993).
TJ	*A Theory of Justice* (Cambridge, Mass.: Harvard University Press, 1971).

Introduction

The aim of this book is to provide a brief but substantive philosophical introduction to one of the most influential texts in the history of European philosophy, Jean-Jacques Rousseau's *Discourse on the Origin and Foundations of Inequality among Men* (1755) or, as it is more commonly called, the Second Discourse. (It is the Second Discourse because it follows an earlier one, *Discourse on the Sciences and Arts* [1751], both of which were written in response to essay writing competitions sponsored by the Academy of Dijon.) This book is an introduction because it presupposes no previous familiarity with the text – apart from one's having read it! – and it is philosophical because rather than being a commentary in the usual sense of that term it aims at distilling and reconstructing the central *argument* of the Second Discourse, a task that turns out to be surprisingly difficult. I decided to write this book one day when, teaching the text to undergraduates for what could have been the hundredth time, I realized that neither I nor any of my students was able to give a concise reformulation of Rousseau's responses to the two apparently straightforward questions he takes himself to be answering, namely, what the source of inequality among humans is and whether it is justifiable. The text, I came to see, is filled with dazzling insights and masterly rhetorical flourishes, but it is also a tortuous maze whose argumentative thread is extremely difficult to keep track of. The consequence is that the Second Discourse is one of the most widely read texts in the Western philosophical canon – a surprisingly large number of undergraduates in the US are required to read it at some point in their studies – and at the same time one of the least philosophically understood. This is a pity – and a condition this book hopes to remedy – not only because the Second Discourse influenced a highly diverse group of philosophers in succeeding centuries (Hegel, Marx, Nietzsche, and

Freud, for example) but also because it contains a coherent argument that offers influential and still relevant answers to a number of questions that ought to be central to contemporary social and political philosophy. As I will argue here, Rousseau's text contains a sustained, comprehensive argument that aims to establish not only what makes social inequalities objectionable (when they are) but also why inequality is so prominent and stubborn a feature of human societies.

Perhaps one reason the Second Discourse has proved to be so difficult to comprehend is that the position it articulates is far more convoluted than its non-technical prose and the apparent simplicity of its questions lead readers to expect. For Rousseau ends up giving surprisingly complex answers to both of his guiding questions. With regard to the first, he argues both that inequality is not a direct or necessary consequence of human nature (or of nature more generally) and that the basic conditions of human social existence make pernicious forms of inequality – along with many other social ills – nearly unavoidable. With regard to the second, he argues that while most (but not all) familiar forms of social inequality are morally objectionable, they are not bad in themselves but only in virtue of certain consequences they tend to produce. Although it is difficult to read this off the surface of the text, Rousseau offers a set of criteria for distinguishing acceptable from inacceptable forms of equality and avoids the simplistic utopian view that social inequality in all its forms is to be criticized.

The contemporary relevance of this topic is difficult to overstate. In the two decades following the end of communism in Eastern Europe, social inequality in nearly every part of the world increased dramatically. (And, contrary to what those who benefit most from capitalism would like us to believe, the end of European communism has something to do with this trend, even if it does not explain it entirely.) The form of social inequality easiest to track is economic inequality, and empirical evidence abounds in support of the claim that not only in poor, developing countries but even in the richest and most technologically advanced – the US provides an especially shocking example – inequality is much greater than at any time in the recent past and that in the absence of forceful political intervention by those harmed by it the gap between rich and poor will only continue to grow wider. Statistics that prove this thesis are easy to find: in 2007 one-third of the US's wealth was owned by just 1 percent of the country's population; in the period between 2002 and 2007 more than 65 percent of the gain in total national income went to those who were already in the wealthiest 1 percent; and in 2010 the average CEO earned 243 times as much as the typical wage earner![1]

Many more statistics could be adduced to show that economic inequality in most of the world has reached catastrophic proportions, but such statements of fact quickly dull one's sensitivity to a phenomenon that has become so obvious that virtually anyone with two eyes and a minimal ability to perceive social reality can recognize it as a cause for alarm. In general, philosophy cannot contribute much to the production of empirical data or to the explanation of particular economic trends of the sort I have just mentioned. What philosophy can attempt, however, is to understand why, very generally, inequality is so pervasive a feature of the societies we live in and to investigate when (and why) social inequalities become morally objectionable and legitimate targets of social critique. This is precisely what Rousseau undertakes in the Second Discourse, and my aim in this book is to show that his answers to both sets of questions remain compelling today. No contemporary philosophical treatment of inequality can afford, in my view, to bypass the explanation and critique of the same phenomenon given by Rousseau more than two and a half centuries ago. Although much about social life in the West has changed since then, not everything has, and we foolishly deprive ourselves of the advantages of our rich philosophical legacy when we adopt the self-flattering view that our forebears have nothing to teach us about the problems that plague contemporary societies.

Rousseau's Second Discourse, as its title tells us, is about the *origin* and *foundations* of human inequality (where, as will become clear below, the latter term refers to the normative status of inequality). The dual focus of Rousseau's text finds expression in the two questions proposed by the Academy of Dijon as the subject matter of the competition for which the Second Discourse was composed, namely: what is the origin of human inequality, and is it authorized by – does

---

[1] These examples come from Joseph E. Stiglitz, *The Price of Inequality* (New York, W. W. Norton, 2012), 2–3. Stiglitz's exhaustive treatment and critique of contemporary inequality makes an excellent empirical companion piece to the Second Discourse.

it have its foundations in – natural law? (*DI*, 130/*OC III*, 129).[2] The greatest obstacle to comprehending the argument of the Second Discourse is the assumption that our own first take on what these questions mean accurately captures Rousseau's understanding of them. In fact, both of the central ideas here – those of "origin" and of "being authorized by natural law" – turn out to be much more intricate and idiosyncratic than they initially appear to be, and for this reason much of the interpretive work undertaken in the following pages will be devoted to figuring out how these ideas are understood in the Second Discourse.

Even before this interpretive work has begun, however, many readers are able to have some sense of the most philosophically perplexing aspect of the Second Discourse: its unexplained assumption that there is a deep connection between these two inquiries – that is, between apparently descriptive or explanatory claims about the origin of inequality and plainly normative claims about whether inequality is legitimate or justified (whether it is "authorized by" or has its "foundation in" natural law). To contemporary readers, the linking of these two questions cannot but seem to rest on a fatal confusion of normative and nonnormative issues: why should determining where a thing comes from be essential to assessing whether it is good or morally permissible or valuable in some way? Normally both philosophy and common sense insist on the logical independence of these questions such that, for example, the (factual) question of under what historical conditions the Electoral College came to be established in the US is mostly irrelevant to the (normative) question of whether one should now regard it as a good procedure for electing a US President and as an institution worthy of continued support. For this reason a central aim of any reconstruction of the Second Discourse must be to give a coherent account of why these questions are as interconnected as Rousseau apparently takes them to be, and one criterion for the success of such a reconstruction must be whether the sense it attaches to the Second Discourse's two central questions allows their alleged interdependence to be comprehended.

To put these points somewhat differently: Rousseau conceives of the Second Discourse as providing a kind of *genealogy* of human inequality that is inextricably bound up with the project of evaluating – more

---

[2] See the conventions used for citing Rousseau's works in the List of abbreviations.

precisely, criticizing – the very phenomenon whose origins his genealogy undertakes to elucidate.[3] In this respect the Second Discourse can be seen as a founding text of a long tradition in modern European philosophy that takes some version of the project of genealogy to be essential to the normative evaluation of the object of genealogical inquiry. To mention only the most obvious example: Nietzsche in the opening pages of the *Genealogy of Morals* defines his task in that work by posing two questions whose similarity to Rousseau's is unmistakable: "*Under what conditions* did human beings devise [the] value judgments good and evil? And *what value* do they themselves possess?"[4] As it turns out, Rousseau has his own distinctive understanding of what it is to provide a genealogy of something such that uncovering its origins is essential to assessing its value. Even though Rousseau's conception of what it is to search for the origins of a social phenomenon such as human inequality – as distinct from purely natural things or processes – differs substantially from those of the philosophical genealogists who follow him, figuring out how Rousseau links the two central questions of the Second Discourse is of great relevance not only for grasping his own, independently valuable views on the legitimacy of inequality but also for understanding how later philosophers have attempted similarly structured genealogies of their own. Thus, answering these two questions and articulating their connection is the principal task I undertake in the pages that follow.

It is possible to make some progress in understanding the coupling of these two questions once one notices that, for Rousseau, seeking the origin of inequality amounts to asking whether inequality *comes from nature*. This realization helps to make some initial sense of the dual character of the Second Discourse's project because nature, even for us, often carries normative connotations. When we say, for example, "it's natural for humans to care more about their own well-being than that of

---

[3] Rousseau himself describes the project of the Second Discourse as a genealogy in a letter to the Archbishop of Paris (LCB, 28/*OC* IV, 936).

[4] Friedrich Nietzsche, *On the Genealogy of Morals*, trans. Walter Kaufman (New York: Random House, 1967), Preface, §3; emphases added. Other versions of this project are essential to Fichte's *Wissenschaftslehre*, Feuerbach's critique of Christian theology, Marx's account of ideology, the *Abbau* of metaphysics proposed by Heidegger in *Being and Time*, and Foucault's genealogies of various social phenomena that define Western modernity. Even more obviously, Hegel's *Phenomenology of Spirit* is inconceivable without the idea that reconstructing the history of our normative practices is essential to assessing their legitimacy.

distant others," we typically mean not only to make a statement about how humans are in fact (by virtue of their nature) inclined to behave but also, perhaps implicitly, to endorse such behavior as justified or acceptable, precisely because it is "natural" and because to expect humans to act otherwise would be to place overly burdensome demands on them, given the kind of creature they are by nature. Saying "it's natural for humans to care most about their own good" normally implies: "It's (most of the time) OK, legitimate, fully in order that they do so." It is worth remembering that this tendency to imbue "nature" and "natural" with normative significance was even stronger for Rousseau and his contemporaries than it is for us. When John Locke, for example, articulated the laws of nature, he attributed to them exactly the dual significance referred to above: they both describe how humans are inclined to (and generally do) act, and at the same time they endorse that "natural" behavior as good.[5] Similarly, Adam Smith's claim that "commercial society" (capitalism) is natural is logically inseparable from his judgment that it is a *fitting* economic system for humans, given their nature.[6] Merely mentioning these examples, of course, does not yet explain or justify the mix of descriptive (or explanatory) and normative elements contained in them – a good deal regarding Rousseau's use of "nature" remains to be said in the pages that follow – but it may help to diminish the initial perplexity that the assumed connection between the Second Discourse's two main questions inevitably arouses.

As I suggested above, nature is not the only central concept of the Second Discourse in need of clarification. "Origin," too, is a potentially misleading term, and understanding what Rousseau is after when he inquires into inequality's origin is essential to appreciating the power and relevance of his argument. The most common misunderstanding is encouraged by Rousseau's own description of his text as a genealogy, as well as by the example I introduced above (the US Electoral College) in order to draw attention to the perplexing character of the presumed connection between the Second Discourse's explanatory and normative ambitions. Usually when one sets out to construct a genealogy in order

---

[5] John Locke, *The Second Treatise of Government*, in *Two Treatises of Government*, ed. Peter Laslett (Cambridge University Press, 1960), Chapter 2.

[6] Adam Smith, *The Wealth of Nations*, ed. Edwin Cannan (New York: Modern Library, 2000), xxiv, 14–18, 54.

to explain a thing's origin, one means to offer a causal, historical account of a succession of actual events that led to the "birth" – the coming into existence – of the specific phenomenon in question. This, however, is *not* what Rousseau is up to when he inquires into the origin of human inequality – despite the fact that he sometimes talks as though it were (*DI*, 133, 186/*OC* III, 133, 191–2), a fact that understandably confuses many readers. Most important, he is not asking how some singular phenomenon (the US Electoral College, for example) came into being at a particular place and time (in Philadelphia in 1787). Instead, his inquiry starts from a general observation about the pervasiveness of inequality in the various human societies known to him – through his own experience, to be sure, but also from the testimony of travelers, the accounts of historians, and so on – and proceeds to ask not how inequality actually came into the world but why, once there, it persists and is so widespread. In other words, the question at the heart of Rousseau's inquiry into the origin of inequality can be formulated as follows: what accounts for the striking fact that nearly all of the human societies known to us are characterized by significant inequalities among their members in wealth, power, and prestige? What forces must be at work – not merely in a specific time and place but more generally – if inequality is so common as to appear to be an enduring feature of the human condition?[7] Much more will need to be said in the following chapters about the kind of genealogical account the Second Discourse undertakes to construct; for now it is sufficient to note that its aim is not to account for the origin of inequality in any straightforwardly historical sense of the term. As we will see below, asking about the origin of inequality need not be construed as a request for an explanation of how this or that particular instance of inequality in fact came to be.

The dual project of the Second Discourse might strike us as a bit less foreign if we see that it is a response to classical Greek treatments of the origin and foundations of social inequality. Both Plato and

---

[7] In this respect Rousseau's genealogy differs importantly from Nietzsche's. The latter's inquiry into the origin of good and evil is, at least to some degree, an inquiry into the actual historical events that issued in the birth of a specific mode of evaluation, alternatives to which are not only possible but have actually been realized in other times and places. And yet, something of Rousseau's project remains in Nietzsche's: insofar as *ressentiment* forms part of his answer to the question of slave morality's origin, Nietzsche, too, aspires to account for the persistence and pervasiveness of slave morality in times and places other than those in which it first came into existence.

Aristotle, for example, ask versions of the same two questions, and both respond by arguing that there is a basis in nature for human inequality. Since nature endows humans with different capacities and talents – differences that imply a natural hierarchy among humans – it qualifies as the source, or origin, of inequality. Moreover, this natural inequality is the foundation of social inequalities; it explains why there should be inequalities in the world and, very generally, who should occupy which positions. Actual social inequalities are legitimate – authorized by nature – to the extent that they reflect natural inequalities. For Aristotle there are natural masters and natural slaves, as well as natural differences, justifying inequalities, between Greeks and barbarians. For Plato there are three types of souls corresponding to three kinds of metal: gold, silver, and bronze. For Aristotle these natural differences justify many existing inequalities; for Plato they show the unnaturalness of existing political arrangements and establish the need for radical political reform if society is to be as reason (and nature) demand. For both, calling the differences "natural" implies that they are not products of human will as well as that they are unalterable; there is nothing human will could or should do to change them.

It is interesting from the modern perspective, by the way, that the differences that justify inequality for Plato and Aristotle are not *deserved* by those who benefit from them; they reflect the natural merits of individuals and are not in any sense earned by those who have them. In contrast, many modern philosophers – the so-called luck egalitarians – are obsessed with the idea that inequalities can be justified only if the better off deserve what they have, where deserved advantages are usually understood as those that depend on one's own (metaphysically) free actions, as opposed to what they have obtained through good luck, for example, from rich parents or good genes.[8] (As we will see, Rousseau does not share this view.) Equally interesting is the fact that for these

---

[8] For a description and critique of luck egalitarianism, see Elizabeth S. Anderson, "What Is the Point of Equality?" *Ethics* 109 (January 1999), 287–337. While I find Anderson's critique compelling (as would Rousseau), one can still ask whether non-luck egalitarians can do completely without the idea that desert plays some role in determining which inequalities are morally legitimate: is it possible, for example, to reject the practice of inheriting advantages of wealth without some appeal to the idea that the sons and daughters in question have done nothing to deserve their parents' property? For a clear example of luck egalitarianism see Robert Dworkin, "What is Equality? Part 2: Equality of Resources," *Philosophy & Public Affairs* (10) 4, 1981, 283–345.

classical thinkers, justified inequalities in power, authority, or prestige do not necessarily translate into justified inequalities in wealth. This is most obvious in the case of Plato, who restricts the pursuit of wealth to those who occupy the lowest place in the natural hierarchy of souls. In today's world it is nearly impossible to imagine that advantages in power or prestige could be separated from great wealth, and Rousseau picks up his pen at a time when this is beginning to be true of his world, too (*DI*, 183–4/*OC* III, 189).

One of the decisive differences between the classical and the modern world is that the latter rejects the view that nature can be appealed to in order to legitimize social inequalities, a position that generally goes hand in hand with asserting the fundamental equality, from the point of view of morality, of all human beings. Just what this fundamental equality consists in and what it implies for social philosophy are vexed issues to which modern philosophers give different answers. Yet no matter how these questions are answered, asserting the fundamental moral equality of humans poses a great problem that the ancients, given their answer to the question of inequality's origin, did not have to face: how can social inequality, a seemingly permanent feature of modern society, be justified if it cannot be traced back to the way that nature (or God) set up the world and if instead there is a prima facie presumption that no individual has any claim to better treatment by society than any other? Does accepting the moral equality of all humans imply that only a society with no inequalities can be justified? And, if so, does that imply that modern societies are hopelessly corrupt?

It is worth considering how modern "common sense" tends to respond to these questions. When asked what explains the pervasiveness of inequality in human societies, the "person on the street" is likely to reply with some version of the claim that inequality is a more or less necessary consequence of basic needs and desires that motivate human behavior everywhere and at all times, which, in conjunction with certain constant features of the human condition, tend "naturally" to produce a wide variety of inequalities. Some who take this position will simply attribute inequalities to an inborn competitive urge – a drive to gain advantage over others for its own sake, merely in order to experience oneself, and to see oneself perceived by those around one, as superior to others. On such a view, inequality is a prominent feature of human societies because proving oneself superior to others satisfies a

universal and fundamental urge of human nature, and for this reason
this response would count as one version of the view that inequality
has – to use Rousseau's terminology – its origin in nature. (Of course,
this appeal to nature – to the competitive urges of human nature – still
differs fundamentally from the classical view.) Perhaps a more common
response would be that, although the desire to achieve superiority for its
own sake is by no means rare, it is neither universal nor intrinsic to
human nature and, so, is not the most fundamental explanation of the
widespread inequality we find around us. Instead – so this second
response – widespread inequality is mostly an unintended but inevitable consequence of a conjunction of several factors, all of which are
more or less constant features of the human condition: an unequal
distribution of natural endowments, the universal desire to do as well
for oneself as possible, and material scarcity. Starting out with unequal
endowments, individuals who seek to maximize their well-being will
inevitably end up in positions that are superior or inferior to others',
even if what they desire most fundamentally is not to outdo their fellow
beings but only to do as well as possible for themselves. In addition to
this, material scarcity provides such individuals with an incentive
actually to seek to outdo their peers, not because they desire superiority
itself but because under conditions of scarcity, achieving superiority is
often the only means of getting what one wants in the first place (to
improve one's own non-comparative level of well-being).

If taken only this far, this second response would also locate the
origin of inequality in nature, as Rousseau understands that idea. Most
who begin down this path, however, are likely to go one step farther
(in the direction of luck egalitarianism) and introduce a further, *non-
natural* element into their account in order to explain why some
individuals develop and exercise their natural endowments more
than others. This additional element is individual "effort," usually
understood as an effect of the individual's free will, and for that reason
this new element extends the explanation of inequality beyond the
realm of the purely natural. (As we will see in the following chapter,
Rousseau accepts this sharp demarcation between natural phenomena and those that depend on free will without, however, appealing
to desert as a source of legitimate inequalities.) On this most sophisticated commonsense view, the pervasiveness of social inequality is
due mostly to natural factors that escape human control – unequal

endowments, natural self-interestedness, and material scarcity – but exactly where particular individuals end up in existing schemes of inequality and how extensive those disparities are depend also on what individuals do with what nature has given them, where what they do is a result of their free choice and therefore not a merely natural cause of inequality.

It is not difficult to see how this answer to the question of inequality's origin, especially its introduction of freedom into the picture, can be taken to have implications for the second of the Second Discourse's main concerns: whether and, if so, to what extent inequality is justified. Insofar as inequality is taken to have its origin entirely in natural factors – in some combination of inborn competitiveness, natural self-interest, unequal endowments, and material scarcity – most (though not necessarily all) of the extensive inequalities characteristic of modern societies are likely to appear as unavoidable or eliminable only through extreme measures that inevitably "do violence to nature." (From this perspective, for example, the socialist goal of eliminating economic class distinctions appears utopian, oppressive, contrary to human nature.) But the introduction of individual effort into this explanation can also serve to justify existing inequalities: because part of where one ends up in the social hierarchy depends on the exercise of freedom, some advantages will appear deserved, or earned, and for that reason legitimate. (As I will argue in Chapter 4, Rousseau's critique of social inequalities has nothing to do with the claim that more advantaged members of society do not deserve their favorable positions; determining which inequalities are legitimate does not involve the hopeless (and moralistic) task of figuring out which individuals deserve what.)

It seems likely that Rousseau expects his readers to approach the Second Discourse already espousing, tacitly or explicitly, some version of this commonsense view, which sees pervasive inequality as fundamental to the human condition (a necessary outcome of both human nature and nature more generally) and views most existing inequalities as legitimate or at least morally unobjectionable. If so, his aim is to convince his readers that most of this commonsense view is mistaken. Instead he will argue that inequality does not come from nature (or, more precisely, nature's contribution to human inequality is so small as to be negligible). For Rousseau this means that widespread inequality is not a necessary, invariable feature of human society and that it therefore cannot be justified merely by appealing to the way human beings and their world are constituted, with the implication that to attempt to eradicate or diminish inequality would be to violate nature. A further implication of the claim that inequality does not originate in nature is that it comes instead (in some complex way to be explicated) from human freedom, which differs from nature in being an unpredictable source of the novel and the contingent. But, Rousseau reasons, if inequality is indeed a contingent phenomenon that humans introduce into the world – if its continued presence is up to us (is our responsibility) – then the question of whether it should exist (whether it is good or justifiable) acquires a significance and urgency that it lacks if in the end very little can be done to alter it. In other words, for Rousseau establishing the non-natural status of inequality has the effect of displacing it from the realm of what is – of what is *necessarily* and of what must therefore merely be accepted – into the normative domain, where it becomes a possible object of evaluation and critique. At the same time, it is important to note that simply viewing inequality as a human creation does not itself answer the normative question for Rousseau. It does not entail, for example, that humans, as creators of the social hierarchy, deserve their places in it, nor does the mere artificiality of inequality – its being the product of human activity – imply its illegitimacy. As we will see in greater detail below, Rousseau's answer to the normative question is unexpectedly elaborate and does not simply dismiss all contingent or artificial inequalities as illegitimate. Ultimately his answer springs from a far-reaching vision of what must be shown about social arrangements in order to establish their legitimacy or moral grounding, a vision that looks beyond mere nature – to freedom (though not to desert) – for its normative criteria.

My account of Rousseau's arguments in the Second Discourse will have the following structure: in Chapter 1 I reconstruct Rousseau's negative claim that inequality – or the sorts of inequality he is most interested in – does not have its source in nature, neither in human nature nor in the natural conditions of human existence. Chapter 2 examines Rousseau's complex positive answer to the question of where inequality comes from: it has its principal origin in a distinctively human but "artificial" passion, together with certain very common but still contingent social circumstances that humans are responsible for creating. Chapter 3 begins to reconstruct Rousseau's answer to the normative question regarding human inequality. It argues that Rousseau has a simple answer to the question of whether most of the inequality we are familiar with is authorized by natural law – it is not – but that this negative answer does not exhaust his position on the legitimacy of inequality. Instead, he provides us with the resources for conceiving of another type of legitimacy, grounded in consent (but also in "nature" in a sense that must be explicated with great care). Chapter 4 shows how the positions articulated in the first three chapters can be used to construct an alternative conception of right – right within society rather than "natural" law – and how this conception can be applied to a specific, especially timely issue concerning the limits of legitimate *economic* inequality. (This chapter concludes with a brief consideration of the methodological issue raised above: how precisely Rousseau's genealogy functions so as to provide answers to both the normative and the explanatory questions that inspired the writing of the Second Discourse.) Finally, Rousseau clearly intended for the Second Discourse to aid us in "judging our present state" (*DI*, 125/*OC* III, 123), and Chapter 5 aims to show that this continues to apply today by considering how contemporary political theory might benefit from incorporating the Second Discourse's insights.

It should be noted already here that in following this plan the present book cannot aspire to deliver a complete interpretation of the Second Discourse. Perhaps no book could rightfully claim to do so, but certainly not this one. The Second Discourse is much too rich for everything that is of value in it to be captured by an approach such as mine that limits itself to answering the two questions that are explicitly announced as its object. My exclusive focus on the theme of inequality, though this is undeniably central to the Second Discourse's concerns, will necessarily leave out of view many important ideas for which the text has rightly become famous. For these reasons my interpretation must be supplemented by others that pay more attention to, for example, the topics of alienation, social pathology, the evils of private property, or the shortcomings of liberal thought and liberal societies. Still, there is much to be gained by concentrating on only the "official" questions posed by the Second Discourse – or at any rate that is what I hope to show here.

Although I have attempted to concentrate here on just one of Rousseau's major texts, the Second Discourse, it has proved necessary to bring in ideas from other texts as well in order to reconstruct the main argument of the Second Discourse. This, in my view, is not a defect of my interpretation but a testimony to the essential unity of Rousseau's philosophical *oeuvre*. Not surprisingly, the supplementary texts I have appealed to most extensively are *The Social Contract*, especially for its vision of the foundations of right within political society, and *Emile*, especially for its treatment of human nature. I have relied throughout on Victor Gourevitch's unsurpassable translations of and introductions to many of Rousseau's texts. (See the List of abbreviations for details.) At times I have made minor emendations of these translations without noting that fact.

More than once, those who have heard or read portions of this text have remarked, and sometimes protested, that my reading of Rousseau has a Hegelian or Kantian bias. It is true that the Rousseau I present here is very much a member of the eighteenth- and nineteenth-century German tradition in social and political philosophy – the founder of it in fact! – but I regard this as a strength rather than a weakness of my interpretation. I regard it as a strength for two reasons: first, there is something illuminating and historically accurate in the claim that Rousseau is the *Urheber* of that great German tradition (Rousseau's influence on Kant, Fichte, Hegel, Marx, and even Nietzsche is both ubiquitous and profound); and, second, the most compelling philosophical positions that can be attributed to Rousseau are, in my view, those that emerge when his texts are read with an eye to how his German successors appropriated and developed his ideas (without, one hopes, making Rousseau indistinguishable from them). I acknowledge that especially the second of these claims is controversial and that many readers of the Second Discourse and of this book will disagree with it. Some will respond (and have responded) that my interpretation of Rousseau is historically inaccurate because it ignores or underappreciates the many non-German influences on his thought – Plato, the Stoics, Machiavelli, and Montesquieu, for example – as well as the historical specificity of the problems his social and political thought addresses. Others will no doubt claim that Hegel's and Kant's appropriations of Rousseau's ideas in fact rid them of their brilliance and originality and obscure their true promise by making them palatable to a philosophical sensibility that places a high value on systematicity and logical coherence. These misgivings about the outcome of my book deserve serious consideration; they contain, no doubt, an element of truth. Rather than respond directly to such criticisms, however, I choose simply to offer in the following chapters my reading of Rousseau, more or less on its own, and to leave it to my readers to decide whether reading the Second Discourse as I do is enlightening, distorting, or – perhaps necessarily – a combination of both.

One further feature of my reconstruction of the Second Discourse needs to be noted. The secondary literature on Rousseau written by philosophers, political theorists, and literary critics is highly diverse, unsurveyably vast, and for the most part very good. Although I have benefited from reading a large part of that literature, it has been impossible to acknowledge my indebtedness to it in detail here. In my previous book on Rousseau[9] I engaged much more extensively with the secondary literature, but I have decided to avoid doing so here in order to produce a leaner and primarily philosophical (argument-focused) introduction to the Second Discourse that concentrates on interpreting and reconstructing Rousseau's classic text. I have attempted to correct for this shortcoming in small measure by providing a very brief "Suggestions for further reading" that is intended to encourage readers to explore some of the secondary literature most relevant to my interpretation of the Second Discourse. No one can pretend to have the final word on any of Rousseau's texts, and my relative neglect of secondary literature in this book should not be understood as an implicit claim to that effect on my part.

---

[9] *Rousseau's Theodicy of Self-Love: Evil, Rationality, and the Drive for Recognition* (Oxford University Press, 2008).

CHAPTER I

Nature is not the source of social inequality

NATURAL AND SOCIAL INEQUALITIES

The present chapter aims to explain what question Rousseau means to be asking when he inquires into the origin of human inequality, as well as the first, negative part of what he takes the answer to that question to be. It seeks, in other words, to reconstruct his argument for the claim that inequalities – or, more precisely, the particular sorts of inequality he is most interested in – do not have their origin in nature, neither in human nature nor in the natural conditions of human existence nor in some combination of the two. By the end of this chapter we will have seen why Rousseau thinks himself entitled to claim at the end of the Second Discourse that he has "proved that inequality is scarcely perceptible in the state of nature and that its influence there is almost nil" (*DI*, 159/*OC* III, 162).

Before reconstructing his argument, however, it is necessary to get clear about the specific phenomenon Rousseau has in view when speaking of inequality in the Second Discourse. The very first pages of the Second Discourse make it clear that Rousseau means to be asking about the origin not of human inequality in general but only of what he calls moral inequality. Moral (or political) inequalities are said to differ from natural (or physical) inequalities in two important respects. First, they are not products of nature but are instead – to use a term Rousseau will invoke repeatedly in the Second Discourse – *artificial*, which is to say: they are established by a kind of convention that rests ultimately on human consent (*DI*, 131/*OC* III, 131). Second, moral inequalities are social in the sense that they consist in one individual (or group) exerting a kind of power or possessing a kind of advantage over another. As Rousseau puts the point, moral inequality consists not in "differences in

16

age, health, or bodily strength" but "in different privileges which some enjoy to the prejudice of others, such as being more wealthy, more honored, more powerful than they, or even getting themselves obeyed" (*DI*, 131/*OC* III, 131). Because "moral" no longer has the same meaning for us that it did for Rousseau,[1] and because "political" is too narrow to capture all the inequalities he means to examine, I will from now on refer to the object of the Second Discourse's inquiry as *social* inequalities. I use this term in order to signal that the inequalities under investigation here both have a social *origin* (in human "conventions") and are social *in nature*, insofar as they consist in relative advantages or privileges that some humans enjoy over others. The first of these points will occupy us for most of this chapter, but it is important not to lose sight of the second as well if we are to have a clear picture of the kinds of inequalities the Second Discourse is concerned with.

It is crucial to bear in mind that for Rousseau social inequalities are always *privileges* – benefits that some enjoy to the prejudice of others – and that his standard examples are differences in wealth, honor (or prestige), power (over others), and authority (the right to command others and to have one's commands obeyed). Rousseau's language and examples here suggest a point whose importance will become clearer later: the characteristics in terms of which social, as opposed to natural, inequalities are defined are robustly relative, or positional, properties rather than "absolute" qualities. Strength of body, mind, and character – differences in which constitute natural inequalities – are properties that individuals can possess, and desire to possess, without regard to whether others possess more or less, or even any amount, of the same. The extent of a person's wisdom, for example, is independent of how wise her neighbors are, and the desirability of her wisdom does not depend on whether others possess or lack it. Social inequalities, by contrast, are made up of disparities in qualities in which the factor of privilege (over others) plays a central role. This is easy to see in the case of authority, where a person can be said to have authority only when

---

[1] "Moral" here contrasts with "physical" and so has a wider sense than "ethical" or "duty-related." Depending on the context, the term can be synonymous with "spiritual," "nonmaterial," or "cultural." A prominent example of this usage is found in Rousseau's characterization of the "public person," or *moi commun*, that issues from the social contract as a "moral . . . body made up of as many members as the assembly has voices" (*SC*, I.6.x). This moral being comes into existence not through physical processes but as a result of the free consent of each of its members.

there is someone else who must obey him. Authority is always authority over some other who (in that specific respect) lacks authority and is therefore (in that specific respect) "beneath" someone else. Something similar is true of power, as long as we mean by that term something more than physical or mental strength, disparities in which count as natural inequalities. A socially powerful individual – one who succeeds in influencing or coercing others to carry out her own wishes and ends – is powerful only insofar as there are less powerful individuals to function as the instruments of her will. The relativity (or positionality) of honor is of central importance to Rousseau's genealogy of inequality and will be discussed in detail below. Finally, privilege over others is constitutive even of riches, at least if Adam Smith's famous account of the "real measure" of wealth "after the division of labor" is to be believed: "every man ... is rich or poor according to the quantity of that labor [of others] which he can command, or ... afford to purchase."[2] In all these cases, possessing a good – wealth, prestige, power, or authority – is inseparable from someone else being disadvantaged by the other's possession of it; the goods that make up the stuff of social inequalities are goods that can be enjoyed only "to the prejudice" of another.

It should be noted that in defining the kind of inequality he is interested in, Rousseau has already told us something important about how he intends to answer the question regarding its origin: social inequality has its origin not in nature but in opinions and practices that come from human activities; it "depends on a sort of convention and is established, or at least authorized, by men's consent" (*DI*, 131/*OC* III, 131). Moreover, he has made it clear that nature as he conceives it stands in opposition to artifice, convention, opinion, and consent. It is worth dwelling a bit on this puzzling claim, for when properly understood it reveals a great deal about how Rousseau conceives of the inequality whose origin and legitimacy the Second Discourse is investigating. The puzzling character of the claim lies in its suggestion that social inequality depends on human consent, presumably the consent of the very individuals who stand in relations of inequality to others. It initially seems wrong, even perverse, to claim that social inequalities exist, even in part, because the propertyless, the oppressed, and the looked-down-upon consent to the wealth, power,

---

[2] Adam Smith, *The Wealth of Nations*, ed. Edwin Cannan (New York: Modern Library, 2000), 33.

and prestige of those above them in the social hierarchy. But Rousseau's exact words are significant here: social inequality is said to be "established, *or at least authorized*," by human consent. That Rousseau replaces talk of how inequalities come to be – how they are first *established* – with talk about how they are *authorized* should alert us to the important fact that the Second Discourse is less concerned with the actual historical origin of inequality than it initially seems to be. In fact, what Rousseau is most concerned with in this statement is how and why, once inequalities have come to exist, they are maintained. Rousseau's fundamental claim, then, is not that social inequalities first come into the world through human agreement but rather that, once present, their continued existence depends on a kind of consent that he calls authorization. That authorization is crucial to the maintenance of social inequalities implies that, in contrast to the "physical," or non-"moral," realm of nature, they are essentially normative phenomena. Social inequalities are normative in the sense that they are embedded in human practices whose existence depends on their participants' belief in the goodness or legitimacy or naturalness of those practices, which in turn implies that we are responsible for social inequalities – they depend on our own doings – in a way that is not true of natural inequalities. To say, however, that social inequalities are authorized by consent does not mean that they are *in truth* legitimate or authoritative; it means only that they are *taken to be* legitimate by those subject to them and that this "authorization" plays a significant role in maintaining them. (It should be noted, then, that "authorized" has a different sense here from its meaning in the second of the Second Discourse's main questions. When Rousseau asks there whether social inequality is authorized by natural law, he is not wondering whether individuals believe in its legitimacy but whether, apart from the actual opinions of humans, natural law in fact makes it legitimate.)

This point brings to light an important sense in which social inequalities for Rousseau are moral rather than physical: the practices and institutions that sustain social inequalities are maintained for the most part not by force but by a (tacit or explicit) consensus that they are justified. When workers in capitalist enterprises perform their eight or more hours of labor, day in and day out, without sabotaging their employers' property or appropriating it for themselves, they typically do so not primarily because they fear the state's power to enforce existing property laws – though one should not forget that such power stands constantly in the background, ready to crush the few who might dare to violate those laws – but because at some level they accept, perhaps unquestioningly, the legitimacy or naturalness of the social arrangements that make it necessary for them to work for their survival, while others have sufficient wealth to live without laboring and to enrich themselves from the fruits of others' labor. By the same token, asymmetric power relations between men and women seldom depend entirely on men's having superior physical power at their disposal; they depend also on the belief of those who participate in those relations, including many women, that patriarchal rule is natural or appropriate. This point is bound up with what Rousseau takes to be a general truth about human social life: institutions that depended entirely on brute, physical force or on the threat of coercion, without any belief in their legitimacy on the part of those who participate in them, would be highly unstable and inefficient, not least because a very large part of the society's resources would have to be spent in maintaining oppressive mechanisms of coercion so that its members would perceive them as ubiquitous and inescapable.

The consent that authorizes most social inequalities, then, is not the consent typical of contracts, where contracting parties negotiate the terms of their relationship and explicitly agree to them before their relationship is established. Instead, the consent that grounds inequalities consists in the holding of more or less conscious beliefs regarding the appropriateness of certain practices and institutions. The reason Rousseau regards this as a type of consent – as a *free* assenting to practices and institutions – is that, as we will see below, beliefs (or "opinions") rest ultimately on our freedom. Believing something requires an active assent to the proposition that such-and-such is the case. It is perhaps more perspicuous to say that holding a belief – for example, that men are naturally suited to rule over women – implies a kind of *responsibility* for what one believes: our beliefs, even if only vague or tacit, are ultimately up to us in the sense that it is within our power as cognitive agents to reflect on their adequacy and then, in light of that reflection, to abandon or revise them (to adjust them according to the evidence we take ourselves to have for or against them). It is for this reason that social inequalities are artificial. They are the sort of thing whose existence requires the active participation of those who are subject to them; they are, if not exactly created intentionally, at least actively perpetuated by the "consent" of their participants, including the very beings who are disadvantaged by them.

While it may seem harsh or unfair to make the oppressed and disadvantaged even partially responsible for their condition, Rousseau's view also implies that the power to alter that condition resides, at least in part, with them. If social inequality were not something that the disadvantaged played some role in maintaining, it would be much more difficult to see how they could ever be in a position to overturn it. Moreover, Rousseau's view implies that philosophy, broadly construed, has an important role to play in progressive social change. For philosophy that refutes our beliefs in the legitimacy of certain inequalities undermines part of the foundations those inequalities rest on. And this is precisely one of the Second Discourse's principal objectives in inquiring into the "origin and foundations [*fondements*] of inequality."[3]

It is impossible to overstate the significance of the opinion-dependent character of social inequality for Rousseau's undertaking in the Second Discourse. It has, for example, profound implications for how he conceives of what he must find in order to uncover the origin of social inequality. When Rousseau poses the question to himself "What precisely is at issue in this discourse?" he responds with the potentially misleading reply: "to mark in the progress of things the moment when, right replacing violence, nature was subjected to law" (*DI*, 131/*OC* III, 132).[4] The central contrast in this reply is that between purely natural beings, on the one hand – for which violence is the rule – and moral, or normatively oriented, beings, on the other, which are governed by law and right (or, better, by law and their *ideas* of what is right).[5] At the core of this obscure but important statement is the following claim: the key to understanding where social inequality comes from lies in explaining how it is possible for opinions

---

[3] I discuss the important term *foundations* of inequality and its implications in Chapter 3.
[4] One potential source of confusion is that Rousseau's language suggests that he will give a historical account of inequality's origin. I have more to say on this vexed topic below.
[5] Readers of *The Social Contract* will recognize this as the same question Rousseau raises there when considering "the remarkable change in man [that] substituted justice for instinct in his conduct and endowed his actions with the morality they previously lacked" (*SC*, I.8.i).

concerning right, as opposed to mere nature, to assume a central role in human affairs. If human societies are typically characterized by social inequalities of diverse sorts (which themselves depend on the opinions, or consent, of their members), then humans must be the kinds of beings that can let opinions (normative beliefs about the goodness or legitimacy of things), rather than mere nature (impulses unmediated by such opinions), determine their behavior and mode of being. One could reformulate Rousseau's question concerning the origin of inequality, then, as follows: what must human beings be like if social inequalities, grounded in opinion, are able to assume so prominent a role in their lives? Assuming that we have understood him correctly so far, it would come as no surprise if Rousseau took his answer to the question concerning the origin of social inequality to depend on uncovering some fundamental feature of human beings that both marks the distinction between the human and the purely natural and explains the capacity of opinion to rule in human affairs. In Part II of the Second Discourse, where the natural creatures of Part I first become genuinely *human* beings, Rousseau will introduce into his account precisely a factor of this sort – the passion of *amour propre* – and, as we should now expect, it will serve as the centerpiece of his answer to the question of where social inequality comes from.

Finally, understanding Rousseau's distinction between natural and social inequalities helps to make clear why he confines his attention in the Second Discourse to the latter. The most obvious reason is that the Second Discourse's two main questions are quickly answered when directed at natural inequalities: these, of course, originate in nature (*DI*, 131/*OC* III, 131) and, so, are authorized – or at least not condemned – by nature's law. It is probably more accurate to say that in the case of natural inequalities the question of authorization – whether they are legitimate or permissible – does not even arise. It seems likely that Rousseau believed that it makes sense to pose the second, normative question only with respect to artificial phenomena, those that depend on human activity (and freedom) in the sense articulated above. In the case of natural phenomena, issues of legitimacy or critique do not arise. It may be unfortunate that nature gave to some individuals stronger bodies, more beautiful voices, or sweeter dispositions than to others, but these differences themselves – as opposed to what human societies make of them – are not unjust, illegitimate, or the proper object of moral critique. Normative assessment and critique for Rousseau are appropriately directed not at nature's (that is, God's) doings but at ours – which is to say, only at those states of affairs for which we bear responsibility. It is important, however, not to overestimate the extent to which Rousseau's view removes nature's effects from the purview of normative critique. The mere fact that one individual is born blind while another comes into the world with perfect sight is not for Rousseau a form of injustice, or any other kind of moral deficiency. But how that natural difference ultimately affects the lives of the individuals concerned is not the result of natural circumstances alone. Since social practices and institutions play a great role in determining the consequences that natural inequalities have for the lives of those disadvantaged by them, these consequences are in large part our own doing – something we, not nature, are responsible for – and are therefore an appropriate subject matter for the Second Discourse's normative question. If natural blindness is not in itself an injustice, the facts that in some societies the blind have little access to educational institutions or public transportation can indeed be unjust (and legitimate objects of critique) since the latter are social, not merely natural, consequences of blindness that it is within our power to change.

This point suggests a further reason why the Second Discourse is concerned exclusively with social inequalities: it is a basic conviction of Rousseau – one for which the Second Discourse means to deliver a kind of argument – that natural inequalities, though real and of some significance, typically end up making very little difference in human affairs compared to the vastly greater effects of artificial inequalities. When an observer of modern society, troubled by the inequalities around him, resolves to inquire into the origin and justifiability of inequality, the phenomena most likely to motivate his inquiry, whether he realizes it or not, are by far more the results of social circumstances than of natural ones. As Rousseau points out at the very beginning of the Second Discourse, it is easy to see once one reflects on the matter that the great disparities in power, wealth, prestige, and authority so prevalent in modern societies are not direct consequences of differences in age, bodily strength, innate talents, or natural intelligence. That wealth, prestige, power, and authority simply reflect the natural superiority of those who possess them "may perhaps be good for slaves to debate within hearing of their masters," but such a hypothesis can have little force for anyone who sincerely seeks the truth about human inequality (*DI*, 131/*OC* III, 132). Of course, that social inequalities cannot simply be traced back to natural differences in no way constitutes proof of their illegitimacy. What it does imply is that the greatest portion of the inequalities found in existing societies are not merely given, natural, or necessary phenomena but instead are due, at least in part, to social circumstances that humans actively maintain and for which they are for that reason responsible; it shows, in other words, not that social inequalities are one and all illegitimate but, more modestly, that they are an appropriate object for moral evaluation and critique.

With these reflections a beginning has already been made in reconstructing Rousseau's answer to the Second Discourse's first question concerning where social inequalities come from. For the initial step in his argument that they do not have a natural origin consists in precisely this claim: the general existence of social inequalities cannot be explained as a direct or necessary consequence of natural inequalities; and, correlatively, natural inequalities play at most a negligible role in determining which individuals in any specific society enjoy the advantages of wealth, prestige, power, and authority. In other words, innate differences among human individuals do not – *pace* Plato and Aristotle – imply the necessity or legitimacy of social hierarchy in general, nor do they authorize any specific assignment of advantages as "in accordance with nature." Moreover, Rousseau insists, even if it turned out that natural inequalities played some role in determining the relative positions of individuals in society, they would not do so of themselves, independently of a host of social practices and institutions – rules of private property, codes of honor, or conventions establishing authority, for example – that give meaning to natural differences and encourage their cultivation in ways that extend their consequences far beyond those they would have "naturally," in the absence of such practices and institutions. Because the practices and institutions that mediate whatever effect natural inequalities might have on social position are variable and depend on human freedom, social inequalities are, at most, *under*determined by nature. Which forms of inequality obtain in a given society, as well as how far they extend, are not natural (and therefore eternal) facts but social (and therefore variable) circumstances that, because sustained by human participation, are up to us and, so, possible objects of both evaluation and reform.

There is, however, more to Rousseau's dismissal of nature as the origin of social inequalities than this, and seeing what more there is reveals a good deal about the nature of the Second Discourse's genealogical project and its central concept, "origin." Immediately after establishing that social inequalities cannot be traced back to natural inequalities, Rousseau poses a further question regarding their possible origin in nature, a sure indication that this first claim does not exhaust his thesis that social inequalities have a non-natural origin. This further question is whether social inequalities might not have their origin – or, as Rousseau sometimes says, their source (*DI*, 124/*OC* III, 122) – in *human* nature. One reason for preferring to speak of inequality's source rather than its origin is that the former term discourages the common but mistaken impression that Rousseau means to be posing a primarily historical question about how inequality actually came into the world. Formulating his question in terms of inequality's source suggests instead that the Second Discourse promises a more general investigation into where inequality comes from than a purely historical account can deliver. When one asks, for example, about the source of the Hudson River or the source of poverty in the US, one normally expects in response not a historical narrative but a synchronic account of, in the first case, the various tributaries whose waters come together to constitute the Hudson and, in the second, the various factors – the export of jobs to countries where labor power is cheaper, laws that discourage union organizing, and so on – that explain not how poverty in the US first came to be but what standing forces contribute to its persistence. Indeed, it is this kind of account Rousseau is after when he inquires into the origin of inequality. Rather than asking when, where, and why social inequality first entered human society, he wants to know instead which of the various aspects of the human condition in general – our biological nature, acquired psychology, history, contingent social circumstances – work together to explain why inequality exists and is so pervasive in most human societies.

Having established that inborn differences among individuals contribute little, if anything, to social inequalities, Rousseau's next concern is to argue, in considerably more detail, that they also do not have their source in human nature (or in nature more generally conceived). Already in the Preface, even before he has properly defined the questions he plans to address, Rousseau makes it clear that developing an accurate picture of human nature is crucial to the Second Discourse's success: "how can the source of inequality among men be known unless one begins by knowing men themselves?" (*DI*, 124/*OC* III, 122). Although it is plain enough from the beginning that he does not intend to explain social inequality as a consequence of human nature, it is much less clear what this position amounts to. Since Rousseau's answer to the question of whether social inequality has its source in human nature turns out to be much more complicated than it initially appears, understanding the argument of the Second Discourse requires devoting considerable effort to figuring out what the question is about and why he answers it negatively.

TWO SENSES OF HUMAN NATURE

The main difficulty here stems from the elusive terms "nature" and "human nature," which, as even a first-time reader of the Second Discourse will notice, Rousseau employs in multiple senses. This multiplicity of meanings is no less evident in the way Rousseau handles the central theoretical construct of Part I, the *state of nature*.[6] It is best to approach the difficulties contained in the related concepts "nature," "human nature," and "state of nature" by examining the passage in which Rousseau first refers to the basic strategy the Second Discourse will employ in order to show that social inequality does not originate in nature:

---

[6] Readers familiar with *The Social Contract* will wonder why the state of nature described there – as a Hobbesian state of war (*SC*, I.6.i) – differs so greatly from its depiction in the Second Discourse. The answer is that Rousseau uses a single term – "state of nature" – to refer to two constructs with very different theoretical functions. The state of nature in Part I of the Second Discourse is an attempt to imagine what human life would be like in the absence of all artificial modifications (those depending on judgment, will, historical developments, and contingent social circumstances), whereas the state of nature in *The Social Contract* is an attempt, similar to Hobbes's and Locke's in their political philosophies, to imagine what human life would be like in the absence of *political* institutions *for humans who have been altered* by the very civilizing processes described in the Second Discourse. Hence (to make matters even more confusing) the state of disorder and domination presented in Part II of the Second Discourse as immediately prior to political society (*DI*, 171–3/*OC* III, 175–8) – and referred to once as "the state of nature" – corresponds (roughly) to the state of nature in *The Social Contract*. One could distinguish these two theoretical constructs by reserving "original state of nature" for the account found in Part I of the Second Discourse, but since my focus here is the Second Discourse alone, I will often simply use "state of nature," with the understanding that it refers to the original state of nature depicted in Part I of that text.

It is no light undertaking to disentangle what is original from what is artificial in man's present nature and to know accurately a state which no longer exists, which perhaps never did exist, which probably never will exist, and of which it is nevertheless necessary to have exact notions in order accurately to judge of our present state.[7] (*DI*, 125/*OC* III, 123)

One point that emerges from this passage is that the state of nature, including its depiction of human nature, represents Rousseau's attempt to distinguish what is original (or natural) from what is artificial in human beings and human society as we know them. In this respect the state of nature can be said to have a descriptive or explanatory function: it aims to reveal which aspects of our existence have their source in nature (and hence in necessary, invariable factors we cannot change) and which have their source in us – which are our creations rather than nature's or God's – and are therefore in principle also alterable by us.

That the state of nature has a second, normative function as well becomes clear at the end of this passage, in its claim that knowing our original condition is necessary if we are accurately to judge – that is, to *evaluate* – our present state. This suggests that answering the main normative question of the Second Discourse – to what extent, and why, are social inequalities justifiable? – depends for Rousseau on acquiring a true understanding of human nature and of our natural condition that enables us to answer the Second Discourse's main explanatory question – where do inequalities come from? – by distinguishing accurately between what in those inequalities originates with us and what is imposed on us by nature. In other words, Rousseau's account of the original state of nature (and of original human nature) is fundamental to the Second Discourse's project as a whole, and it will play a major role in both the normative and the non-normative tasks undertaken there. For this reason it is necessary to examine in detail what kind of theoretical tool the state of nature is for Rousseau and how it functions both to explain and to evaluate (and, eventually, to criticize) the "artificial" social arrangements whose legitimacy he is ultimately interested in. In the course of doing so it will also be necessary to arrive

---

[7] Careful readers will note that Rousseau here uses "nature" (of humans) in yet a different sense from the two senses I distinguish below: "man's present nature" refers to what humans are currently like and, so, is distinct from "human nature" in both its explanatory and normative senses as I define them here.

at an understanding of the most bewildering claim in the passage cited above: that the state of nature may never have actually existed and probably never will but must nonetheless be known if we are accurately to evaluate our present condition. Because the present chapter is devoted to answering the first of the Second Discourse's two questions – where does social inequality come from? – I will restrict my attention here to the state of nature's descriptive and explanatory functions. In Chapter 3, when beginning to reconstruct Rousseau's view on the legitimacy or justifiability of inequality, we will need to return once more to the state of nature and attempt to understand the role it plays in the normative assessment of society and in social critique.

To repeat: Rousseau's elaboration of the state of nature in Part I of the Second Discourse is meant to play a central role in explaining where social inequalities come from. More precisely, it aims to establish where social inequalities do *not* come from: neither from human nature nor from nature more generally (nor, as we have already seen, from natural inequalities themselves). The content of Rousseau's claim that social inequalities do not have their source in human nature or in nature more generally can be summarized in two general claims (beyond the claim that they do not come from natural inequalities): first, that human nature provides no psychological incentives that explain why humans would be motivated to seek out the inequalities they in fact create; and, second, that there are no fixed features of the external world to which humans must relate in order to satisfy their natural needs that necessitate or even encourage the creation of inequalities beyond the relatively insignificant natural inequalities imposed on them by nature. Rousseau's negative answer in Part I to the Second Discourse's first question – nature is not the source of social inequalities – prepares the way for his positive, and very complex, answer to the same question in Chapter 2, where new, non-"natural" elements are introduced into the psychological constitution of humans and into their social relations. The remainder of this chapter will be taken up with a reconstruction of the two claims I have just summarized. Before turning to this task, however, it is necessary to say a bit more about Rousseau's highly confusing use of the term "nature" more generally.[8]

---

[8] For a good discussion of these issues, see Ludwig Siep, "Rousseau's Normative Idea of Nature," in *Finnish Yearbook of Political Thought* 4 (2000), 53–72.

Corresponding to the two main functions I have ascribed to the state of nature, the concept of nature in general has both a normative and an explanatory sense in the Second Discourse (and, indeed, throughout Rousseau's corpus).[9] That is, "natural" sometimes refers to the kind of existence that humans and other beings *ought* to have, despite the fact that (in the case of humans) their actual lives often bear little resemblance to those that nature prescribes. In the Second Discourse this normative function is most apparent in the quotation from Aristotle that serves as the text's epigraph – "One must seek what is natural not in depraved beings but in those that live well in accordance with nature" (*DI*, 113/*OC* III, 109) – as well as in statements that depict the inhabitants of the state of nature as enjoying the "way of life prescribed to [them] by nature" (*DI*, 138/*OC* III, 138), which implies that their way of life is *uncorrupted* or *good* or *appropriate*, given the kind of beings they are (*DI*, 157/*OC* III, 160). This use of "natural" is common in other texts of Rousseau's as well – for example, in *Emile*, where the goal of Emile's education is said to be to make him into a natural man (*E*, 205, 254/*OC* IV, 483, 549), which means that he is to be educated into a way of being that is "suitable for man and well adapted to the human heart" (*E*, 34/*OC* IV, 243). When used in this normative sense, the opposite of natural is corrupted, or degenerate, or unbefitting the kind of being one is.

In its non-normative meaning, "natural" contrasts not with "corrupt" or "unbefitting" but with "artificial." When Rousseau employs "natural" in this sense, he associates the artificial with the intervention of human opinions, or judgments, such that a thing counts as artificial if it has been in some way "modified by . . . opinions" (*E*, 39/*OC* IV, 248). This is why, as we saw above, he classifies social inequalities, which depend on human consent, or beliefs regarding their legitimacy, as artificial and distinguishes them from natural inequalities. Another way of defining the artificial is to say that it is the result (or

---

[9] Rousseau himself distinguishes between descriptive (or explanatory) and normative senses of nature when discussing the natural law tradition and the various ways in which natural law has been understood by previous thinkers. He invokes the former sense when speaking of natural law as "the general relations established by nature among all animate beings [to insure] their common preservation"; he invokes the latter in speaking of the law that nature "prescribes" to rational beings (*DI*, 126/*OC* III, 124). Natural laws in the first sense describe or explain the behavior of animals by relating it to the end of all animate beings, the preservation of life; natural laws in the second sense tell us how we ought to act (if we want to achieve the ends nature has set for us).

partial result) of human action, where action, as distinct from mere animal behavior, is informed by an opinion or judgment concerning the purpose or good of what one does. Simply being moved by a disposition to avoid what is painful, for example, does not yet take one beyond the realm of nature (*E*, 39/ *OC* IV, 248), whereas behavior informed by a judgment – say, a judgment of what it is good to do – counts as an expression of agency, an instance of human, as opposed to merely natural, doings. Examples of the natural in this sense are the purely "mechanical" effects that self-love and pity have on humans' animal-like behavior in the state of nature, "prior to reason" (*DI*, 127/*OC* III, 126); its defining characteristic, as Rousseau explains more clearly elsewhere, is the "absence of knowledge and will" (*E*, 61/*OC* IV, 280). When, in contrast, humans intervene in the world in ways shaped by their judgments and will, they introduce artificiality into it, and a world that has been altered by intervention of this sort ceases to be fully natural in this second, non-normative sense of the term.

Although Rousseau says this less explicitly than he might have, the reason the intervention of judgments counts as artificial is that judging involves *freedom*.[10] Following the Stoics who so impressed him in his youth, Rousseau takes both willing and judging to involve a spontaneous act of consent or endorsement, either to a proposition (in which case the result is a judgment) or to something's appearing to be good (in which case the result is an action) (*E*, 270–3, 280/ *OC* IV, 571–6, 585–6). This is why, as we saw above, belief in the legitimacy of a form of social inequality – a kind of judgment – counts for him as a species of consent. At root, then, what divides the natural from the artificial – as well as the purely animal from the human (*DI*, 141/*OC* III, 141–2) – is the absence or presence of freedom. A world modified in some way by human freedom – by human judgment and will – is no longer completely natural. According to this standard, only the original and "hypothetical" (*DI*, 132/*OC* III, 133)[11] state of nature described in Part I of the Second Discourse is a truly natural world, whereas the world depicted in Part II – where *human* beings first appear – is always in some measure artificial.

---

[10] Rousseau expands on this idea at *E*, 280/*OC* IV, 586. Although he expresses this point in the voice of the Savoyard vicar, I see no reason for thinking it is not his own view as well.

[11] I defend this interpretive claim in detail below.

It is worth noting an implication of the two meanings of "natural" just elaborated that will be of great importance when we consider Rousseau's critique of inequality: contrary to what readers often assume, "artificial" is a normatively neutral term for Rousseau. There is for him no conceptual – or any other – reason that something artificial (something informed by opinion or will) must also be unnatural in the sense of bad or depraved.[12] Rousseau's point when he later calls society (and the passion that accompanies it, *amour propre*) artificial is not that social relations (or *amour propre*) necessarily corrupt humans, nor that they are foreign to our "true," or ideal, nature. His point, rather, is that society is something humans help to *make*, which is to say, something that is always partly the product of human belief and will. The important claim in thinking of society as artificial is that even though real humans must have social relations of one kind or another, the specific forms those relations actually take are highly variable and dependent on many contingent factors, including human will. It is not up to humans to live in society or not, but since nature dictates no determinate social arrangements for us as it does for bees and ants, it *is* up to us how our social relations are configured. Contrary to how the Second Discourse is commonly read, Rousseau does not envision human existence without enduring social relations any more than he envisions it without love, reason, language, or the drive to be esteemed by others (*amour propre*) – all of which are just as artificial as society but, as we will see, no less essential to a good human existence.

Bearing in mind these two senses of nature – one contrasted with the artificial, the other with what is depraved or corrupted – it is possible to begin to make sense of what it means for Rousseau to deny that human nature is the source of moral inequality. It will come as no surprise that "human nature" has precisely the same duality of meanings as "nature" more generally. Because Rousseau takes there to be important connections between these normative and explanatory senses of human nature – a topic I return to in Chapter 3 – it is probably more accurate to say that he employs a single conception of human nature that has two related aspects. Still, it is important to the logic of Rousseau's argument

---

[12] The social contract is, of course, artificial (*SC*, I.6.x), and Rousseau explicitly praises a variety of artificial phenomena at *SC*, I.8.i, I.9.viii, and II.7.iii, as well as in the Second Discourse (*DI*, 164, 167/*OC* III, 169, 171).

to distinguish the normative from the non-normative aspects of his conception of human nature, even if later it will be just as important to ask how he sees the two as fitting together. (For ease of expression I will continue to refer to two conceptions of human nature, though it should not be forgotten that Rousseau takes them to be intimately connected.)

In the Second Discourse Rousseau's normative conception of human nature appears mostly in conjunction with his talk of the "corruption" and "debasement" of human nature that accompany the changes in human beings and their society depicted in Part II (*DI*, 133, 178–9, 203/*OC* III, 133, 183–4, 207).[13] In *Emile* the normative sense of human nature is more prominent, especially in its central claim that the proper task of education is to form humans so as to realize their true nature. The conception of human nature that enables Rousseau to speak in both texts of human corruption and debasement is normative because it specifies the characteristics human beings ought to possess but frequently do not, the lack of which is precisely what Rousseau means by a debased human existence. I will postpone discussion of this sense of human nature until Chapter 3, when reconstructing Rousseau's normative position with respect to social inequality. In this chapter, where my concern is the origin of inequality, I will examine his descriptive or explanatory conception of original human nature, which is contained in his account of the state of nature in Part I. One reason for beginning here is that Rousseau's non-normative conception of human nature is more difficult to understand and typically engenders more confusion than his relatively straightforward conception of true (or ideal) human nature.

THE NON-NORMATIVE CONCEPTION OF ORIGINAL
HUMAN NATURE

Rousseau's descriptive or explanatory conception of original human nature offers an account of what human beings are like – or, since, as I argue below, the state of nature is a hypothetical construct (*DI*, 125, 132/*OC* III, 123, 133) – what they *would* be like in a world completely

---

[13] The normative conception is also apparent in those aspects of what Rousseau calls his "study of original man" that are concerned with "his true needs and the fundamental principles of his duties" (*DI*, 128/*OC* III, 126).

untouched by the artificial, a world in which nature, including our own (animal, or biological) nature, were completely unmodified by the effects of human agency. I will call this conception, with Rousseau, *original* human nature (*DI*, 124–5, 128/*OC* III, 122–3, 126), although it is important to remember that, since it abstracts from all effects of human agency, this original human nature will in important respects not be recognizably human at all. (In Chapter 2 I will contrast this original human nature with another non-normative conception of human nature that can be attributed to Rousseau – consisting essentially of original human nature plus *amour propre* – which I will call human nature in the expanded sense.) Although much more will need to be said about this idea, what Rousseau means to capture in his conception of original human nature is the human being's "original constitution," or what the human is like "as nature formed him," apart from "what circumstances and his progress have added to or changed in his primitive state" (*DI*, 124/*OC* III, 122).

Before exploring the content of Rousseau's account of original human nature, however, it is necessary to confront an interpretive issue that has generated much controversy among readers of the Second Discourse and that is of considerable importance for reconstructing and evaluating the position it sets forth. I have already indicated that in my view it is crucial to regard the state of nature depicted in Part I as a hypothetical construct, not as a thesis that purports to describe an actual state of affairs that really existed sometime in our distant past.[14] One reason for espousing this interpretation is that doing so makes the most *philosophical* sense of the Second Discourse, which is to say that it renders Rousseau's argument more coherent and more compelling than alternative readings. A second reason, though, is that Rousseau himself says clearly – or so it seems to me – that this is how he intends for the original state of nature to be understood. Since many interpreters disagree with me on this fundamental exegetical claim,[15] however, it is worth pausing

---

[14] For an extensive discussion of this and related issues, see Victor Gourevitch, "Rousseau's Pure State of Nature," *Interpretation* 16 (Fall 1988), 23–59.

[15] For example: Roger D. Masters, *The Political Philosophy of Rousseau* (Princeton University Press, 1979) 115–18; and Marc F. Plattner, *Rousseau's State of Nature: An Interpretation of the Discourse on Inequality* (DeKalb, Ill.: Northern Illinois University Press, 1979), 17–25. Tzvetan Todorov espouses a view similar to mine in *Frail Happiness: An Essay on Rousseau*, trans. John T. Scott and Robert Zaretsky (University Park: Pennsylvania State University Press, 2001), 10. I am grateful to John Scott for pressing me to think more about this issue.

to consider in some detail the textual evidence relevant to deciding the matter.

I have already cited the passage most important for settling this controversy, Rousseau's reference to the original state of nature as a condition "which no longer exists, which perhaps never did exist, which probably never will exist, and of which it is nevertheless necessary to have exact notions in order accurately to judge of our present state" (*DI*, 125/*OC* III, 123). This statement is relatively plain in revealing both that Rousseau takes his hypothesis of the state of nature to be of fundamental importance to his undertaking and that whether or not it refers to an actual historical state has no relevance for his argument: if the state of nature might never have existed but our ideas about it are nevertheless essential to answering the Second Discourse's questions, then what is of interest to Rousseau in this thesis can have nothing at all to do with its representing an actual state of affairs. Apart from all other complications, this in my view is the fundamental point to be kept sight of in the matter, and it plays a major role in my reconstruction of the Second Discourse's argument.

Even if one grants this point, however, one might argue that there is still room for the possibility that Rousseau in fact believed in the historical veracity of the original state of nature, or at the very least was agnostic about it, even if its philosophical importance is independent of that point (what he says, after all, is that *perhaps* the state of nature never existed). But even these weaker possibilities appear to be excluded, and just as plainly, by the following statement:

Let us begin ... by setting aside all the facts, for they do not affect the question [as to whether the state of nature ever existed].[16] The inquiries that

---

[16] That this passage is referring to the original state of nature is evident from the sentence immediately preceding it, where what is at issue is whether "men were ever in the pure state of nature," a question that Rousseau answers once again in the negative. The explicitly theological context in which the question is raised here – Rousseau is clear that taking the state of nature as a historical reality would be seen by many as contradicting the Biblical account of human origins – has encouraged some to conclude that his explicit denials of that state's historical character can be explained by his desire to avoid the consequences of religious controversy. (I am indebted to Christopher Brooke for impressing on me the importance of this possibility.) While Rousseau was fully aware of the real dangers involved in contradicting Church doctrine, the claim that this was his only or main reason for denying the historical character of the state of nature requires more positive evidence than the text in fact supplies. For: (1) not all of his denials occur in the context of theological discussions (*DI*, 125/*OC* III, 123); (2) there is no strong positive evidence for the contrary interpretation (that he intends to

may be pursued regarding this subject ought not to be taken for historical truths but only for hypothetical and conditional reasonings, better suited to elucidate the nature of things than to show their genuine origin and similar to those our physicists daily make regarding the formation of the world. (*DI*, 132/*OC* III, 132–3)

Here Rousseau says about as clearly as one could hope for that the state of nature is not a historical thesis, and contrary to what one might think, his subsequent reference to the hypotheses of physicists does not undercut but instead reinforces his denial of the state of nature's historical status. The hypothetical reasonings of physicists to which Rousseau is referring here are attempts, such as Descartes' in *The World* (and perhaps those of other eighteenth-century Cartesians), to construct coherent narratives with no pretensions of being factually true that depict how an ordered world such as ours could in principle emerge out of initial conditions of chaos in accordance only with a circumscribed set of mechanical laws of motion.[17] The point of such attempts was not to establish any claim regarding the actual temporal origin of the universe but – without making any assumption about *actual* initial conditions – to investigate the relation between different levels of orderedness in the world and to show that it was possible for higher levels of order to come about even if the only principles governing nature were mechanical laws of motion. The point of such hypotheses, in other words, was (exactly as Rousseau says) "to elucidate the nature of things" – to reveal relations of continuity between mechanical phenomena and those that appear to be of an entirely different order – rather

be making a historical point); and, most important, (3) construing the state of nature historically saddles Rousseau with a highly implausible view that must have appeared as such even to him.

[17] René Descartes, *The World and Other Writings*, trans. Stephen Gaukroger (Cambridge University Press, 1998), 23. Like Rousseau, Descartes too describes his account as a "fable" that makes no claim to being literally true (32). Rousseau's descriptions of his project echo Descartes' in other respects as well, as the following passage demonstrates: "With regard to the things which cannot be perceived by the senses, it is enough to explain their possible nature, even though their actual nature may be different. However, although this method may enable us to understand how all the things in nature could have arisen, it should not therefore be inferred that they were in fact made in this way . . . I shall think I have achieved enough provided only that what I have written is such as to correspond accurately with all the phenomena of nature"; René Descartes, *The Philosophical Writings of Descartes*, trans. John Cottingham, Robert Stoothoff, and Dugald Murdoch, vol. I (Cambridge University Press, 1985), 289. I am indebted to Allen Wood and David Hills for pointing out this connection to me and to Elliot Paul for explaining it and suggesting further similarities between the two thinkers' genealogical projects.

than "to show their genuine origin." Similarly, the Second Discourse's project is to show that the range of complex human phenomena that we are familiar with in highly developed societies can be accounted for by assuming a very small number of "first principles," namely those embodied in Rousseau's account of original human nature (and, as I explain in the following chapter, supplemented in Part II by the fundamental "principle" of social existence, *amour propre*). As I argue more extensively below, those principles are important to Rousseau because they represent the fundamental "building blocks" of human reality and indicate the very general limits that nature imposes on human variability. This way of putting the point suggests yet another way of describing the theoretical function of the state of nature that finds an echo in one of the passages cited above: hypotheses concerning our original nature have an *analytic* function that consists in "disentangling what is original from what is artificial [and due to society][18] in man's present nature" (*DI*, 125/*OC* III, 123) – or, equivalently, in "separating what, in the present constitution of things, divine will has done from what human art has pretended to do" (*DI*, 128/*OC* III, 127) – even if in reality neither the natural nor the artificial ever appears detached from its counterpart.

In any case, it is important to see that denying the historical veracity of the original state of nature is consistent with regarding it, as I do, as making a truth claim, even a claim to be in a certain sense *empirically* true. For Part I of the Second Discourse purports to reveal the truth about the basic elements of human nature, even though these elements cannot be directly apprehended by sense perception alone (because the object of our inquiry, "original" human nature, never appears in reality in that pure form). This does not mean the thesis is metaphysical in the sense of being empirically unfalsifiable – it is always possible in principle to discover human phenomena that cannot be explained on the basis of the minimal elements Rousseau attributes to human nature – but merely that it is not an immediate "fact" of the sort 'The tree before me is green' might be taken to designate. (Recall in this context Rousseau's call for us to "set aside all the facts" when considering the state of nature (*DI*, 132/*OC* III, 132).) Nor are claims about original human nature unscientific in the sense

---

[18] I explain the connection between the artificial and the social in Chapter 2.

of being hypotheses of a completely different sort from those made by natural science, which is why it is not entirely out of line for Rousseau to suggest that "experiments," in the broadest possible sense, might help to decide the question of our original nature (*DI*, 125/*OC* III, 123–4). Indeed – to invoke yet another analogy with physics – it is likely that Rousseau thinks of his theses about human nature as having a similar theoretical status to that possessed by Newton's first principles of motion: though neither empirical generalizations nor directly observable facts, Rousseau's theses derive their support from the success with which, on the assumption of a very small number of basic principles regarding "the first and simplest operations of the human soul" (*DI*, 127/*OC* III, 125), they account for the vastly diverse forms of human behavior we know from our own experience as well as from other empirical sources, such as biology, history, and what we would now call anthropology. (And this explains why the empirical evidence adduced in the Second Discourse concerning the great diversity of human forms of life, both "primitive" and developed, is relevant to Rousseau's undertaking even though the original state of nature is not a historical thesis. I return to this issue in the Coda to Chapter 4.)

Let us now return to setting out the content of Rousseau's account of original human nature.[19] The most important part of this account is what Rousseau calls our "natural faculties," those simplest operations of the soul that function in us "prior to reason" (*DI*, 127–8/*OC* III, 125–7). In other words, original human nature for Rousseau is made up of the natural endowments of human individuals, the "original dispositions" (*E*, 39/*OC* IV, 248) and capacities they receive from nature alone, apart from how contingent social or historical circumstances might form them. Given what has been said above regarding nature in general, it makes sense to think of these dispositions and capacities, in their purely natural form, as existing and functioning independently of human judgment and will. This is precisely how Rousseau describes the two original dispositions he attributes to human beings, love of self (*amour de soi-même*) and pity, both of which he takes to be dispositions we have

---

[19] For an interesting, slightly different reading of the picture of human nature set out in the Second Discourse, see John Scott, "Rousseau's Unease with Locke's Uneasiness," in Christopher Kelly and Eve Grace, eds., *The Challenge of Rousseau* (Cambridge University Press, 2012), 302–11.

from birth that lead us to respond to the world without the intervention of opinion or will and, so, prior to reason. Insofar as these dispositions operate independently of judgment and will, they are no different in kind from animal dispositions; in fact, Rousseau regards both as dispositions that humans and (at least some) other animals have in common.

As its name indicates, *amour de soi-même* (or, equivalently, *amour de soi*)[20] is a form of self-love, or self-interestedness, the defining characteristic of which is that it "leads us to care intensely about our [own individual] well-being and self-preservation" (*DI*, 127/*OC* III, 126). (In Part II of the Second Discourse Rousseau introduces a second form of self-love, *amour propre*, whose aims are importantly different from those of *amour de soi-même*. Because this distinction plays so large a role in Rousseau's thought, and because no English terms adequately capture the contrast, I will use the French expressions from this point on.) In its completely natural form, before any opinions of what our well-being consists in can guide our self-interestedness, *amour de soi-même* operates in a purely animal fashion, which means that natural human beings are disposed to respond to the world, more or less "mechanically" and "prior to all reflection" (*DI*, 152/*OC* III, 154), with behavior that furthers their individual preservation and well-being.[21] What Rousseau has in mind here is surely that humans, like other animals, are born with dispositions to seek sensations of pleasure and to avoid sensations of pain. These dispositions lead the beings that have them to seek – or in the case of pain, to avoid – the objects in the world that tend to produce those sensations in them (*E*, 39/*OC* IV, 248). Moreover, nature is so arranged – it is in this modest respect *teleologically* structured – that the unreflective responses of such beings issue for the most part in behavior that ultimately promotes their good *qua* natural beings, which is to say: their survival and well-being.

---

[20] In this book I use the first of these equivalent expressions. In French one would normally refer to *l'amour de soi-même* and to *l'amour propre*. Instead I follow here the established practice in English writings on Rousseau of omitting the definite article, even though this will sound odd to readers who know French.

[21] In Chapter 2, once *amour propre* has been introduced into the picture, we will see that a more general and more accurate description of what *amour de soi-même* strives for is: one's *own non-relative* (non-positional) well-being.

The second disposition Rousseau ascribes to our original nature, one that humans also share with other animals, is pity (*pitié*), which consists in "a natural repugnance to seeing any sentient being, and especially any being like ourselves, perish or suffer" (*DI*, 127/*OC* III, 126). This natural repugnance at the suffering of others has behavioral consequences for natural beings because repugnance, as a type of pain, provides them with a motivation to avoid others' suffering. Fleeing the presence of another's suffering is one response that pity is capable of producing, but alleviating that suffering, especially when doing so is not burdensome, is clearly another. Rousseau's thesis that pity belongs to our original nature amounts to the claim that humans are not by nature solely self-interested creatures. Instead, they are capable of feeling pain merely on the basis of their perception of others' pain, and this serves as the basis for a kind of natural concern for the well-being of others that in more developed human beings provides the motivating force behind moral virtues such as mercy, benevolence, and generosity (*DI*, 153/*OC* III, 155). Not surprisingly, then, the presence of pity is an important factor in accounting for the mostly benign character of the original state of nature: "as long as [natural man] does not resist the inner impulsion of commiseration [or pity], he will never harm another man or even any sentient being, except in the legitimate case when, his preservation being involved, he is obliged to give himself preference" (*DI*, 127/*OC* III, 126).

Yet, as this quote makes clear, even though pity often serves to balance out and soften the natural self-interestedness of human beings, the two dispositions do not have equal motivational force. In cases of serious conflict – for example, where one's preservation is at stake – the ends of *amour de soi-même* take priority over those of pity since, as Rousseau unambiguously asserts, the latter makes itself felt only "under certain circumstances" and then merely in a "gentle voice" relative to that with which *amour de soi-même* makes itself heard when its basic interests are threatened (*DI*, 152–4/*OC* III, 154–6). Rousseau's view, then, is that original human nature is characterized by two independent sources of motivation – *amour de soi-même* and pity – but that, despite our capacity to be moved to alleviate the sufferings of others independently of the benefit to ourselves of doing so, we remain fundamentally self-interested beings in at least the relatively weak sense that ultimately our own pain matters more to

us than others' and our inclination to relieve others' suffering tends to
be trumped by self-love when helping our fellow beings would result
in significant harm to ourselves. In the ends of these two original
dispositions, together with their relative strength, Rousseau finds in
nature the basis for a "maxim of natural goodness" that provides the
general rule for "natural" human behavior "in all men": "*Do your good
with the least possible harm to others*" (*DI*, 154/ *OC* III, 156). Of course,
the sense in which this maxim constitutes a rule for human behavior
differs significantly depending on whether we are thinking of behavior
in the state of nature or of human action within developed social
conditions. In the former – where, in the absence of countervailing
tendencies due to artificial conditions, "no one is tempted to disobey"
it – the maxim describes how humans *in fact* behave, while in the
latter it takes the form of a genuine imperative, instructing humans
who in fact may or may not obey it how they *ought* to act. (Moreover,
as Rousseau notes, the "naturalness" of the maxim implies that most
civilized beings feel a "repugnance to evil-doing" when they encounter
it in the world, including when that evil-doing is their own.)

That humans are by nature first and foremost self-interested beings is
a claim that Rousseau, together with most of his predecessors and
contemporaries, takes to be sufficiently obvious as to require little
argumentation. Most of us are likely to agree. Still, it is worth articulating the two, mostly implicit considerations that ground Rousseau's
claim. The first is entirely empirical: merely observing the behavior of
those around us, together with what we know about how men and
women in other times (and places) have lived (and live), makes it clear
that self-interest is a central element of human psychology – or, in other
words, that human individuals are by nature highly motivated to pursue
their own good as they conceive it. A second, less banal argument
reinforces the first: the widely observed self-interestedness of individuals
can plausibly be regarded as serving a purely biological end of nature,
namely, the survival and physical well-being of the very organisms that
are "programmed" by nature to seek their own good. Thus, the thesis
that *amour de soi-même* belongs centrally to human nature is based not
only on empirical observations of actual behavior – which, as Rousseau
points out, can easily mislead us into taking contingent but widely
observed characteristics of humans to be part of their invariable nature
(*DI*, 125, 132/ *OC* III, 123, 132) – but also on a more general conception of

the kinds of ends (in this case, physical survival) that nature's creatures must be equipped to achieve if they are to satisfy the most basic strivings of life itself.[22]

The claim that pity, too, belongs to original human nature is no doubt more controversial, both for us and for Rousseau's contemporaries, and perhaps for this reason he devotes more attention to the arguments in support of it. First, Rousseau makes a point of presenting various examples of familiar human behavior that are very difficult to explain without the thesis of natural pity. One obvious example is the readiness of mothers to subordinate their own interests – in extreme circumstances, their lives – to the well-being and comfort of their infants. But since his readers might be inclined to regard this as a special case limited to women or to the very close relation parents have to their own offspring, other examples are needed, and these Rousseau finds in the scenario, adapted from Mandeville, of the personally disinterested (and male) spectator of a child being torn from his mother's breast by a ferocious beast, as well as in the well-known fact that theater audiences are commonly moved to weep for unknown and even fictitious characters whose sufferings they see portrayed on the stage. Second, as in the case of *amour de soi-même*, these considerations are reinforced by speculations about how pity, too, helps to achieve nature's ends: if *amour de soi-même* promotes the preservation of individuals, our natural sensitivity to the pains of others serves an even larger purpose of nature: by "carrying us without reflection to the assistance of those we see suffer," it "contributes to the mutual preservation of the entire species" (*DI*, 154/ *OC* III, 156). This consideration is closely related to Rousseau's claim that, in the original state of nature at least, all human behavior is guided by a single, very general end: "love of well-being is the sole spring of human actions" (*DI*, 163/ *OC* III, 166). In the case of *amour de soi-même* the well-being that is sought is our own; in the case of pity, it is that of others.

Some pages after Rousseau has set out the basic elements of original human nature and shown that the state of nature is peaceful and good,

---

[22] That such a consideration is at work when Rousseau thinks about original human nature is evident in his reference to the "relations established by nature among all animate beings *for their common preservation*" when characterizing natural law in its descriptive or explanatory function (*DI*, 126/*OC* III, 124; emphasis added). See note 9.

he introduces what can look like a third natural disposition: sexual passion (*DI*, 154–7/*OC* III, 157–9). Much of his discussion is devoted to making the plausible point that, because it is unshaped by opinions and imagination, the merely animal desire for sex (what is "physical in the sentiment of love") is a much less powerful and destructive force than the sexual passion – the "moral" element of love, bound up with love for a specific individual and judgments of personal worth, of both the lover and the beloved – that is the cause of so much jealousy and sexual rivalry among "civilized" beings. The more puzzling aspect of Rousseau's discussion of sex arises at a more fundamental level, however.[23] It is difficult to know, partly because he says nothing about it, how sexual desire fits into the two categories of natural dispositions distinguished earlier: is the desire for sex a prompting of *amour de soi-même* or of pity? The initially more plausible alternative is to regard it as a subspecies of *amour de soi-même* since the pleasure sexual behavior brings to the individual creatures that engage in it is clearly central to what motivates it. But sexual desire is also different from the other natural urges associated with *amour de soi-même* – hunger, thirst, the desire for sleep – in that its satisfaction is useless to the being that has acted on it. That is, acting on sexual desire produces no good, beyond the pleasure it brings, for the satisfied individual herself. Obviously, sexual desire does serve a natural end of the species (biological reproduction), but in this respect it is more like pity than *amour de soi-même*. Perhaps it is best to conclude that purely natural sexual desire is motivationally similar to *amour de soi-même* – the promise of their own pleasure is what prompts natural beings to seek sex – but more like pity with respect to the natural good it leads those beings to realize ("mechanically," of course, without their necessarily intending or caring about that good). (Both *Emile* [*E*, 211–15/*OC* IV,

---

[23] This is not the only place in the Second Discourse (or in his other texts) where issues of sex and sexual difference cause Rousseau problems. One obvious example is how gender-differentiated lifestyles are introduced without explanation in Part II of the Second Discourse (*DI*, 164/*OC* III, 168), even though Part I treats the two sexes as virtually indistinguishable by nature. The position of Part I seems to demand an explanation of gender difference in the civilized state as due to contingent social and historical factors. Instead, Rousseau introduces the sexual division of labor – housework for the women, hunting or gathering for the men – as if that arrangement were dictated by nature. He is more consistent in his treatment of gender-related issues, however, when criticizing Locke (*DI*, Note XII). For more on this topic see Joel Schwartz, *The Sexual Politics of Jean-Jacques Rousseau* (University of Chicago Press, 1984).

489–94] and Part II of the Second Discourse [*DI*, 165/*OC* III, 169] make clear that human sexual passion, as distinct from animal desire, is necessarily bound up with *amour propre*, the form of self-love Rousseau introduces only in Part II.)

In addition to these two dispositions, original human nature includes two capacities – one cognitive, the other voluntative – the existence of which is independent of all social and historical development. It is best to speak of these capacities' presence rather than their functioning as natural (or innate), for, as we will see, in the absence of all social relations one of them would be completely latent and the other would be reduced to the very thinnest of functions. It is worthy of note that Rousseau regards both of these as distinctively human capacities, whereas he takes the two dispositions of original human nature discussed above to be shared by both human and non-human animals. This implies that whatever eventually distinguishes human from merely animal existence must have its ultimate source not in *amour de soi-même* or pity but in these two capacities and the modifications they undergo under artificial conditions created by society and history.

The first of these natural capacities is perfectibility, the human species' "faculty of perfecting itself" (*DI*, 208/*OC* III, 211). At its core, perfectibility consists in an ensemble of latent, species-specific cognitive faculties – including the faculties of language, thought, and imagination – which, though present as capacities from birth, remain dormant until more complex circumstances stimulate their development (*DI*, 141, 159/*OC* III, 142, 162).[24] In discussing perfectibility Rousseau is careful to distinguish between latent faculties, on the one hand – the purely natural endowments that make the acquisition of a certain skill or competence in principle possible for a given creature – and actualized faculties, on the other (which include the actual ability, acquired through a process of development, to perform the cognitive functions in question). He is equally careful to include only the former within perfectibility and, so, to ascribe only these bare, unrealized capacities to original human nature: "although the organ of speech is

---

[24] Examples of how external circumstances stimulate the development of a latent faculty can be found in Rousseau's discussion of how new needs, created by changing external conditions, awaken the understanding (*DI*, 142/*OC* III, 143) and at the beginning of Part II, where natural changes in the environment stimulate development of the capacities to compare and to reflect (*DI*, 161–2/*OC* III, 165).

natural to man, speech itself is . . . not natural to him" (*DI*, 207/*OC* III, 210). As Rousseau emphasizes again and again, whatever development of these natural capacities actually takes place in humans depends on "the fortuitous convergence of several foreign causes that might never have arisen and without which [man] would have remained eternally in his primitive condition" (*DI*, 159/*OC* III, 162). The difference, then, between humans and other animals with respect to the cognitive capacities that belong to perfectibility is not, to take a specific example, that humans always possess or inevitably develop language skills, whereas other animals do not; the difference, rather, is that humans have the inborn potential, given the right external circumstances, to develop and use language, whereas other animals lack this potential entirely, regardless of the circumstances they live under.[25]

As many commentators have already pointed out,[26] perfectibility – a term of art that Rousseau himself introduced into philosophical discourse (*OC* III, 1, 317–18) – is a potentially misleading name for what it is meant to designate. It does not, for example, refer to some innate tendency or drive humans have to improve themselves and their condition over time, to come closer and closer to a state of "perfection." Whatever type of perfection is at issue here, it is manifestly not *moral* perfection. On the contrary, Rousseau takes very seriously the possibility – and in a limited sense affirms this speculation in Part II – that "this distinctive and almost unlimited faculty [might be] the source of all of man's miseries" and the cause of "his errors and vices" (*DI*, 141/ *OC* III, 142). In other words, ascribing perfectibility to original human nature is not in any way an expression of optimism about the fate of humans, nor is it a claim about their inherent goodness or tendency to actualize their natural potential. Instead, the obviously teleological connotations of the term must be construed very weakly: human beings by nature possess a number of latent cognitive faculties that are in principle capable of being perfected in the relatively meager sense of

[25] The pre-Darwinian aspects of Rousseau's view hardly need to be pointed out: (1) with respect to the capacity for development and change the human species is fundamentally different from all other species; and (2) the latent capacities of the human species are themselves given by nature for once and for all, prior to any actual development, even if how these pre-set capacities manifest themselves concretely depends on historical and natural contingencies.
[26] See, for example, Victor Gourevitch's remarks in his introduction to the Second Discourse (*DI*, xxix–xx).

undergoing qualitative development from the simpler to the more complex.[27] Again, "perfection" does not imply that there is a single, determinate form or telos that each faculty ought under ideal conditions to develop towards, nor that there is some disposition internal to human nature that makes such development necessary or even probable.

Strictly speaking, perfectibility involves slightly more than the various specific cognitive faculties discussed above; it is itself said to be a faculty – a "faculty of perfecting oneself" (*faculté de se perfectioner*). What Rousseau has in mind in attributing to humans a general faculty of self-perfection, over and above their specific cognitive capacities, is far from obvious. It is not, to repeat, an internal drive towards development since Rousseau insists that in the absence of contingent external conditions, human development might well never have occurred. If one looks carefully at the paragraphs surrounding his statements that perfectibility is itself a faculty (and not just a collection of specific latent capacities) (*DI*, 141–2, 208/*OC* III, 142–3, 211), one gets the impression that what is most important in this claim is the general point that the human species, in contrast to all other animal species, is highly malleable in the sense that social and historical circumstances are able to transform it in numerous and fundamental ways, making the human being of today similar to the statue of Glaucus invoked in the very first paragraph of the Second Discourse. Like this time- and storm-ravaged statue, contemporary humans have been so altered "by all the changes that the succession of times and of things [has] wrought in [their] original constitution" that their original nature is now "almost unrecognizable" (*DI*, 124/*OC* III, 122). (That in present circumstances our original natural is *almost* unrecognizable is important, for otherwise the task of discerning that nature, so crucial to Rousseau's undertaking, would be

---

[27] It is possible, though hard to determine with certainty, that Rousseau did have something more robust in mind than the position I attribute to him here – something like the view that there is a more or less set pattern (or a small number of possible patterns) that human development, once external circumstances set the process of development in motion, must take and that the capacities in question are sufficiently determined in advance by nature that it makes sense to speak of a latent faculty being perfected in the sense of being fully actualized, or developed in the manner and to the extent "intended by nature." It may be possible to find this more robust view of natural development in *Emile* (though, as far as I know, the term "perfectibility" appears nowhere in that text). In any case, the meager view I attribute to Rousseau here is all that the Second Discourse requires or explicitly invokes in its explanation and critique of social inequality.

impossible.) Understanding Rousseau's claim in this way does not add much new content to the thesis of perfectibility, but it is not difficult to see why it merits special attention: this aspect of perfectibility is essential to the Second Discourse's principal undertaking, for the enormous malleability of the human species – its astounding ability to develop in a nearly limitless variety of ways and to acquire fundamentally new characteristics and capacities – is crucial to the claim of Rousseau here that social inequality, though pervasive in the world we know, is not a necessary product of nature (or of human nature) itself.

The second capacity Rousseau ascribes to original human nature is a primitive form of free will – a "power . . . of choosing" – which he describes as the ability to follow or resist what could loosely be called instinct[28] or the promptings of nature: "Nature commands every animal, and the beast obeys. Man experiences the same impressions but recognizes himself as free to acquiesce or to resist" (*DI*, 141/*OC* III, 141–2). When Rousseau introduces this feature of original human nature, he makes it clear that to ascribe freedom of this sort to human beings is to ascribe to them a "metaphysical" property (*DI*, 140/*OC* III, 141), by which he means a property that lifts humans above the realm of pure nature (and hence above all other animals), understood as a domain governed entirely by deterministic causal laws: "in the power of willing . . . are found purely spiritual acts about which nothing is explained by the laws of mechanics" (*DI*, 141/*OC* III, 142).

The ascription of free will to beings that lack language and reason is, as Rousseau recognizes, a tricky matter. This is why he is careful to characterize the free will of original human nature as thinly as possible. Usually he characterizes our original capacity for free agency merely in terms of something we lack, namely, the instincts that determine with strict necessity the behavior of other, non-human animals: whereas "the beast cannot deviate from the rule prescribed to it" by nature, the human being, even at his most primitive, can choose – freely, without being determined to do so – to act on or to disregard the urges nature supplies to him (*DI*, 140/*OC* III, 141). In including free will as part of original human nature Rousseau means to ascribe to us an innate

---

[28] Another way of formulating the difference between humans and mere animals is to say that the latter have instincts, which determine their behavior with necessity, whereas the former ("perhaps") have none (*DI*, 135, 141/*OC* III, 143).

capacity for spontaneous choosing that is undetermined by either causes or reasons, a spontaneity best characterized as a not being necessitated to respond to nature's stimuli in specific, predetermined ways. Of course, free will, like the other original characteristics of humans once they have undergone development, will look much different in civilized conditions from the bare form it takes in primitive beings. Free will as it appears in Part II of the Second Discourse will amount to choosing which of one's desires to satisfy in accordance with one's own "opinions" concerning who one is and what one's good consists in.[29] (And in *The Social Contract* Rousseau will point to a yet more complex form of freedom available only to humans living under just political institutions: a species of autonomy that consists in determining one's actions in accordance with laws that come from oneself (*SC*, I.8.iii). The Second Discourse, in which autonomy does not appear, delivers the negative part of Rousseau's argument for the claim that this most elevated form of freedom is impossible except within a legitimate republic.)

Whereas Rousseau's ascription of perfectibility to original human nature is relatively unproblematic – since the latent capacities he is interested in are capacities we already find realized in actual human beings – his position regarding free will in the state of nature is more controversial, especially its claim that free choosing is possible in the absence of language and reason. Before rejecting Rousseau's claim, however, it is important to be clear as to what exactly it asserts. Above all, it is important to remind oneself – and to be prepared to do so again and again while interpreting the Second Discourse – that the state of nature has a purely hypothetical status for Rousseau, that it aims not to describe actual or actually possible human beings but to develop a picture of what humans *would* be like in the absence of all modification of their original nature by (contingent) social or historical circumstances. Rousseau is not claiming, then, that at some time *before* they lived in societies, and *before* they possessed language and thought, actual human beings inhabited primeval forests like animals, spontaneously choosing which of their urges to act on. Instead, his

---

[29] Elsewhere Rousseau describes this form of freedom as "my being able to will only what is suitable to me, or what I regard as such, without anything foreign to me determining me" (*E*, 280/*OC* IV, 586).

account of original human nature – one part of his vision of the state
of nature more generally – is meant to function as an analytic device
that separates out the different independent and fundamental endowments of human individuals (in abstraction from all social circumstances) that must be presupposed and brought together in order to
comprehend the basic features of all actual forms of human life as we
know it in its astounding variety. Just as pity was introduced into the
set of natural dispositions because *amour de soi-même* alone could not
explain certain forms of human behavior that we know to be real, so
the hypothesis of free will is required in order to do justice to some
basic features of human reality as we know and understand it. To
attribute free will to original human nature, then, is to claim that some
fundamental element would be missing from a theory of human
nature that attempted to grasp the human condition in all its complexity while restricting itself to the cognitive capacities of perfectibility and the dispositions of *amour de soi-même* and pity. What such
a theory would be unable to accommodate in its picture of the human
condition is the realm of the voluntary – the entire range of phenomena that we take to be bound up with the human will, the
capacity of humans to determine their own actions rather than be
determined from without. Rousseau's thought is that if we are to end
up with a picture of civilized humans that has room for free agency,
some basis for that freedom must be located in original human nature
itself. This is because anything that counts as genuine freedom for
Rousseau must incorporate an element of metaphysical independence
from the causal laws of nature (*DI*, 140/*OC* III, 141),[30] and this aspect
of human action can never emerge from a developmental story based
solely on a theory of human nature that, having at its disposal only
perfectibility and natural dispositions, is restricted to purely naturalistic

---

[30] It is an interesting question, raised to me by Paul Guyer, whether Rousseau actually needs this
strong conception of metaphysical freedom in order to sustain the claims about human
freedom most important to him in the Second Discourse (and elsewhere). In other words,
does the social conception of freedom that matters most to him there – the absence of
domination by others – require the metaphysical thesis of free will? Or, in Kantian terms,
does Rousseau's moral and political project require transcendental freedom in addition to
practical freedom? (Immanuel Kant, *Critique of Pure Reason*, trans. Paul Guyer and Allen
W. Wood [Cambridge University Press, 1998], A802/B830). In distinction to Rousseau (and
in agreement with Hegel), I am inclined to answer these questions negatively. See also note 14
of Chapter 3.

explanations. If spontaneity is to be found at some advanced point in the civilizing process, Rousseau reasons, it must be present in some form among the original endowments that undergo development in civilization since a metaphysical difference of this kind – between causally determined nature and self-determining freedom – cannot emerge from the development itself.

Of course, the "phenomena" that we take to be manifestations of free will are not phenomena in the same sense as the examples of behavior appealed to above in support of the hypothesis of natural pity. More precisely, the evidence that grounds the latter is found in empirically observable behavior (and in a general thesis about the natural reproductive ends of living beings), whereas no strictly empirical evidence exists for the hypothesis of free will. That is, the human actions we take to be free can be empirically observed, but that they arise from free self-determination rather than being the necessary effects of antecedent causes explainable by deterministic laws is not in any way suggested by empirical facts themselves. Rousseau is fully aware that his "metaphysical" hypothesis of free will is grounded neither in empirical observation nor in purely theoretical considerations concerning what is required in order to explain empirically observed phenomena (since deterministic laws of nature might well satisfy those ambitions). This is why in other places he calls the hypothesis of free will an "article of faith" and attempts to ground his belief in human freedom in the testimony of his "inner voice," a voice that all humans who will but attend to it are capable of hearing and that evokes in every listener the same "sentiment of [his] freedom": "One may very well disagree with me about this; but I sense it, and this sentiment that speaks to me is stronger than the reason that combats it . . . I consent or I resist; I succumb or I conquer; and I sense perfectly within myself when I do what I wanted to do" (*E*, 280–1/*OC* IV, 585–7).[31] It should be clear, then, that the considerations that motivate Rousseau to include free will among the elements of original human nature are of a different kind from those that motivate the inclusion of perfectibility, *amour de soi-même*, and pity. It is not on the basis of empirical (or any other theoretical) evidence that we take

---

[31] Here, too, Rousseau expresses these points in the voice of the Savoyard vicar, but echoes of the same claims can be found in other texts where Rousseau is clearly speaking in his own voice.

humans to be free; rather, support for this hypothesis comes from a different source, from a "looking within" that is available only from the first-person perspective and that delivers a kind of evidence one can have only in relation to one's own actions.[32]

Properly understood, then, Rousseau's ascription of free will to original human nature is not distant, with respect to both content and the grounds that support it, from Kant's well-known claim that humans possess a freedom to choose, an *arbitrium liberum*, that distinguishes them from non-human animals, which possess only an *arbitrium brutum*, where the difference consists in the fact that the former is *affected* (or influenced) but not *determined* by natural impulses, whereas the latter is always simply determined by the natural impulses it has.[33] The most significant respect in which Rousseau's position diverges from Kant's – a substantial difference, to be sure – lies in its claim that the undetermined character of the will is prior to – existentially independent of – reason. (For Kant, as I read him,[34] the absence of foreign determination that characterizes the *arbitrium liberum* is possible only for creatures that also possess pure practical reason – that is, for creatures that can understand themselves as obligated by, and can determine their wills in accordance with, the supreme principle of pure practical reason, the moral law. If this is correct, then free will, even in the minimal sense in which Rousseau ascribes it to original human nature, cannot exist independently of reason.) Despite his similarities to Kant on other issues, with respect to the relation between freedom and reason Rousseau stands in the other great tradition of thinking about the will, voluntarism, according to which free choice does not require the exercise of reason. For the latter tradition there is something akin to spontaneous, unguided "picking," and this is precisely the type of freedom of will that Rousseau attributes to original human nature.

A further issue on which readers of the Second Discourse sometimes disagree is how freedom and perfectibility are related. If the account of original freedom given above is correct, then, strictly speaking, the two

---

[32] In Note II Rousseau even hints, citing Buffon, that an "internal sense" of this sort is necessary for achieving the knowledge of human nature that the Second Discourse requires (*DI*, 189/*OC* III, 196).

[33] Kant, *Critique of Pure Reason*, A802/B830.

[34] In understanding Kant's position in this way I have been influenced by Henry E. Allison, *Kant's Theory of Freedom* (Cambridge University Press, 1990), 136.

endowments are completely independent of each other: the spontaneity of the will does not require reason or language, and the mere existence of the latent cognitive capacities does not in any way depend on the presence or exercise of will. The question becomes trickier, however, when one asks whether the *development* of perfectibility – the actual unfolding of our latent capacities – depends on free will. Rousseau's view is that it does, but it is important to be clear about what this claim entails. The development associated with perfectibility requires the exercise of freedom, but in a very specific sense: the development itself is not willed (consciously intended) by the being that undergoes it but is an unintended consequence of freely chosen actions directed at other ends. When adverse climatic conditions and increasing competition from animals led primitive humans to fashion fishing hooks and to invent bows and arrows, which in turn developed their capacity to perceive relations among things, these creative deeds – free, because, although motivated by *amour de soi-même*, they were spontaneous deviations from "instinct" – were aimed at satisfying their hunger, not at perfecting their capacities. Getting clear on the interplay between freedom and perfectibility is important because it enables us to understand how the contingent development of human beings and their society that plays so large a role in the Second Discourse both is and is not the product of human will: it is the result of free human activity – a state of affairs that we, not god or nature, introduce into the world – but it is not an intended product of our will. In other words, the process of civilization (and consequent degradation of the human species) depicted in Part II is to be understood as our own doing – as something we are responsible for in the sense that it is the product of our own free choices and, as such, could have turned out differently – but not as a development we can be morally blamed for (since we did not intend it and could not, in the less developed stage, have foreseen its consequences). Even if "most of our ills are of our own making" (*DI*, 137/*OC* III, 138), they are not the effects of evil wills (or of original sin). The importance of this doctrine for Rousseau's project is obvious: it enables God and nature – and us, too – to emerge free of blame, or "justified," from the account of the human species' decline (*DI*, 197/*OC* III, 202), and it shifts the responsibility for reforming the world we inhabit onto us, the free creators (or re-creators) of the very features of the world that the critique of social inequality tells us ought to be changed.

There is a prominent feature of Rousseau's state of nature (and its concomitant account of human nature) that has elicited much criticism from his readers and that I have barely touched on thus far. This is the thoroughly individualistic character of original human nature, as reflected in the repeatedly emphasized circumstance that the state of nature is completely void of social relations and that original human nature lacks all capacities and dispositions that concern or depend on social existence. This atomistic perspective is so fundamental to Rousseau's vision of the state of nature that his conception of original human nature could also be characterized as an attempt to capture the basic dispositions and capacities that nature bestows on all human beings *qua individuals*, in abstraction from all relations they might have to other humans. In other words, in ascribing *amour de soi-même*, pity, perfectibility, and free will to original human nature, Rousseau is claiming that all are features of human beings that individuals could in principle possess on their own, that is, even were they to exist outside all society (even though real humans never do in fact exist in that isolated state). Rather than reject this individualistic conception of human nature out of hand, it is worth trying to understand why Rousseau proceeds in this way, given that, as I argue here, he does not ultimately fall into the error most readers take him to be guilty of, namely, regarding all that belongs to our social being as external to our "true" nature (in the normative sense).

One way of understanding Rousseau's individualistic conception of the state of nature is to see it as an attempt to avoid the Stoic principle of sociability (*DI*, 127/*OC* III, 126), which later natural law theorists, especially Grotius and Barbeyrac, included in their pictures of human nature. For these thinkers sociability was understood as an innate sentiment, intrinsic to all human individuals, that inclined them both to care about the welfare of others independently of its relation to their own particular good and to seek out social relations of various kinds for more than merely instrumental reasons. Rousseau's most important reason for rejecting sociability appears to be that it encloses too much of the social within the realm of the natural, blinding us to the artificial and, above all, the malleable character of our social institutions and our desires to have bonds to others. For him the desires that lead us to establish families, states, and economic relations are cultural and historical products, and no "natural" blueprints for these institutions can be read off any innate human drives of the sort sociability was taken to be. While Rousseau's relation to the thesis of sociability is complex, it would not be too far off the mark to say that what replaces it in his picture of human psychology is the combination of pity, a "natural" sentiment, and *amour propre*, an "artificial" passion. The former helps to explain how individuals can be positively disposed to willing the good (or the absence of suffering) of other individuals, whereas – as will become clearer in the following chapter – the latter accounts for the persistent need civilized humans experience to establish and maintain social relations.[35]

Perhaps the best way to make sense of Rousseau's individualistic approach is to see how it follows from his more basic aim of determining what humans would be like in a wholly non-*artificial* state. The key here is to understand why he posits so close a link between the natural (that which is devoid of artificiality) and asociality. The basis for this connection lies in the thought that social relations are indispensable to and inseparable from the development and exercise of the very capacities that artificiality depends on. Given that the mark of artificiality is the intervention of human actions mediated by opinion, then artificiality necessarily goes hand in hand with social relations if it is the case that humans can develop and exercise their capacity to judge only in society. This is precisely Rousseau's view, for he takes language and thought – two prerequisites of judgment and agency – to be possible only for social beings. At the same time, he holds that enduring social relations bring with them, more or less automatically,[36] the development of capacities such as language and reason, which inevitably introduces opinion into human affairs. His view, in other words, is that there could be no genuinely social existence without language and thought and, conversely, no language or thought for beings that lived as isolated an existence as those fictional inhabitants of the original state of nature. From this it

---

[35] See also Chapter 2, note 18. For more on pity and its relation to sociability in the Second Discourse, see Charles L. Griswold, "Smith and Rousseau in Dialogue: Sympathy, *Pitié*, Spectatorship and Narrative," in Vivienne Brown and Samuel Fleischacker, eds., *The Philosophy of Adam Smith: Essays Commemorating the 250th Anniversary of "The Theory of Moral Sentiments"*, vol. V of *The Adam Smith Review* (Oxford: Routledge, 2010), 59–84.

[36] The thesis I am attributing to Rousseau is that language and reason develop more or less automatically *in the presence of social relations*. This is not the same thesis rejected above in the discussion of perfectibility, namely, that human individuals by nature possess an inner drive or tendency to actualize their latent capacities.

follows that in order to get at what humans would be like "as nature formed" them, before our "original constitution" was "altered in the lap of society" (*DI*, 124/*OC* III, 122), it is necessary to look at them in abstraction from social relations.

Yet, even if this explains why Rousseau links the natural with the asocial, it merely pushes our original question back a step: if humans never do exist in a condition void of language, thought, and social relations, and if (as we will see in Chapter 3) such a condition is incompatible with what Rousseau regards as a fitting existence for humans, why is he so intent on figuring out what original human nature is like? Rousseau's full answer to this question is complex, and laying it out will occupy a large portion of the rest of this book. Still, it is possible now to grasp part of that answer. Since the idea of original human nature is an analytical device intended to separate out nature's contribution to what we are actually like from our artificial features – those due to social and historical circumstances (and, hence, to circumstances produced by our own intervention in the world) – the question above can be reformulated as follows: why is Rousseau so intent on figuring out what in our current condition comes from *nature* and what originates in our own *freedom* (since society and history are our own, if usually unintended, creations)? The answer to this reformulated question is contained in what has already been said about the significance of the distinction between the natural and the artificial for Rousseau, namely, that it marks the dividing line between what is imposed on us necessarily and invariably by nature and what, because it depends ultimately on our free choice, is contingent, variable, and up to us in the sense that it is in principle alterable by our own activity. In view of this, it is of great importance that the dispositions and faculties that Rousseau ascribes to original human nature are relatively meager in both number and content. For part of the aim of his account of human nature is to explain the nearly limitless diversity of forms of life that historical and anthropological observations show to be possible for human beings. Yet, even though Rousseau is among the most radical proponents of the variability of human culture and the mutability of our original dispositions, his account of original human nature also sets some very broad natural limits to human variability – limits that will function to dismiss certain responses to the evils that arise in Part II of the Second

Discourse as utopian and that will have important normative implications for the kinds of behavior it is appropriate to expect of human beings, given the constraints of their original nature.

SOCIAL INEQUALITIES DO NOT HAVE THEIR SOURCE IN HUMAN NATURE

Let us return now to the main thesis that the original state of nature, together with its picture of human nature, is supposed to establish, namely, that social inequalities do not have their source in nature. As I indicated above, one part of this thesis consists in the claim that original human nature alone provides no psychological incentives that explain why humans would be motivated to seek out the inequalities they in fact create. In other words, neither of the two species of motivation that arise from the original dispositions of humans inclines them or gives them reason to seek out inequalities (other than perhaps very short-term advantages that special circumstances might make instrumentally desirable). In the case of pity this is obvious: although it is conceivable that short-term advantage might in unusual circumstances serve the end of alleviating others' suffering – for example, when an aggressor who seeks to inflict pain on a weaker third party has great physical power – there is no reason to think that sensitivity to others' pains should systematically motivate natural human beings to seek out inequalities, either for their own sake or as a means to pity's distinctive end (reducing the pains of others).[37] The situation is more complicated in the case of *amour de soi-même*. Here too, however, Rousseau's claim is that there is nothing in purely natural self-interestedness that would lead humans in the state of nature to seek out inequalities for their own sake: the goods sought by *amour de soi-même* – food, shelter, and sleep, for example – are all non-relative (or non-positional) goods and, so, neither consist in nor intrinsically depend on advantages over others. How well my good night's sleep satisfies my own need for rest is completely independent of how well

---

[37] One should ask, though: could there be such an aggressor in the pure state of nature? Regardless of how one answers this question, one should bear in mind that what is most important to Rousseau throughout is the claim that, even if possible in isolated instances, such scenarios would have to be rare and inconsequential in the natural state; in other words, nothing in nature systematically encourages the establishment of inequalities.

or poorly those around me have passed the night, so the mere wish to sleep well gives me no reason to want to sleep better than others.

But might not *amour de soi-même* provide creatures that possess it with a standing incentive to seek inequalities as a *means* to its ends? Many philosophers are inclined to answer affirmatively – Hobbes is the most famous example and surely the main interlocutor Rousseau has in mind here[38] – and common sense is quick to agree, for it is easy (for us) to imagine plausible scenarios in which getting what one wants or needs for oneself requires outdoing others. It is important to be clear, though, about the background assumptions that inform such scenarios. One situation philosophers often appeal to when thinking about self-love in general is that of several self-interested individuals who face the task of cutting a pie and distributing its pieces among themselves and whose self-interestedness motivates each to seek to maximize the size of the piece she receives.[39] Given these two assumptions – the desire to maximize one's lot without limit and a fixed amount of the good to be distributed – it is easy to see how humans could be motivated to strive for conditions of inequality. One way of understanding what Rousseau is up to in painting such a meager picture of original human nature, however, is to see him as calling into question the naturalness of these assumed conditions. With respect to the first, Rousseau would counter that nothing internal to purely natural *amour de soi-même* can explain the desire to *maximize* some good that one desires or needs (as opposed to merely acquiring enough to satisfy a given need or urge). In other words, although extremely common in human societies we are familiar with, the desire to maximize – and especially the desire to maximize without limit – is not a desire that nature imposes on humans, which is to say: it is not

---

[38] Thomas Hobbes, *Leviathan* (Oxford University Press, 1998), Chapter 11, §§1–3; Chapter 17, §7.

[39] Normally no distinction is made in such examples between different species of self-interestedness. It is important to bear in mind that Rousseau's precise way of distinguishing between *amour de soi-même* and *amour propre* is unique to him and a philosophical innovation of fundamental significance. Even though some figures before Rousseau distinguished these two forms of self-love, his specific understanding of the contrast is new. For more on the history of conceptions of self-love, see Christopher Brooke, *Philosophic Pride: Stoicism and Political Thought from Lipsius to Rousseau* (Princeton University Press, 2012); and Pierre Force, *Self-Interest before Adam Smith: A Genealogy of Economic Science* (Cambridge University Press, 2003).

implicit in the ends of self-preservation and purely animal well-being alone. Instead, the desire to get as much as one can depends on opinions concerning what one's good consists in, as well as on acquired habits and dispositions, and these for Rousseau belong not to the domain of nature but to the realm of what is artificial, variable, socially shaped, and the result of human freedom. The desires and needs that come from natural *amour de soi-même* alone have a natural and relatively easily reached satiation point, beyond which they cease to make demands on their bearers, until, of course, the regular cycles of nature reignite them. The (to us) familiar phenomena of desires that exceed natural needs or that have no clear satiation point originate for Rousseau in contingent social and historical circumstances rather than in nature, and getting clear on the conditions under which they arise is a main task of Part II.

One might think that all that is needed to derive from *amour de soi-même* an incentive for seeking inequality is to switch examples and focus instead on the equally familiar scenario in which, say, four shipwrecked individuals find themselves on a lifeboat that can support only three. Here, it might be thought, is a plausible scenario that, in showing how *amour de soi-même* can give rise to a desire for advantage over others, derives a disposition to create inequality from nature itself. This second example comes closer to achieving its goal than the first, insofar as it avoids presupposing an artificial impulse to maximize one's goods and attributes to individuals only an aim internal to natural *amour de soi-même*, self-preservation. It is important to note, however, that this example works only by building the assumption of scarcity into its imagined scenario: the environment into which individuals are placed is by hypothesis lacking in sufficient resources to satisfy the biological needs of all. Rousseau does not deny that such scenarios are possible even in a world completely untouched by the artificial conditions that human opinion and will introduce into the world. For this reason it is not incorrect to say that *under certain special circumstances*, the desire to gain advantage over others – the impulse to create inequalities – is a possible consequence of purely natural *amour de soi-même*. It is significant, however, that even here individuals desire inequality only instrumentally (in order to secure their own survival) and that this end, like all ends of *amour de soi-même*, is ultimately indifferent to the success or failure others have in pursuing the same end. Even if achieving one's end in this scenario requires securing advantage over another (the one who finds no room on the lifeboat), this advantage is not internal to *amour de soi-même*'s final end of survival but is desired only because external conditions make it impossible to survive without it. A similar conclusion is suggested by the less extreme example of ordinary hunger: the only conditions under which *amour de soi-même* alone provides a hungry creature with an incentive to seek more of something than others – more food, more force, or more influence, for example – is when having *more* is necessary to satisfying its only ultimate concern, having *sufficient* food, regardless of what others have, to still its own discomfort. As both examples show, seeking advantage over others is a rational strategy for *amour de soi-même* only under conditions of scarcity.

This leads us directly into what I labeled above the second part of Rousseau's thesis that social inequalities do not have their source in nature: the claim that there are no necessary or invariable features of the external world to which humans must relate in order to satisfy their natural needs that necessitate or encourage the creation of inequalities beyond those they are born with. What has become plain from the preceding considerations is that Rousseau's denial that social inequalities have their source in nature depends on an assumption regarding the extent and significance of natural scarcity, an assumption expressed in his depiction of the original state of nature as a condition of plenty that makes labor, conflict, and private property both unnecessary and undesirable (*DI*, 134–5/*OC* III, 134–5). Many readers are inclined simply to dismiss Rousseau's claims about the natural fertility of the earth as manifestations of a naïve and unjustified faith in the goodness of nature. In order to assess the appropriateness of his assumption, however, it is necessary to be clear about precisely what it entails and what role it plays in his account of inequality's origin.

By assuming a natural condition of plenty Rousseau does not mean to deny that scarcity of some sort generally plays a prominent role in human affairs and therefore must be taken seriously by social philosophy. The point of his assumption, rather, is to make a claim about the kind of scarcity that plays so prominent role in human society and to, as it were, locate its source. Rousseau's claim is that the vast majority of the scarcity that affects actual human societies has not natural but social origins. It is, in other words, not a necessary consequence of general facts about human and non-human nature but is instead socially created – which is to say: it results from social arrangements that are themselves the (mostly unforeseen) consequences of human actions and opinions, which, because free, could also have had different outcomes. Although Rousseau can admit that natural scarcity is possible, he is committed to denying that it is an invariable or fundamental feature of the human condition. Moreover, when it does exist – in cases where actual scarcity is due in some part to purely natural factors – it nearly always plays a negligible role in comparison to scarcity that has its source in social, humanly created circumstances. When Rousseau describes with enthusiasm the abundance of the state of nature, he should not be understood to be making a factual claim about the natural availability of the resources required for human survival but to be proposing instead a sort of theoretical abstraction. (Here, again, it is important to bear in mind the hypothetical, analytical function of the state of nature.) The assumption of natural plenty, by eliminating from view nature's contribution to scarcity, serves to direct our attention away from the type of scarcity that common sense normally, and mistakenly, takes to be the only or most significant kind in order to focus exclusively on the type that Rousseau – this is the substantive claim underlying his assumption of natural abundance – takes to account for the by far greatest part of the scarcity that plays a role in producing inequalities in actual societies. In this respect Rousseau's position on scarcity exemplifies a general tendency of his thought towards *de-naturalizing*, and thereby de-mystifying, *the social*.[40] In this case de-naturalizing scarcity consists in showing that scarcity does not come from nature in either of two possible senses: there is nothing, first, in the constitution of nature itself – in the relation between human biological needs and the earth's natural resources – or, second, in the character of unsocialized pity and *amour de soi-même* that would explain why scarcity is a necessary or widespread feature of human social life. Much of the force of this argument depends on seeing

---

[40] Rousseau's most explicit reference to his project of de-mystifying the social occurs in a remark criticizing earlier attempts to describe human nature: "philosophers ... have all felt the necessity of going back as far as the state of nature, but none of them has reached it . . . [A]ll of them, continually speaking of need, greed, oppression, desires, and pride, transferred to the state of nature ideas they had taken from society. They spoke of savage man and depicted civil man" (*DI*, 132/*OC* III, 132).

how, in Part II, the introduction of both artificial social conditions and a "non-natural" passion enables Rousseau to explain the powerful tendency of humans to produce scarcity – of many types and of great magnitude – and hence to explain why extensive inequalities are nearly unavoidable in the social state.

We are now in a position to summarize the main elements of Rousseau's argument in Part I of the Second Discourse that nature is not the source of social inequality. His argument can be understood as a rejection of three possible natural explanations of social inequality (as well as all combinations of the three). First, social inequalities are not the direct or necessary consequences of natural inequalities. Although the latter exist, they explain neither the existence of social inequalities in general nor why particular individuals end up where they do within existing hierarchies. If natural inequalities matter at all in the constitution of social inequality, they play only a very minor role and make themselves felt, if ever, only within a context of social practices and institutions that humans, not nature, are responsible for creating and that therefore could in principle be otherwise than they are. Second, the two natural passions of humans – pity and *amour de soi-même* – provide no incentives for humans to seek to establish inequalities (except in certain conditions of scarcity) since the final ends of each are indifferent to how well or how poorly other individuals fare in achieving their own natural ends. Third, there is no reason to believe that the conditions under which pity and *amour de soi-même* could lead humans to seek advantage over others as a means to achieving their final ends – the conditions of scarcity – would necessarily or typically obtain in a world where desires remain untransformed by unnatural passions and where artificial social institutions have not made scarcity a systematic necessity.

The thought that leads us into the topics covered in the next chapter is the following: if social inequality is to be understood as our creation rather than nature's, we need some way of understanding what motivates us to create it, and, as we have seen, *amour de soi-même* and pity provide no such explanation. In Chapter 2 we will examine the positive part of Rousseau's view on the origin of inequality, his account of how systematic social inequalities are made possible, and nearly unavoidable, once a certain "artificial" passion, *amour propre*, is added to his picture of original human nature.

Amour propre *is the source of social inequality*

The aim of this chapter is to reconstruct the positive part of Rousseau's answer to the Second Discourse's first main question: where does social inequality come from? Its task is to uncover the various "non-natural" factors that, according to that account, must come together in order to explain the pervasiveness of inequality in actual human societies, and in carrying out this task it explicates one part of the Second Discourse's well-known thesis that "most of our ills are of our own making" (*DI*, 137/*OC* III, 138). Rousseau's positive answer to the question of inequality's origin is surprisingly complex and difficult to reconstruct, in part because the logic of his position – how the various elements of his account work together to explain inequality – is buried within a developmental narrative that, as I suggested in the preceding chapter, ought not to be understood literally, as a recounting of actual historical events. The narrative structure of Part II; Rousseau's repeated emphasis on the search for "origins"; his description of his project as a genealogy (*OC* IV, 936); his insistence that the "events" he describes "could have occurred in several ways" or "might never have arisen" at all (*DI*, 159/*OC* III, 162) – all these factors tend to obscure the systematic, atemporal, in short, the philosophical,[1] character of the Second Discourse's explanation of inequality.

Indeed, it seems likely that most readers when confronted with the question this chapter attempts to answer – if nature is not the source of social inequality, then what is? – will be tempted to locate Rousseau's response in *history*, not least because the opposition between nature and history occupies a prominent place in the Second Discourse, the very

---

[1] Which is to say, philosophical according to Rousseau's (and most of the tradition's) understanding of what a philosophical explanation consists in.

first page of which highlights the contrast between "man ... as nature formed him" and "the transformations that the succession of times and things ... produced in his original constitution" (*DI*, 124/*OC* III, 122). History, to follow up on this suggestion, is presumably something that humans, given their free will, have a hand in shaping. If history, unlike nature, is in some sense up to us, then making it the source of social inequalities would certainly fit with Rousseau's claim that those inequalities are created by us rather than imposed by nature. Moreover, if history were the source of social inequality, it would be easy to understand why Rousseau undertakes a project of genealogy: if we could trace the historical record back to the point where social inequalities first arose, we might be able to see not only where, but also perhaps why, they came about – and maybe even whether they are justified.

The obvious problem with this suggestion is that Rousseau's genealogy is manifestly not a history in any straightforward sense. As we saw in the previous chapter, Rousseau denies that the state of nature depicted in Part I is to be understood as factually true (*DI*, 125, 132/*OC* III, 123, 132–3). In addition to this, he also denies – and just as explicitly – that the "developments" that lead humans beyond that state are to be taken for real historical events. Instead, he describes the narrative of Part II as a "hypothetical history" (*DI*, 128/*OC* III, 127) that is grounded not in facts but in "conjectures based solely on the nature of man" (*DI*, 132/*OC* III, 133). Rousseau repeats this claim at the end of Part I (*DI*, 159, 160/*OC* III, 162, 163), and, finally, as if to dispel any doubts that might linger about the historical status of his narrative, he emphasizes the point once more in the Second Discourse's closing paragraph: "I have tried to give an account of the origin and the progress of inequality ... insofar as these things can be deduced from the nature of man by the light of reason alone" (*DI*, 188/*OC* III, 193). It is not, then, only the original state of nature but also the "events" depicted in Part II that are to be understood as hypothetical and conjectural posits rather than as attempts to write a factually true history of human development. At the same time it must not be forgotten that the Second Discourse abounds with empirical examples from historical and anthropological sources that appear to be offered as evidence for the hypothetical history it proposes. Before ending our reconstruction of the Second Discourse, then, we must take up the matter of why empirical facts of this kind are nevertheless relevant to a history that takes itself to be only conjectural and hypothetical. (I return to this issue in Chapter 4.)

These initially bewildering features of Rousseau's narrative merely underscore the importance of figuring out what kind of project he takes himself to be engaged in when inquiring into inequality's origin. If progress is to be made here, it is best to begin by paying attention to Rousseau's own description of the task that faces him at the end of Part I: "Having proved that inequality is scarcely perceptible in the state of nature and that its influence there is almost nil, it remains for me to show its origin and progress in the successive developments of the human mind (*l'esprit humain*)" (*DI*, 159/*OC* III, 162). The important, but also startling, claim of this passage is that the key to explaining inequality's origin lies in discovering how *the human mind* must differ from what it is like in the original state of nature if social inequality is to assume a significant place in human affairs. If Rousseau is not concerned with the actual history of human development, it is plausible to suppose that the question that interests him instead is analytic in character: which new element (or elements) of *human psychology* must be added to his account of original human nature in order to explain why humans create inequalities beyond those that nature bestows on them? That this psychological question is indeed Rousseau's primary concern is borne out by the story he goes on to tell in Part II. Yet saying that psychology is his primary concern does not imply that it his only concern, and, as we will see, much of the difficulty in reconstructing the Second Discourse's argument lies in understanding how psychological and non-psychological factors interrelate in explaining widespread social inequality. For now, however, as a first step, I focus exclusively on the "developments of the human mind" that Rousseau himself singles out as the most important element of his account.

AMOUR PROPRE

Although Rousseau notes a number of developments that take humans beyond their original state – the beginnings of leisure, of language, of families and even nations[2] – what he explicitly points to

---

[2] These are nations without states, peoples united not by political institutions but by ties of blood and a shared way of life.

as "the first step towards inequality" (*DI*, 165–6/*OC* III, 169) is a
psychological phenomenon: the emergence of an artificial, inherently
social passion that he calls (later in the text) *amour propre*. Here is the
important passage in which *amour propre*, without being named as
such, makes its first appearance in the Second Discourse:

> It became customary to gather in front of their huts or around a large tree;
> song and dance ... became ... the occupation of idle men and women
> gathered together. Each began to look at the others and to want to be looked
> at himself, and public esteem acquired a value. The one who sang or danced
> the best, the handsomest, the strongest, the most skillful, or the most
> eloquent came to be the most highly regarded, and this was the first step
> towards inequality and at the same time towards vice. (*DI*, 166/*OC* III, 169)

If my interpretive claims above are correct, the point of this passage is
to reveal the core of Rousseau's answer to the first of the Second
Discourse's two questions: it isolates *amour propre* – a passion to be
looked at, to be highly regarded, to acquire public esteem or respect –
as the principal source of social inequality.[3]

What, then, is *amour propre*, and why is it the principal source of
social inequality?[4] As its name indicates, *amour propre* is a kind of self-
love, and as we saw in our earlier discussion of *amour de soi-même*,
'self-love' in this context means simply self-interestedness. In the
case of humans, to love yourself (in general) is simply to care about
your own good and to be disposed to pursue whatever you take
that good to be. Yet clearly *amour propre* is something more specific
than self-interestedness in general since, as Rousseau makes clear in
the supremely important Note XV, it differs in both its nature and
its consequences from the other, "natural" form of self-love, *amour de
soi-même*:

> One must not confuse *amour propre* and *amour de soi-même*, two passions
> very different in their nature and effects. *Amour de soi-même* is a natural
> sentiment that leads every animal to attend to its own preservation and that,
> guided in man by reason and modified by pity, produces humanity and

---

[3] Although there are often good reasons to distinguish esteem from respect, for the most part I
abstract from those differences here. I devote extensive attention to this distinction as it is
relevant to Rousseau's theory of *amour propre* in *Rousseau's Theodicy of Self-Love: Evil,
Rationality, and the Drive for Recognition* (Oxford University Press, 2008), 61–70, 114–15.

[4] Niko Kolodny provides a provocative set of answers to these questions in "The Explanation of
Amour-Propre," *Philosophical Review* 119 (2010), 165–200.

virtue. *Amour propre* is but a relative sentiment, artificial (*factice*) and born in society, that leads each individual to set greater store by himself than by anyone else, inspires in men all the evils they do to one another, and is the true source of honor . . . [I]n the true state of nature *amour propre* does not exist. For, since each man in particular regards himself as the sole spectator who observes him, as the sole being in the universe who takes an interest in him, as the sole judge of his own merit, it is not possible that a sentiment that has its source in comparisons that he is not led to make could spring up in his soul. (*DI*, 218/*OC* III, 219)

This passage, Rousseau's most explicit definition of *amour propre* anywhere, distinguishes the two forms of self-love along four dimensions. The first of these concerns the object, or good, that each inclines those who possess it to seek: *amour de soi-même* aims at self-preservation and one's own well-being,[5] whereas *amour propre* pursues the intrinsically non-material ends of honor, merit, or the regard of others. A being that possesses *amour propre*, then, is moved by the desire to be esteemed, admired, or thought valuable in some respect by those it regards as its spectators. One could also say – to adopt a term adopted later by Fichte and Hegel – that what *amour propre* seeks is some form of *recognition*, an acknowledgment by others of one's status as a valued subject.[6]

The second dimension along which the two forms of self-love differ concerns their consequences: whereas *amour de soi-même* is mostly benign, *amour propre* is the source of evil – indeed, as Rousseau says, of *all* the evils that humans, as opposed to nature, introduce into the

---

[5] It is important that the aims of *amour de soi-même* are not restricted to self-preservation or even to physical well-being. In civilized humans, the good that *amour de soi-même* inclines one to seek varies with one's self-conception, so to the extent that one thinks of oneself as more than a physical being, the good one seeks will extend beyond the mere necessities of life. (See N. J. H. Dent, *Rousseau: An Introduction to His Psychological, Social and Political Theory* [Oxford: Blackwell, 1988], 98–103.) It is more precise to distinguish the two passions by saying that the goods sought by *amour de soi-même* are always non-relative (or absolute), and in precisely the same two senses in which the ends of *amour propre* are, as explained below, always relative.

[6] It would be foolish to claim that Rousseau operates, even implicitly, with precisely the same conceptions of recognition that Fichte and Hegel develop later. At the same time, Rousseau's account of *amour propre* – of its nature, its aim, its lamentable effects – is clearly the source of these later conceptions. Despite the fact that Rousseau never uses the term in connection with *amour propre*, it is not going too far to say that he (alongside Hobbes perhaps) is the first "philosopher of recognition" in modern Western philosophy. I discuss some of the differences between Rousseau's and Hegel's theories of recognition in "Rousseau und Hegel: Zwei Begriffe der Anerkennung," in Stefan Lang and Lars-Thade Ulrichs, eds., *Subjektivität und Autonomie: Grundprobleme der praktischen Philosophie nach Kant* (Berlin: de Gruyter, 2013).

world. Of course, *amour propre* is not the cause of purely natural evils, such as diseases and earthquakes,[7] but the artificial evils with which the Second Discourse is most concerned – social inequality, for one, but also enslavement, domination, unhappiness, vice, and alienation – are all to be explained as having their psychological source in the desire to be well regarded by others. It is worth noting that Rousseau does not say here, or anywhere else, that *amour propre* has these effects *necessarily* but only that when they do exist, *amour propre* is their cause. Nor does he believe that there are *no* good things that owe their existence to *amour propre*; on the contrary, many do, and they include love, appropriately tempered ambition, and the disposition to behave honorably. In fact, Rousseau is much more ambivalent about *amour propre* than this passage or the Second Discourse in general leads readers to assume. The positive potential of *amour propre* is most visible in his later work *Emile*, but even in the Second Discourse Rousseau admits that the "universal desire for reputation," the "ardor to be talked about" – in other words, *amour propre* – is responsible for "what is best and worst among men: our virtues and our vices, our sciences and our errors" (*DI*, 184/*OC* III, 189). Moreover, one of "the sweetest sentiments known to man," conjugal love, is unthinkable without the desire for mutual regard, which only *amour propre* can generate (*DI*, 164/*OC* III, 168). That the Second Discourse is largely silent about the possible benefits of *amour propre* is explained by the fact that, in contrast to *Emile* and *The Social Contract*, its task is mostly diagnostic in character, and in this context – when the point is to explain where the ills of human society come from rather than to devise a remedy for them (*DI*, 201/*OC* III, 205) – it is only fitting that *amour propre* appears in a predominantly negative light. Understanding why Rousseau regards *amour propre* as the principal source of one of the main ills of human society (inequality) is the central undertaking of this chapter; once we have finished explaining what *amour propre* is and how it differs from *amour de soi-même*, we will return to this claim and reconstruct it in detail.

---

[7] Though even here, as Rousseau argues in his letter to Voltaire on the Lisbon earthquake, the harmful effects of natural disasters often depend on artificial circumstances, such as the shabby construction of houses for the poor, which usually distribute the harm of natural disasters unequally, disproportionately burdening those who are already disadvantaged in other ways (*LV*, 232f/*OC* IV, 1059f).

The final two dimensions along which Rousseau distinguishes *amour propre* from *amour de soi-même* involve complex issues that demand somewhat lengthier discussions. These differences concern the *relativity* and the *artificiality* of *amour propre*, in contrast to the non-relative and natural character of *amour de soi-même*. Let us begin with relativity. "Relative" here means relative to other subjects, and Rousseau's point is that the good that *amour propre* leads us to seek requires, even consists in, certain relations to others. In fact, *amour propre* is relative in two respects, each of which distinguishes it from *amour de soi-même* and contributes to explaining why the two passions differ so greatly in their effects. First, the good sought by *amour propre* – a kind of status or esteem – is relative, or comparative, in nature. To desire status or esteem is to desire a certain standing in relation to others. For this reason comparison is essential to *amour propre*'s workings, which is why the passage cited above characterizes it as "a sentiment that has its source in comparisons." In other words, the esteem or standing that *amour propre* strives for is always a positional good, where doing well for myself (finding the standing I seek) consists in doing well in relation to others (acquiring a standing defined in relation to theirs). This means that the extent to which I am satisfied in my desire for esteem depends on how well, or how badly, those around me fare with respect to their desire for the same.

It is important to note, however, that a relative standing is not necessarily a superior or inferior one. If what *amour propre* leads one to seek is simply the respect one deserves as a human being – a respect one is willing to grant to others in return – then the standing one seeks is comparative (or relative) but not superior; in other words, equal standing is still standing relative to others.[8] Interestingly, the possibility of seeking equal standing appears to be raised in the paragraph immediately following the entry of *amour propre* into the Second Discourse's narrative,[9] where, as we saw above, it first assumes a non-egalitarian

---

[8] Joshua Cohen makes this point especially well in *Rousseau: A Free Community of Equals* (Oxford University Press, 2010), 101–4.

[9] Understandably, many interpreters deny that Rousseau regards *amour propre* as having the egalitarian potential I ascribe to it here. Admittedly, the evidence for such a potential in the Second Discourse is thin. (I present it in the text immediately following this note.) In *Emile*, however, this is clearer: a successful domestic education is predicated on forming individuals' *amour propre* so that they understand themselves as the moral equals of all other human beings and are able to find some satisfaction of their *amour propre* in being recognized as such.

guise, as a desire to be regarded as the *best* in some respect (as the handsomest, most skillful, etc.). Just after this, however, Rousseau explicitly notes the possibility – perhaps even the inevitability – of a quite different manifestation of *amour propre*:

As soon as men had begun to appreciate one another and the idea of consideration had taken shape in their mind, each one claimed a right to it, and one could no longer deprive anyone of it with impunity. From here arose the first duties of civility, . . . and from it any intentional wrong became an affront because, along with the harm that resulted from the injury, the offended man saw in it contempt for his person that was often more unbearable than the harm itself. (*DI*, 166/ *OC* III, 170)

The duties of civility referred to here involve a species of regard importantly different from the acknowledgment humans seek in wanting to be esteemed as the handsomest or the strongest. For the demand to be respected as a "person" expresses a desire to be treated in accordance with standards of dignity or civility that apply equally to all persons, rather than to be esteemed as someone who stands out in some way as better than others. Despite the important difference between the demand to be respected as an equal and the desire to be valued as superior in some respect, both – so Rousseau suggests – are capable of helping to satisfy the general aim of *amour propre* "to have a position . . ., to count for something" in relation to others (*E*, 160/ *OC* IV, 421).

In this respect the relativity of *amour propre* contrasts sharply with the absolute, or non-comparative, character of *amour de soi-même*. Here it is helpful to recall one of Rousseau's reasons, explained in Chapter 1, for denying that social inequalities have their source in human nature: there is nothing in purely natural *amour de soi-même* that motivates humans to seek out inequalities for their own sake since the goods it strives for – the requirements of self-preservation, for example – satisfy its needs and desires irrespective of the level of satisfaction achieved by others. (Recall from Chapter 1 that for beings still unaffected by the relative desires of *amour propre*, the extent to

(Accomplishing this is the tutor's principal undertaking in Book IV.) Moreover, the state's equal respect of its citizens is a major theme in *The Social Contract*, and it is difficult to believe that Rousseau did not regard this as responding in part to the problems generated by *amour propre* as depicted in the Second Discourse. I discuss this issue in greater detail in *Rousseau's Theodicy of Self-Love*, 33, 39–40, 59–60, 65–6, 166–9, 174–9.

which one's sleep or nourishment satisfies oneself is independent of how much sleep or nourishment those around one enjoy.) As it is possible to begin to see already, the fact that *amour propre* seeks only relative goods will play a major role in Rousseau's explanation of where social inequality comes from.

The second sense in which *amour propre* is relative to other subjects is that the good it seeks depends on, even consists in, the judgments or opinions of others. As Rousseau expresses it in the note cited above, *amour propre*, in contrast to *amour de soi-même*, requires the idea that there are other "spectators who observe" one and other "judges of one's own merit" beyond oneself. Another way of putting this point is to say that the aim of *amour propre* – some form of esteem or respect from others – is intrinsically social in character. Here, too, *amour propre* contrasts sharply with *amour de soi-même*: since the opinion of one's fellow beings is not constitutive of the goods sought by *amour de soi-même*, it does not *necessarily* motivate us to establish relations to other subjects. *Amour propre*, on the other hand, because it seeks standing *in the eyes of others*, provides humans with a permanent motivation – an urge sufficiently strong and enduring to be considered a *need* – to enter into relations with others. (This is why I said in the previous chapter that *amour propre* was a partial replacement for the Stoic principle of sociability: it impels us to seek social relations, and not merely for instrumental reasons.) Since its needs cannot be satisfied in isolation, the passion to count as something for others is a direct and permanent source of human dependence and sociality.

The final dimension along which *amour propre* differs from *amour de soi-même* is that the latter is natural, whereas the former is artificial (*factice*). A careful reading of Note XV reveals that "natural" refers to three qualities of *amour de soi-même*, all of which were topics of discussion in Chapter 1: first, it is a sentiment we share with other animals (and so is part of our biological nature); second, it is benign (or good), not itself a source of inequality or of other human ills; and, finally, it is not "born in society" but is (or would be) operative even in the absence of all social relations. *Amour propre* has the three opposite qualities: it distinguishes humans from other animals insofar as it relies on faculties – the capacities to compare, to form opinions, and to care about the opinions of others – that non-humans lack; it is the psychological source of all human-made ills; and it is an inherently social passion (because relative in the two senses discussed above). Picking up on a point I made in Chapter 1, this last claim can be reformulated as follows: whereas it would make sense to attribute *amour de soi-même* even to human beings who lacked all social relations, the same is not true for *amour propre*, since its goals depend directly and necessarily on relations to others, who must serve both as objects of comparison and as subjects who take the seeker of esteem or respect as the object of their regard. It is important to recall that by labeling *amour propre* artificial, Rousseau does not mean to suggest that it is a merely accidental feature of human reality or that humans would be better off without it. Nothing in his claim that *amour propre* is artificial implies that humans can or should exist without it. Contrary to popular primitivist readings of the Second Discourse,[10] Rousseau does not envision human existence without *amour propre* any more than he envisions it without love, reason, or language – all of which are just as artificial as *amour propre* and no less essential to human reality. Indeed, Rousseau's view is that there can be no genuinely *human* beings without *amour propre*, a view that finds expression in the fact that in Part I of the Second Discourse, before *amour propre* has entered the world, he seems unable to decide whether to refer to the beings he describes there as humans or animals. In truth, they are both (or neither): although they possess capacities that other animals do not (free will and perfectibility), they lack most of the attributes – language, reason, passion – that we generally take to be central to *human* existence. This is an indication that for Rousseau the desire to compare oneself to others and to be the object of their evaluative gaze is so fundamental a part of all distinctively human phenomena – including the need to live with others – that it would not be going too far to define humans as "recognition-seeking animals."[11]

---

[10] The term *primitivist* comes from Arthur O. Lovejoy, who convincingly rebuts the common perception of Rousseau as calling for a return to, or in some other way nostalgically idealizing, the original state of nature. See "The Supposed Primitivism of Rousseau's Discourse on Inequality," in his *Essays in the History of Ideas* (Baltimore: Johns Hopkins Press, 1948), 14–37.

[11] This is closer to Aristotle's definition of humans as rational animals than it appears, since it is possible to read Rousseau as claiming that rationality itself relies on *amour propre* (and in this light it is interesting to recall that Aristotle also defines the human being as a *zoon politikon*, a social or political animal, as if the rationality of humans were connected to their social character). For the connection between rationality and *amour propre* in Rousseau, see my *Rousseau's Theodicy of Self-Love*, Chapter 7.

It is important to be clear about why Rousseau insists on calling *amour propre* artificial rather than simply social. Why think of *amour propre* as something humans *make*? One reason is that, unlike *amour de soi-même*, *amour propre* cannot move human beings in the absence of comparisons and judgments that ultimately rest on the freedom of the judging subject. It is not only that *amour propre* seeks the (free) judgments of others; it is also the case that it can yield no determinate desires for recognized standing unless informed by some conception, or opinion, of what makes someone worthy of being esteemed, whether this is being the best singer, possessing the most property, or simply being a member of the human species. In short, *amour propre* requires that both the giver and receiver of esteem be valuing subjects, and valuing is possible only on the basis of judgments that themselves presuppose the free participation of the subjects that make them.

Another way of understanding the claim that *amour propre* is artificial is to recall Rousseau's reasons for considering society and the phenomena that depend on it – social inequalities, for example – artificial. His thought is that even though *human* beings must have social relations of one kind or another (since the distinctively human is impossible outside society), the particular forms that social relations take are highly variable and, more to the point, dependent on human will – though not, of course, on the will of any single individual. It is not, in general, up to humans to live in society or not, but it is up to them, in some sense at least, how their social relations are configured. In other words, the social world is artificial in the sense that the practices and institutions that characterize any particular society are the (mostly unintentional) products of the collective actions of humans and, as we saw in Chapter 1, are sustained only by the ongoing participation and "consent" of their members. *Amour propre*, then, is artificial in the same sense and for similar reasons: although humans cannot exist as such without *amour propre*, the particular forms it takes – how, by whom, and on what basis individuals seek to be valued by others – are highly variable and depend on the kind of social world its possessors inhabit. Processes of socialization, for example, give particular shape to the desires and ideals that motivate individuals, and real social institutions inevitably encourage certain ways of finding public esteem while ruling out others. (Modern capitalism affords its participants different forms of social recognition from those available under medieval feudalism or in ancient societies; states that safeguard individual rights accord their citizens a species of recognition unavailable in despotic regimes.) If social institutions are human-made in the sense explained above, and if concrete expressions of *amour propre* depend on them, then there is an important sense in which *amour propre* is human-made as well: with respect to *how* it manifests itself in the world, *amour propre* is just as dependent on human doings as the social institutions that shape it.

The extreme plasticity of *amour propre* – its susceptibility to being formed and re-formed through human interactions of many different kinds – is of crucial importance to Rousseau's account of inequality and must be borne in mind when encountering passages, such as Note XV, that appear to ascribe a fixed and usually pernicious character to *amour propre*. When Rousseau says that *amour propre* "leads each individual to set greater store by himself than by anyone else [and] inspires in men all the evils they do to one another," he must not be read as claiming that the inclination to think of oneself as better than others or the evils that can result from the desire for superior standing are necessary consequences of *amour propre* but, instead, only that they are possible or likely effects of it. Although Rousseau does hold that *amour propre* is the principal source of the evils that beset human beings, he does not believe that it leads to those evils necessarily, in all its possible forms. Thinking more highly of oneself than of others is one way that *amour propre* commonly manifests itself, but because the forms it actually assumes are always influenced by contingent circumstances that ultimately depend on human will, it is by no means necessary that it do so.[12] Of course, one reason the plasticity of *amour propre* is so important to Rousseau (even if these ambitions are more visible in *The Social Contract* and *Emile*) is that it opens up the possibility that the various evils diagnosed in the Second

---

[12] Great care must be taken here. I am distinguishing phenomena such as setting greater store by oneself and thinking more highly of oneself, on the one hand, from the broader phenomenon of striving for superior standing, on the other. As I read Rousseau, the latter is, in some form, a necessary part of human existence, whereas the former are not. This means that there are forms of the desire for superior standing that do not have pernicious consequences for social life, for example, the desire to be "loved best" by one other person or the desire to be esteemed as a superior, even the best, singer or dancer. I expand on this crucial point in *Rousseau's Theodicy of Self-Love*, Chapter 3.

Discourse are susceptible to being remedied. If the particular forms that *amour propre* takes are shaped by conditions that depend, at least to some extent, on our own wills, then it is conceivable that certain kinds of human intervention – education or institutional reform – might be able to transform individuals such that they are able to satisfy their desire to have value in the eyes of others in ways that do not result in the ills that plague modern societies.[13]

In sum, then, *amour propre* is a form of self-love that is the source of the enduring, though highly malleable, need that human beings have to count as someone of value, both in the eyes of others and relative to the value of others. As such, it occupies a prominent place in Rousseau's theory of the fundamental motivators of human action. His psychological thesis is that *amour propre* and *amour de soi-même* are the sources of two distinct kinds of motivation, each of which plays a central role in human life – a thesis that finds expression in his claim that "all our labors are directed at only two objects: the comforts of life for oneself and consideration among others" (*DI*, 219/*OC* III, 220). (The mention here of only two objects of human activity bears further witness to the relative weakness of the third source of motivation, pity.) Distinguishing two *sources* of motivation does not, however, imply that an action can be a manifestation of only one species of self-love at the same time. On the contrary, most human behavior aims at satisfying both *amour de soi-même* and *amour propre* at once. The homes we construct, the clothing we wear, the food we eat and serve to guests – all are typically motivated not only by physical need but also by opinions concerning how our homes, clothing, and food reflect our standing for others, both as individuals and as human beings in general.

It is important to bear in mind that by classifying one of these passions as natural and the other as artificial, Rousseau is not making a

---

[13] According to Axel Honneth, my optimistic reading of the potential of *amour propre* is hard to reconcile with Rousseau's later, more autobiographical writings; see his "Die Entgiftung Jean-Jacques Rousseaus," *Deutsche Zeitschrift für Philosophie* 60 (2012), 625. But perhaps we are to understand these later writings as belonging to a different philosophical project from the one set out in *Emile, The Social Contract*, and the Second Discourse. My suggestion is that the later project turns away from social, political, and moral philosophy in their traditional guises and investigates how one is to live, as happily and with as much integrity as possible, in a world that is hopelessly corrupt and therefore insusceptible to the remedies proposed in Rousseau's earlier work.

claim about their relative strength or significance as a source of human motivation, nor about their relative value for human beings. His point, rather, is to highlight the necessarily social character of *amour propre*, in contrast to the (in principle) individualistic character of *amour de soi-même*. The point of this, in turn, is to draw our attention, in Part II, to the variable and fateful effects that contingent, human-made social arrangements have on how *amour propre* manifests itself in specific social contexts. The fact that *amour de soi-même* precedes *amour propre* in the Second Discourse's narrative is not an indication of temporal, logical, or normative priority; it is a sign instead of the different sources the two passions have – biology on the one hand, social relations on the other – and of the differences in structure, malleability, and possible effects that Rousseau sees as following from this difference. Understood in this way, his theory of *amour propre* asserts the following: in one form or another the esteem, regard, or approval of others is a universally desired end of human beings; the drive to acquire a recognized standing for others cannot be extinguished in human beings (except perhaps through measures of extreme repression); and social, moral, and political philosophy must therefore take very seriously the implications of this fundamental human need. Moreover, the twofold relativity of *amour propre* implies that the impulse to compare one's condition with others', as well as the need to have one's comparative standing confirmed by them, are basic and permanent features of the human condition (*DI*, 183/*OC* III, 189) that remain at work even in the best of societies.[14]

As in the case of *amour de soi-même* and pity, Rousseau's thesis regarding the fundamental status of *amour propre* is based in part on empirical evidence. As I have suggested, his claims concerning all three basic sources of human motivation derive much of their support from the success with which these few hypotheses about human psychology make sense of the diverse forms of human behavior we are familiar with from experience. In placing *amour propre* alongside *amour de soi-même* in his psychological theory, Rousseau is in effect claiming that reflection on our general acquaintance with human reality suffices to show that the desire for public esteem plays a major role in human behavior

[14] For evidence of this external to the Second Discourse, see *E*, 235, 245, 339, 436/*OC* IV, 523, 536, 670, 806.

and social existence, such that the urge to count in the eyes of others is every bit as pervasive in human affairs as the drive to preserve oneself and to secure one's own non-relative well-being. Moreover, Rousseau's texts suggest that this more or less empirical claim finds further support in a more philosophical consideration concerning the centrality of comparison in general to various kinds of distinctively human phenomena and activities.[15] Reflection, for example, "is born of the comparison of ideas" (*OL*, 268/*OC*, 396), while language, concept formation, and reason itself are no less dependent on the capacity to distinguish and compare (*DI*, 147–8/*OC* III, 149–50; *OL*, 254/*OC* 5, 381). Once the capacity (and tendency) to compare is awakened and the basic fact of social intercourse is introduced into the picture in Part II, it is no mere accident that creatures of self-love come to notice and to care about how their positions compare to others'. Indeed, within the narrative of the Second Discourse the newly acquired ability to make simple comparisons is immediately followed by "the first movement of pride (*orgueil*)"[16] – a consciousness of one's superiority that, though at first only a pride in one's species, eventually turns into *amour propre*'s concern for one's standing as an individual (*DI*, 162/*OC* III, 166). Then, once humans develop a more settled existence in which they come into repeated contact with the same individuals,[17] they inevitably apply their capacity for making comparisons to the qualities of individuals, which makes "sentiments of preference" possible and, immediately thereafter, the desire to be preferred – and hence compared and evaluated – by others (*DI*, 165–6/*OC* III, 169). (I go into the complex relation among comparing, preferring specific others, and concern for one's own rank as an individual in more detail below, in explaining the "origin" of *amour propre*.) The clear implication is that the tendency to

---

[15] Nietzsche espouses a similar view when he locates the origin of civilization in relations in which one person "measures himself against another" and when he claims that establishing equivalences through comparison "constitute[s] thinking *as such*" (*On the Genealogy of Morals*, Essay II, §8). Related views about the importance of comparison can be found in Adam Smith, *The Wealth of Nations*, ed. Edwin Cannan (New York: Modern Library, 2000), 14.

[16] This is pride, not yet *amour propre*, because, first, it is a looking at oneself that does not seek the opinion of others; and, second, the comparative standing of *individuals* is not at issue. In other words, the two species of relativity that define *amour propre* are lacking.

[17] Recall that these developments are not best understood as temporal events, as if Rousseau were asserting that social relations actually came into being at some point in human history. The introduction of social existence in Part II should instead be thought of as the taking back of an abstraction undertaken in Part I for analytic purposes.

compare the merits of individuals, although artificial in Rousseau's technical sense, is no less basic to human life than the foundations of reason and language.

Finally, even though Rousseau himself does not speak in this way, I will treat the picture of human psychology presented in Part II, where *amour propre* is added to the sentiments of *amour de soi-même* and pity discussed in Part I, as furnishing us with what I call an *expanded* conception of human nature in the non-normative or explanatory sense. The fundamental and ineradicable character of *amour propre* – that it in some form motivates all *real* human beings regardless of time and place – qualifies it as a basic disposition or endowment of the human soul, even if, unlike *amour de soi-même* and pity, it could not operate in the absence of social relations or in the absence of distinctively human cognitive activities such as judgment and comparison. Like *amour de soi-même* and pity, *amour propre* is essential to an adequate account of human psychology because a very large part of real human behavior would remain inexplicable if the desire to acquire standing in the eyes of others were left out of the picture. This means that social and political philosophy must take at least as much notice of *amour propre* in devising standards for criticizing and endorsing social institutions as it does of the two sentiments that define original (non-social) human nature. There is, of course, an important sense in which human nature in the expanded sense no longer qualifies strictly as nature for Rousseau, which is no doubt why he avoids speaking of *amour propre* as a part of human nature: this distinctively human passion depends on judgments, and hence on human freedom, in ways that *amour de soi-même* and pity do not. What I am calling the expanded (explanatory) conception of human nature is, one might say, a conception of *human* nature, not of human *nature*.

In invoking the idea of an expanded conception of human nature that adds the passion of *amour propre* to "original" human nature, I take myself to be denying one of the theses most commonly associated with Rousseau, namely that humans are by nature *radically asocial*. Of course, if "nature" is taken in the idiosyncratic sense that Rousseau gives to the term "original nature" – denoting what individuals would be like in the absence of all social relations and historical development – then, more or less by definition, humans are indeed "naturally" asocial. But this is not what those who interpret Rousseau as espousing the radical asociality of humans mean to be claiming. Perhaps the view they attribute to Rousseau is best understood as a flat-out rejection of every version of the thesis of sociability, according to which in the absence of extensive artificial formation – by powerful social institutions or the intervention of a great educator (such as the legislator invoked in *The Social Contract* [*SC*, II.7]) – humans would be naturally inclined to avoid enduring social relations, experiencing no desire or need for them, and would prefer instead to exist in something like the solipsistic condition depicted in Part I of the Second Discourse. It will come as no surprise that the interpretation I am proposing here breaks fundamentally with this common understanding of Rousseau's position. As I explained in the previous chapter, on my view Rousseau rejects the thesis of *natural* sociability and replaces it with the combination of *amour propre* and pity – one natural and one artificial element – regarding both as passions (or sentiments) that motivate all real human beings wherever they are found. (The most important difference between the two, recall, is that the latter could in principle motivate human beings independently of the social relations in which they find themselves, whereas the former is a highly malleable, intrinsically social passion that requires comparison, judgments of merit and value, and the idea that (a part of) one's good depends on – consists in – something irreducibly "moral," namely, the opinions others have of them.) It is true that the solution proposed jointly in *Emile* and *The Social Contract* to the problems articulated by the Second Discourse require extensive educational measures, but these measures are best understood not as directed at transforming asocial creatures into social beings but at forming the *amour propre* and pity of beings that are already social – in the sense that they desire the good opinion of others as an important part of their own good – in such a way that their social intercourse avoids the evils depicted in the Second Discourse.[18] Again, this aspect of

---

[18] When Rousseau, in discussing the task of the legislator, says that "anyone who dares to institute a people must feel capable of . . . changing human nature" (*SC*, II.7.iii), his idea is not that the legislator must take beings who lack *amour propre* and make them sensitive to the good opinions of others, in this case of their fellow citizens. His emphasis, rather, is on "instituting a people," that is, on bringing *self-interested* individuals to see their own good as bound up with the good of a social group, including the good of all its individual members. Both *amour propre* and *amour de soi-même* must be "socialized" in this sense if a people as

Rousseau's view is much more visible in texts other than the Second Discourse, most notably in *Emile*, where Rousseau states repeatedly that the task of good domestic education cannot consist in preventing *amour propre* from taking hold of individuals,[19] but only in forming *amour propre* in ways that foster rather than destroy human freedom and happiness. If the Second Discourse is to be made consistent with Rousseau's other major texts – and Rousseau himself encourages us to seek such consistency – the thesis of the radical asociality of humans must give way to the more complex picture of his position that I am proposing here.[20]

AMOUR PROPRE AS THE SOURCE OF SOCIAL INEQUALITY

Once *amour propre* has been introduced into Rousseau's picture of human psychology, it is no longer difficult to understand where social inequality comes from – or, more precisely, how it can be our creation rather than nature's. For whenever humans conceive of their good in comparative terms – whenever our own satisfaction depends on how much or how little of the same good those around us find – the possibility exists that we will seek to do well for ourselves by trying to outdo others. In other words, the concern for relative standing is susceptible to becoming a desire for superior standing, and as soon as one takes the view that an affirmation of one's own worth requires being esteemed not merely as good but as better than others, *amour propre* requires inequality in order to be satisfied. It is primarily the comparative nature of *amour propre*, then, that explains why the

Rousseau understands it is to come into being. In other words, two things must be distinguished, both of which are included in traditional conceptions of sociability: the natural ability, even in the absence of educational measures, to will the good of a social group as one's own; and the possession (by virtue of one's nature) of certain desires that can be satisfied only in intercourse with others, such that such intercourse is sought for its own sake, not merely as a means to satisfying the ends of *amour de soi-même*. Rousseau attributes the second to the fundamental character of all real human beings but not the first.

[19] For example: "I would find someone who wanted to prevent the birth of the passions almost as mad as someone who wanted to annihilate them; and those who believed that this was my project . . . would surely have understood me very badly" (*E*, 212/*OC* IV, 491); see also *E*, 215/ *OC* IV, 494. And see Rousseau's own unsuccessful attempt to rid himself of the desire for affirmation from others (*RSW*, 71, 73/*OC* I, 1,077, 1,079).

[20] Rousseau himself stated that his books "form a coherent system" (*RJJ*, 209, 213/*OC* I, 930, 934–5). See also Gustav Lanson, "The Unity in Jean-Jacques Rousseau's Thought," in John T. Scott, ed., *Jean-Jacques Rousseau: Critical Assessments* (Oxford: Routledge, 2006), 11–29.

human desire to be looked at favorably by others constitutes "the first step towards inequality," for it alone explains how humans can be led to seek out inequalities for their own sake, as public demonstrations of the superior standing they are out to achieve. The range of human phenomena that depend on such an impulse towards inequality is extensive and familiar: the endless pursuit of wealth, ostentatious consumption, the relentless drive to compete and outdo, scurrying to "keep up with the Joneses" – all are manifestations of "the fervor," inspired by *amour propre*, "to raise one's relative fortune, [not] out of genuine need [but] in order to place oneself above others" (*DI*, 171/ *OC* III, 175). In other words, *amour propre* has the potential to drive humans to improve their relative condition for the sole purpose of appearing superior to others, and a passion of this sort is precisely what is needed to explain why artificial inequality is so prevalent in the large majority of the actual societies we know, both present and past.

Thus, the core of Rousseau's answer to the first of the Second Discourse's questions, though frequently overlooked, is relatively straightforward. It consists in a psychological claim concerning where the impulse to inequality comes from in humans, and the specific "development of the human mind" that is said to be responsible for social inequality is the awakening and strengthening of *amour propre*.[21] That Rousseau means to single out *amour propre* as the main source of social inequality is evident not only in his claim that its workings represent "the first step towards inequality" (and "at the same time towards vice") but also in his description of that passion as the "leavens" whose "fermentation . . . produced compounds fatal to happiness and innocence" (*DI*, 166/*OC* III, 169–70).[22] At the same time, as the latter statement suggests, if *amour propre* is the principal cause – and a necessary condition – of social inequalities, it is far from being sufficient by itself to produce them. It is important here to take the analogy with bread-making seriously: the drive to be esteemed by others is the cause of social inequality in exactly the sense in which it is yeast that causes a loaf of bread to rise. To say that yeast is the cause of the bread's rising is

---

[21] It is important, though difficult, to bear in mind that the "awakening" of *amour propre*, like the "birth" of social relations, is not best understood as a temporal event. See note 17.

[22] Further assertions of the causal primacy of *amour propre* can be found at *DI*, 184, 188/*OC* III, 189, 193.

not to claim that it has that effect all by itself, in the absence of other conditions it needs – warmth, moisture, flour – in order to do its work. The same holds for the production of inequality. For, as the Second Discourse makes clear, a number of other, non-psychological conditions must be added to the mix – leisure, the division of labor, private property, for example – if the fermenting of *amour propre* is to be activated and its leavening powers unleashed.

Despite these auxiliary conditions – the number and interdependence of which account for the ultimate complexity of the Second Discourse's complete answer to the question of inequality's origin – what makes *amour propre* the source of social inequality is that, like yeast in the making of bread, it supplies the force, or power, that drives a certain process of growth or transformation: it is to *amour propre* that "inequality, being almost nonexistent in the state of nature, owes its force and growth" (*DI*, 188/*OC* III, 193). In other words, the passion to be esteemed by others is what fuels the spread of inequality, since it alone among the elements of human psychology provides humans with a motive to create inequalities beyond those that nature itself produces. It is the principal cause of inequality, then, because it is capable of moving humans to devise a nearly unlimited variety of new, artificial opportunities for satisfying the desire to acquire a valued standing in the eyes of others, whenever a valued standing is understood to imply superior standing. But if the core of Rousseau's account of the origin of social inequality is relatively simple, its supplementary details, as any reader can see, are anything but straightforward. For the story told in Part II of how inequality comes to play a dominant role in human affairs also appeals to a wide and complex array of non-psychological factors, which include socio-political phenomena – the division of labor, private property, the state, and class stratification – as well as very general features of civilization, such as leisure, luxury, and technological innovation. As I suggested above, these non-psychological factors figure in Rousseau's account as auxiliary conditions that must be present in some combination if *amour propre* is to have the leavening effects it is capable of producing. Unfortunately (but perhaps to Rousseau's credit), it is very difficult to determine exactly how and in what combination, according to the Second Discourse, these conditions work together to unleash *amour propre*'s latent power. Disentangling these densely woven strands of Rousseau's account is a delicate and time-consuming enterprise, and the remainder of this chapter will be dedicated to this task.

It is best to begin by attempting to determine why the mere presence of *amour propre* is insufficient to explain the diverse and pervasive forms of social inequality that the Second Discourse is most concerned with. The first reason is that, although always a comparative passion, *amour propre* need not, under all conditions, manifest itself exclusively or primarily as a desire for superior standing. For, as I suggested above in considering the demand to be treated in accordance with standards of civility, it is also possible for the quest for standing in the eyes of others to take the form of wanting to be respected as an equal – as simply a "person" or "human being," for example – who has the same rights and dignity as every other individual. This means that in order to account for widespread social inequality, the Second Discourse must also have something to say about why *amour propre* so frequently takes the form of a desire for superior standing if in principle it can also seek equal standing (in which case it would supply no motive for creating inequalities beyond those established by nature). One of the puzzling features of the Second Discourse is that it seems to give no answer to this crucial question. Instead, as we saw above, already in its first appearance in the Second Discourse, *amour propre* manifests itself as a desire to be esteemed more highly than others – as "the handsomest, the strongest, the most skillful, or the most eloquent" (*DI*, 166/*OC* III, 169) – and this fact, so crucial to the Second Discourse's explanation of the origin of social inequality, appears to be left unexplained (though, as I argue below, a careful reading of Rousseau's texts provides the resources needed to dispel this appearance).

The second reason *amour propre* by itself is insufficient to generate widespread inequality is that, even when it is configured in many individuals primarily as the desire for superior standing, a number of other, non-psychological conditions must obtain before that desire can translate into the enduring systems of advantage that Rousseau is concerned with when inquiring into the origin of social inequality. As long as the quest for superiority is confined to the simple desire of primitive beings to be regarded as the most handsome or the best singer, significant social inequality cannot arise. This can be seen in the fact that in the Second Discourse's narrative the desire to be esteemed as better than others in certain respects establishes itself well before society achieves its "happiest and most durable epoch" in the so-called Golden Age (*DI*, 167/*OC* III, 171).[23] This is one reason the auxiliary conditions mentioned above must enter into the Second Discourse's complete answer to the question concerning inequality's origin, as can be seen, to take just one example, in Rousseau's remark at the end of the Second Discourse that whereas "inequality . . . owes its force and growth" to *amour propre*, "property and laws" are needed to make artificial inequalities "stable and legitimate" (where with the latter term he means only that those inequalities *appear* to be legitimate to those who are subject to them). In some way, most of the "developments" invoked in Part II of the Second Discourse – technological advancement; the perfection of cognitive faculties; specialization occasioned by the division of labor; the origin of private property, states, and codes of justice – serve to institutionalize and give permanence to the various inequalities that beings with the desire for superior standing are driven to create. Yet here, too, Rousseau appears to have little to say about why these conditions arise or, more important, about the extent to which they represent necessary, or non-accidental, features of human civilization in general. Instead, he tends to emphasize the contingency or even the inexplicability of these crucial conditions, claiming, for example, that inequality's gaining a foothold in human existence "required the fortuitous convergence of several foreign causes that might never have arisen" (*DI*, 159/*OC* III, 162), and implying that the development of latent capacities for language, reason, and other basic cognitive functions (including the knowledge required for metallurgy) cannot in the end be explained (*DI*, 143–9, 168/*OC* III, 144–51, 172).

Let us begin with the first of these qualifications to Rousseau's core thesis that *amour propre* is the principal cause of inequality. It is possible, although only with considerable effort, to extract from Rousseau's corpus as a whole – especially with help from *Emile* – a complex answer to the question of why, when *amour propre* first appears in the Second Discourse, it takes the form of a desire for superior rather than merely

---

[23] In fact, Rousseau never uses this term in the Second Discourse; nevertheless it has become customary to refer to the stage of civilization depicted here as the Golden Age.

equal standing (or, if we abstract from the apparent historical character of Rousseau's narrative, why *amour propre* is so likely to appear as a desire for superior standing, independently of the specific social conditions under which it appears).[24] As I have noted, however, the Second Discourse itself provides surprisingly little help in explaining this crucial feature of its account. Yet the question of why *amour propre* first appears, or is so likely to appear, as a desire for superior standing is of great importance to the Second Discourse's project. For if the desire for superior standing were merely a product of contingent social conditions, or if, independently of social conditions, it were no more likely to be present than the desire for equal standing, Rousseau's account of social inequality would be affected in two significant ways: his thesis that *amour propre* is the principal cause of inequality would be considerably weakened (since it would be *amour propre* only *as formed by contingent social circumstances* that gave rise to the desire that fueled the spread of inequality); and pervasive social inequality would be shown to be a possibility for human societies but hardly a probable or nearly universal phenomenon. Just to be clear on this crucial but very complex point: Rousseau, to his credit, does not make the problems he is addressing easier to solve by believing that desires for superior standing can be completely eliminated from human psychology or that the social inequalities that result from such desires can be completely eliminated from human societies, and this aspect of his view is expressed in the (unexplained) fact that *amour propre* makes its first appearance in the Second Discourse in the form of a desire to be regarded by others as, in some very specific respect, superior to others.

In other words, the fact that certain forms of the desire to be accorded preference by others are present already in the Golden Age, and therefore predate the perversion of *amour propre* by social conditions, should be taken to imply that the desire for some kind of superior standing in the eyes of others is a non-accidental manifestation of *amour propre* and that it would therefore be unrealistic to want to construct a society in which all forms of that desire were lacking or in which no social inequality of any kind existed. Other passages in the Second Discourse support this interpretation, and it is further

---

[24] For a detailed explanation of this important feature of *amour propre*, see my *Rousseau's Theodicy of Self-Love*, Chapter 4.

confirmed by *Emile*'s description of the awakening of *amour propre* in an adolescent boy: "the first glance he casts on his fellows leads him to compare himself with them. And the first sentiment this comparison arouses in him is the desire to be in the first position" (*E*, 235/*OC* IV, 523). The more difficult question is not whether Rousseau believes that *amour propre* has an inherent tendency in humans, independently of social circumstances, to appear as the desire for superior standing but why he believes this. One passage in the Second Discourse relevant to this question is its description of how at first comparison and then pride accompany the very earliest advances of civilization, still prior to the awakening of *amour propre* (or, translated into non-historical language: how, independently of particular social arrangements, the basic practice of making comparisons implies, or tends to lead to, a concern for the *rank* among the items compared). According to this passage, the capacity to compare distinct things, a component of natural perfectibility, is awakened and developed in humans by natural circumstances in which the ability to make certain comparisons – Is that beast before me faster or slower, stronger or weaker, than I? – is valuable for survival and therefore crucial to the ends of *amour de soi-même*. Once the ability to compare is in place, the development of pride is said to follow in its train:

The new enlightenment that resulted from this development increased [man's] superiority over the other animals by acquainting him with it. He practiced setting traps for them, he tricked them in a thousand ways, and . . . in time he became the master of those that could be useful to him and the scourge of those that could be harmful. This is how the first look he directed at himself produced the first movement of pride [*orgueil*] in him; this is how, while still scarcely able to discriminate ranks, and considering himself in the first rank as a species, he was from afar preparing to claim the first rank as an individual. (*DI*, 162/*OC* III, 165–6)

Although there is much of interest in this short passage – the awakening of self-consciousness, the first taste of mastery over other creatures, the move from comparing to ranking – it is the final point that is most important here: how and why these more primitive phenomena lay the groundwork for the disposition, attributed later to *amour propre*, to claim for oneself "the first rank as an individual." Insofar as Rousseau has an account here of where this disposition comes from, it seems to proceed as follows: the ability of humans to make comparisons, together with their natural interest in certain circumstances in knowing who is faster or stronger, lays the groundwork for them to become aware of their own superiority (as a species) over other animals – a superiority that pre-exists that awareness but grows even larger once humans become aware of it and interact with their environment in ways that increase it. Moreover, these developments presuppose no new source of motivation; because superiority over other species is advantageous for survival, even consciously intended increases in that superiority can be understood as motivated by (non-relative) *amour de soi-même*.[25] Something new enters this story, however, when humans' experience of their superiority – including, interestingly, their experience of *mastery* over the less advantaged – brings with it a feeling of pleasure in occupying the higher rank,[26] a pleasure identified here as "the first movement of pride." The view towards which Rousseau seems to be struggling, then, is that three things – the capacity to make comparisons, a concern for certain forms of superiority relevant to survival, and the experience of their actual superiority – collaborate to introduce humans to the pleasure that can be had from the awareness of oneself as belonging to a higher rank. This new and unanticipated pleasure then awakens in them a taste for superiority, perhaps even whets their appetite for more of the same, but it does not yet (as far as can be told from the text) furnish them with a positive incentive intentionally to produce conditions of superiority for the sake of enjoying even more of that pleasure. Although it is here still only the superiority of the species that humans have learned to delight in, it is not difficult to imagine how this could be

---

[25] Even though such humans aim in the short term at a relative end (increasing their superiority over other species), theirs is still a non-relative form of self-love because the final end of their actions is a good – survival – that is neither defined nor valued in relation to other beings' survival. Superiority is sought only because it serves as a means to achieving an absolute end; how well others do with respect to survival is irrelevant to the end they ultimately value.

[26] In order to explain why being first (rather than last) should evoke pleasure it may be necessary to appeal to the very weak form of self-preference (preferring one's own good to others') built into all forms of self-love, including *amour de soi-même*. Although this aspect of *amour de soi-même* manifests itself only rarely in purely natural conditions, it surfaces whenever a zero-sum conflict of basic interests arises: when my survival is incompatible with yours, it becomes clear that, independently of *amour propre*, there is a sense in which I prefer myself to you (*DI*, 197/ *OC* III, 126). This element of self-preference does not make *amour de soi-même* a relative sentiment, for the good sought is not defined in relation to how well others fare with respect to the same good.

transformed into a taste for individual superiority in more complex circumstances, once differences among individuals are noticed, multiplied, and then consciously cultivated.

Something like this is indeed what Rousseau goes on to describe in the next phases of human development. It is an intriguing feature of his account, however, that a further important stage intervenes between pride (humans' pleasure in belonging to a superior species) and the first appearance of *amour propre* (the desire to be looked at by others and esteemed as the handsomest or strongest). Once differences among individuals have developed and become salient – which itself requires a certain degree of regular intercourse among individuals, as well as a level of productivity that provides them a degree of leisure – a further step seems to be necessary:

> they grow accustomed to attending to different objects and to making comparisons; imperceptibly they acquire ideas of merit and beauty that produce sentiments of preference. The more they see one another, the less they can do without seeing one another more. A tender and sweet sentiment steals into the soul and at the least obstacle becomes an impetuous fury; jealousy awakens together with love. (*DI*, 165/*OC* III, 169)

It is only after this scene – though immediately thereafter, in the very next paragraph – that we are presented for the first time with creatures that, looking at their companions and wanting to be looked at themselves, long to be regarded as better than others. In short, it is only after the capacity for sexual love has awakened that we are presented for the first time with *human* beings who are moved by *amour propre* – or, more precisely, moved by the specific but hardly contingent form of *amour propre* that, because it seeks recognition of one's superiority as an individual (in some respect), counts as the principal – that is, the psychological – source of artificial inequality.

The intriguing feature of Rousseau's account, then, is that intervening between pride and the birth of the desire to be esteemed as better than other individuals is a stage in which humans get practice in a form of according first place *to others*: they attach "sentiments of preference" to specific objects of sexual love. (This is not the only place in which Rousseau suggests, without really articulating, a deep connection between sexuality and *amour propre*; in *Emile*, too, the two passions emerge in tandem, and it is clear there as well that this connection is not accidental.) Assuming that we are to regard this passionate love for a specific other as a condition of the *amour propre* that comes on the scene immediately after it – and assuming that this point is to be brought together with the earlier discussion of pride – Rousseau's view appears to be the following: already in noticing their superiority to non-human animals, humans gain experience of the pleasure to be had in occupying a position of superiority. This pleasure is what Rousseau calls pride (although it should be noted that, in contrast to the *superbia* of Eve and Adam, this pride is thoroughly benign, even good). This first lesson in pride, however, falls short of furnishing humans with an incentive to seek out superiority for its own sake, nor does it yet suggest to them that individuals might also stand in relations of superiority or inferiority to other individuals of the same species. The latter idea comes to them, rather, only through their experience in the context of sexual love of the relative merits, including the beauty, of specific individuals. One individual perceives another as the most beautiful, the sweetest, the most tantalizing – in short, as the *best* – and he (or she) falls passionately in love with him (or her). According to Rousseau's account, it is in this experience of passionate need for the single individual one values above all others that the desire to be valued oneself as better than others arises, for my own passion will be satisfied only if I succeed in getting my beloved to see me in turn as more desirable than my competitors.[27] The claim, then, is that once this concern to count as more desirable than my rivals in the eyes of another subject has gained a foothold in human psychology, some form of it remains a permanent acquisition,[28] manifesting itself often and most likely (but not necessarily, in every situation) as the desire to count, not merely as good, but as better – even best – in the opinions of at least some other human individuals. Once the aspiration to superior standing that is internal to sexual passion has been generalized and dispersed into other domains of human reality, *amour propre*, in the very form

[27] Similar ideas concerning the relation between sexual love and the desire to be recognized as best can be found at *E*, 214–15/*OC* IV, 494.

[28] Presumably in the case of real as opposed to merely hypothetical human beings, this drama of sexual desire – together with the birth of *amour propre* – is enacted already in the infant's longing to be loved by the mother (or parent?). Some passages of *Emile* appear to confirm this suggestion (*E*, 65/*OC* IV, 286).

it takes when beings of leisure assemble before their primitive huts, has entered the world and become a permanent and fundamental motivator of creatures that are no longer merely animal but now genuinely human beings. (At the end of this chapter I will return to these claims in order to ask what remains of Rousseau's basic thesis that social inequality does not come from nature, once the desire that fuels it – the longing to achieve some kind of superior standing in the eyes of others – is accorded so fundamental a role in human reality.)

AUXILIARY CONDITIONS REQUIRED TO EXPLAIN SOCIAL INEQUALITY

Having explained why, in general, the desire to be regarded as better than others (in some respect) is no merely accidental manifestation of *amour propre*, I turn now to the second and more complicated qualification of Rousseau's core thesis that *amour propre* is the principal cause of inequality, according to which various non-psychological conditions must obtain if that desire is to give rise to enduring and consequential schemes of inequality. It is easy enough to grasp Rousseau's general point, that as long as the drive for superior standing does not exceed the simple desire of beings in primitive circumstances to count as the handsomest or strongest, significant social inequality cannot arise. It is just as easy to see how each non-psychological condition, taken on its own, serves to promote, shore up, or "legitimize" the inequalities that the impulse to achieve superior standing leads humans to create. It is considerably more difficult, however, to figure out how the various elements of his account fit together and, once this is accomplished, to determine what implications that account has for assessing the extent to which social inequalities, especially those that will be shown to have pernicious consequences, are ineliminable features of human society.

That private property is to play a major role in this account is signaled clearly in the famous opening lines of Part II, where Rousseau attributes responsibility for countless "crimes, wars, murders, miseries, and horrors" – as well as the origin of civil (or political) society – to "the first person who enclosed a piece of land and came up with the idea of saying *this is mine*" (*DI*, 161/*OC* III, 164). It is easy to understand how rules regulating private property, especially when backed up by the power of a state, contribute to the growth and institutionalization of inequality by opening up a domain of social intercourse in which new types of comparative standing – differences between rich and poor – are made possible and rendered visible to all. But it is equally clear that Rousseau does not mean for private property to be the only (or explanatorily primary) non-psychological condition that his account of the origin of inequality relies on, for in the very passage in which he highlights the pernicious consequences of private property, he also points out that the idea of property in turn "depends on many prior ideas that could only have arisen in succession." In other words, private property, once established, plays a major role in creating and stabilizing social inequalities, but it is not the explanatorily primary element in his account of which (and how) non-psychological social conditions interact with *amour propre* – or, more precisely, with the impulse to achieve superior standing – in order to produce widespread and enduring social inequality.

Once this is recognized, it is natural to ask: which non-psychological factor *is* then explanatorily primary? Much of the Second Discourse's bewildering complexity is due to the fact that Rousseau refuses to pick out any of these factors as the single, primary, non-psychological cause of social inequality. This makes his account more difficult to reconstruct than it might have been, but also more interesting and plausible (because more adequate to the complexity of the phenomena it aims to understand). In light of this complexity, my reconstruction of this part of Rousseau's account of the origin of social inequality will have to address several interrelated questions at once: (1) Which are the various non-psychological conditions that play a role in explaining social inequality? (2) How does each of these conditions, taken alone, contribute in its own way to the creation and spread of social inequality (assuming some desire for superior standing is already present)? (3) To what extent are these various conditions causally or existentially interdependent, and what does their interdependence imply about which, if any, has explanatory primacy? (As we will see, some of these non-psychological factors also condition and are conditioned by the appearance and development of *amour propre*, which adds even further to the complexity of Rousseau's account.) (4) How are we to understand Rousseau's repeated and perplexing claims regarding the contingent character of these conditions and, sometimes even, the unlikelihood or impossibility of their ever coming about, and what implications do these claims have for his position on the extent to which artificial inequality is an ineliminable feature of human society in general?

The first task is to attempt to distinguish the various conditions that play some independent role (without being completely independent of one another existentially) in explaining the ubiquity and permanence of social inequality. The Second Discourse seems to invoke six such conditions, which appear in its narrative in roughly the following order: (1) *leisure*, or recurring lengths of time in which humans are not forced by natural need to seek or produce the goods required for physical survival; (2) leisure's counterpart, *luxury*, which is best understood as habituation to goods and pleasures that are not biological necessities but that quickly come to be perceived as needs; (3) *individual differentiation* with respect to character, circumstances, and abilities that is far in excess of natural differences among individuals and the result of differences in luck, effort, and natural endowment; (4) a *division of labor*, manifested most strikingly in the invention of metallurgy and agriculture and their being practiced as separate branches of production, that increases individuals' dependence on others for the satisfaction of needs;[29] (5) codified rules of *private property*, especially in the means of production, such as land; and (6) *political institutions* (the state). Although in the real world once even minimal conditions of civilization are achieved, these six factors cease to be causally independent of one another – perhaps they never are entirely – it still makes sense to rank them with respect to how fundamental they are in explaining social inequality. Not surprisingly, their "chronological" order in the Second Discourse, given above, corresponds exactly to their order when ranked according to explanatory primacy. (This is a good example of how the apparently

---

[29] Although Rousseau emphasizes the material division of labor in his claim that metallurgy and agriculture "civilized men and ruined the human species" (*DI*, 168–9/*OC* III, 171–3), he also alludes to the pernicious effects of the first *class* divisions: "as soon as . . . [men] learned that it was useful for a single person to have provisions for two, equality disappeared, property was introduced, labor became necessary, and the vast forests changed into laughing fields that had to be watered with the sweat of men, and in which slavery and misery were soon seen to sprout and grow with the crops" (*DI*, 167/*OC* III, 171). As I discuss in more detail below, the existence of distinct economic classes depends on private property – more precisely, on the unequal private ownership of the means of production.

historical features of the Second Discourse's narrative can be translated into non-historical, philosophical claims concerning relations of conceptual or existential dependence.) Thus, for example, Rousseau makes it clear that both private property[30] and the state presuppose some level of leisure, individual differentiation, and the division of labor, and that leisure, as defined above (and in small amounts), presupposes none of the others.

That leisure is among the most fundamental of these conditions can be seen in the fact, already noted above, that it precedes even the birth of *amour propre* in the Second Discourse's narrative. We are now in a position to see that this chronological feature of Rousseau's story reflects his belief that a concern for how one appears to others can be a significant source of motivation for humans only if they have achieved a level of material productivity that not merely allows them to think about something other than how to satisfy their hunger and thirst – a condition they had already enjoyed in their most primitive state – but that also, and more important, has awakened some of their latent natural capacities for "enlightenment" (*DI*, 164/*OC* III, 167), including no doubt a curiosity for things beyond the merely necessary or useful. (A small degree of individual differentiation seems to be a condition of *amour propre* as well, for without it there would be no distinguishing features among individuals for the passion to be admired or esteemed to latch on to, but perhaps purely natural differences suffice for this.) That leisure precedes *amour propre* in the Second Discourse's narrative is also an expression of the view that it can be explained independently of the desire to achieve standing in the eyes of others, as a direct consequence of *amour de soi-même*, together with minimal technological advances that enable humans to produce more than mere subsistence requires. (And as this point suggests, the Second Discourse's mode of explanation has much in common with forms of materialism, like Marx's, that attribute great

---

[30] Though, strictly speaking, this holds only for codified forms of private property since "a sort of property" – each family's informal claim to the hut it has constructed for itself – is said to precede the division of labor occasioned by metallurgy and agriculture (though it does not precede the division of labor that comes with gender differentiation and that Rousseau treats as a quasi-natural feature of human social life). These qualifications point out the nearly unmasterable complexity of Rousseau's account and the necessity of simplifying his claims in reconstructing it.

explanatory weight to social changes brought about by technological advancements, which themselves are responses to challenges humans face in reproducing themselves materially.[31] For Rousseau, growth in productive forces also plays a role in explaining individual differentiation and the further development of the division of labor, and ultimately therefore private property and the state as well.)

Leisure is important to Rousseau's account of social inequality, then, because it is a precondition of the very psychological force that gives rise to the impulse of humans to create inequalities. This is not, however, the only role it plays in that account. Leisure is also what makes luxury (or "conveniences") possible, which, by increasing humans' perceived needs beyond those that nature imposes on them, gives them incentives to produce and to possess (though not yet to *own*) more than purely natural beings could ever imagine desiring.[32] Although luxury itself does not necessarily imply inequality, the farther humans move away from a condition in which their desires are limited to a circumscribed set of relatively easily satisfied needs, the more room there is for differences in luck, circumstances, and natural characteristics to enter the picture and increase the distance between individuals with respect to skills, possessions, and (artificial) needs. Once these differences are in place, the way is open for forms of *amour propre* that seek superior standing, eventually abetted by codified rules of private property, to join up with the taste for luxury so as to insure that a mania for amassing goods, and the inequality that inevitably results from it, are unavoidable consequences. (It should be noted that these considerations do not exhaust the significance Rousseau attaches to luxury, as suggested by the ominous statement accompanying the first appearance of luxury in the Second Discourse: "This was the first yoke that, without being aware of it, they imposed on themselves and the first source of evils they prepared for their descendants" (*DI*, 164–5/*OC* III, 168). Luxury plays this central role in the

---

[31] This is best seen in the fact that what starts the whole train of developments in Part II is difficulties humans face – the height of trees, competition with animals – in satisfying their biological needs (*DI*, 161/*OC* III, 165).

[32] In unpublished lectures István Hont has fruitfully examined the importance of luxury for Rousseau. For related themes in other Enlightenment thinkers, see his "The Luxury Debate in the Early Enlightenment," in Mark Goldie and Robert Wokler, eds., *The Cambridge History of Eighteenth-Century Political Thought* (Cambridge University Press, 2006), 377–418.

Second Discourse because, as the source of new needs – "these commodities, by becoming habitual, ... degenerated into true needs" (*DI*, 165/*OC* III, 168) – it is also a principal source of human *dependence* (on others). Because this point is less important for explaining inequality than for explaining the evils bound up with inequality, discussion of it will be postponed until the following chapter.)

It is obvious how social inequalities presuppose some differences among individuals beyond those that would be present in a purely natural state. Perhaps the only point worthy of further discussion is the following: although Rousseau is generally consistent in treating such differences as artificial – as the results of contingent and often random processes that depend on human consciousness and will – there is one important difference among individuals that, while conspicuously absent in the original state of nature, appears very early and without explanation in the narrative of Part II and then appears to assume a fixed, essentially natural status for the rest of the Second Discourse. After initially emphasizing the similarities that men – *males*, not human beings in general – perceive in "their" females, Rousseau very quickly introduces an extremely consequential form of differentiation, "the ways of life of the two sexes" (*DI*, 164/*OC* III, 168), that seems to be due entirely to a natural distinction, the biological difference between male and female. Clearly, this quasi-natural difference in the habits and characters of men and women functions in the Second Discourse as the unexplained basis (and justification) of profound social inequalities that, in this text at least, Rousseau has little interest in investigating or even noticing. Apart from illustrating how differentiation among individuals helps to make social inequalities possible (as well as pointing out a significant defect in Rousseau's treatment of inequality here), the example of gender also serves to highlight the connection between differentiation in general and the next major phenomenon in the Second Discourse's genealogy of inequality, the division of labor. Although Rousseau emphasizes the division of labor occasioned by the development of metallurgy and agriculture as separate branches of production, a significant form of the division of labor in fact creeps into his story much earlier, as soon as men go out to hunt and gather while women stay at home to cook, clean, and take care of the children. Like many men who have never done such work, Rousseau imagines that these tasks are consistent with a "sedentary" way of life (that contrasts with men's more vigorous hunting and gathering), and the fact that he seems not to regard women's tasks as work probably explains why he fails to see this aspect of gender differentiation as another fundamental form of the division of labor.

Like the phenomenon of luxury discussed above, the division of labor is important to Rousseau because of the role it plays in making humans dependent on one another for the satisfaction of their needs. (And, as in the case of luxury, I will return to the pernicious consequences of this aspect of the division of labor in the following chapter.) Yet the division of labor, especially that involved in the development of metallurgy and agriculture, clearly plays a part in explaining social inequality as well:

> Things in this state could have remained equal if . . . the use of iron and the consumption of foods had always been exactly balanced; but this proportion, which nothing maintained,[33] was soon upset; . . . the worker of fields had greater need of iron, or the smith greater need of wheat, and in working equally, the one earned much while the other was barely able to stay alive. (*DI*, 169–70/*OC* III, 174)

Rousseau's general point is that the more individuals become differentiated from one another and occupy specialized and mutually dependent positions within society, the greater the possibility that through entirely random, unintended occurrences what was once merely qualitative difference will eventually turn into difference coupled with inequality.

In Rousseau's explanation of this point, the phrase "which nothing maintained" is significant. It expresses a philosophical outlook that deeply informs the Second Discourse's approach not only to artificial inequality but to social phenomena in general. Rousseau tends to think of nature, unadulterated by human intervention, as an ordered and harmonious realm governed by the eternal, beneficent laws its Creator imposed on it. Human action – the intervention of the artificial – invariably disrupts this order, however, and unintentionally introduces into nature (which from this point on is never again *merely* nature) contingency, discord, and evil. In the present example, the

---

[33] This qualification is one of many examples in the Second Discourse where the absence of conscious control or organization plays an important role in explaining social ills.

more extensive division of labor occasioned by the development of metallurgy and agriculture results ultimately in social inequality because, once humans have interfered with the natural order, there is no natural law or power to guarantee that the initial equilibrium that might have existed between metalworkers and farmers remain in place. In the absence of such a guarantee, the maintenance of equilibrium depends entirely on good fortune, and as time progresses, the disruption of that equilibrium is virtually assured. Left to run its own course, the balance between the two separate but interdependent branches of production is bound to become skewed: too many ironworkers and too few farmers, for example, means that the former are barely able to live from what they produce, whereas the latter profit nicely from their highly demanded products.[34] Although the Second Discourse itself does not tell this part of the story, the only hope Rousseau sees for restoring a benign order to a world that has been modified by human freedom is for humans themselves to impose (artificial) laws on the social world – laws that order the very disorder they have unintentionally produced – which leads to the reproduction of *some version* of the same goods that characterized the natural world (freedom, survival, and the unproblematic satisfaction of needs and desires) before their own deeds ruined nature's design. Articulating what such laws must look like is the task of *The Social Contract*, not of the Second Discourse, but as we will see in the following chapter, the Second Discourse's account of how (and why) the original state of nature is *good* helps to lay the normative foundations (*fondements*) on top of which *The Social Contract* will construct its vision of a legitimate state and a healthy society.

Once leisure, luxury, differentiation, and the division of labor have been introduced into the Second Discourse's narrative – alongside, of course, *amour propre* – private property and the first rules of justice are said, somewhat abruptly, to follow necessarily (*DI*, 169/*OC* III, 173–4). Presumably this is the point at which Rousseau takes himself to have run through the various conditions – the "many prior ideas" – without which the land-grabbing described in the first paragraph of

---

[34] In fact, as Note IX makes clear (and as István Hont has emphasized), Rousseau thought the more likely scenario to be one in which farmers, not metalworkers, were disadvantaged (*DI*, 202/*OC* III, 206).

Part II would not have been possible. It is not difficult either to see why those prior phenomena might be necessary conditions of private property, or to understand how the introduction of private property advances the Second Discourse's account of the sources of social inequality, since it opens up a major new domain in which economic inequality can grow. Beyond this, however, the establishment of private property and the state enables other forms of social inequality to flourish as well. For example, once the state is in place, a new possibility for inequality arises between the governed and those who govern; in other words, political domination (as I call it in Chapter 4), backed up by the coercive power of the state, becomes a possible way of satisfying the desires of some to achieve publicly recognized positions of superiority. Along with this, new possibilities for non-political forms of domination emerge from inequalities in wealth when they are buttressed by the state, ultimately through the threat of violence, and conjoined with increasing economic dependence. These conditions make it possible for *amour propre* to seek new kinds of satisfaction and to establish more enduring inequalities than were possible when individuals were self-sufficient and roughly equal in terms of the resources available to them (*DI*, 167/*OC* III, 171). For alongside the old strategies of striving to be the best singer or dancer, new opportunities for achieving superiority arise, including the possibility of exploiting others' dependence and economic disadvantage for the purpose of subjugating them. Those who own land, for example, can easily impose unreasonable demands on those who, because they own no land themselves, must labor for them. Although exploitation of this sort – the exploitation of one *class* by another – clearly brings economic benefits to the exploiters, it also yields recognitive advantages: establishing oneself as the exploiter of others, especially when the roles of exploiter and exploited are sanctioned and enforced by social institutions, can be seen as just one more way of finding public confirmation of one's high standing in the eyes of others.

What is less clear in Rousseau's account, however, is why the private ownership of things should be a necessary or even likely consequence of leisure, luxury, individual differentiation, and the sort of division of labor necessitated by metallurgy and agriculture. Serious difficulties arise already in the paragraph's first claim: "From the cultivation of land, its division necessarily followed; and from property, once recognized, the first rules of justice necessarily followed." It is immediately striking that, just as in the first sentence of Part II, it is the private ownership of land, not of just any commodity, that Rousseau seems most interested in. This is surely because land itself, in distinction to the consumption goods produced by working the land, belongs to what Marx would later call the means of production (those basic goods, such as land, raw materials, machinery, and workplaces, that are materially necessary for production of any kind to take place). This concept is of fundamental importance to Marx because it lies at the center of his definition of economic class: the principal distinction between the two main classes in capitalism is that the capitalist class owns, and therefore controls, the means of production, whereas workers own no productive forces other than their own labor power, which, because they must eat, they are obliged to sell to the capitalist in exchange for wages. Although Rousseau lacks these precise concepts – the capitalism of his time was a much less developed and less visible phenomenon than that of Marx's, almost a century later – he is more interested in land than in its products for very similar reasons: owning land, a basic prerequisite of production, is potentially a source of great social power, especially when there are other members of society who own no productive forces other than their own labor power. The situation in which some individuals own land (or factories or stocks of raw materials) and others do not is of great interest to Rousseau because it is a situation in which *dependence* (requiring the cooperation of others to satisfy one's needs) is joined with *inequality,* and this combination, as we will see in the next chapter, produces a noxious brew out of which the various evils of society described in Part II inevitably arise.

As I suggested above, however, it is far from clear why the cultivation of land should necessarily lead to its being divided up and privately owned. One unanswered question is why land, once partitioned, should be owned by individuals. For if cultivation is carried out collectively – by far the most likely scenario – why would land, if owned at all, not belong instead to the groups that work it? A second problem is that the principle Rousseau appeals to in explaining (and apparently justifying) ownership of the land's products – that the person who labors to produce the good is its "natural" owner – is, as he himself sometimes seems to be on the verge of admitting, hardly applicable to land, which of course no human being has produced. It is little help to claim, as Rousseau seems to do, that the right to the goods one produces on the land also gives one a right to the continuous possession of that land. For this argument is surely fallacious – how can a right to exclude others from means of production that one has not produced oneself arise out of the mere right to own what one has produced *using* those means of production? – and, in any case (and as Rousseau admits), continuous possession would fall short of genuine ownership. Further, if the argument extending the natural law of property to land were not fallacious, it is very hard to see how its conclusion, *ex hypothesi* soundly deduced from what Rousseau regards as a natural law (and therefore in harmony with the fundamental interests of humankind [*DI*, 127/ *OC* III,125]), could be made consistent with the opening sentence of Part II, which appears to characterize the private ownership of land as an arbitrary innovation and unambiguously decries it as the source of "many miseries and horrors [that without it] the human species would have been spared" (*DI*, 161/*OC* III, 164).

In light of these difficulties, my proposal is to attempt to understand this tortured paragraph by beginning with its final sentence, in which Rousseau clearly distinguishes property that "follows from natural law" – ownership of the goods one has produced with one's own labor – from "a new kind of . . . property right different from the one that follows from natural law," namely, the right to own land itself. Rousseau is most plausibly interpreted as endorsing the former conception of property as natural, just, and valid in all societies in which labor is carried out (which is to say, in all human societies), while regarding the latter as an artificial and not strictly necessary innovation that can be explained as one possible way humans might understandably try to extend the natural law governing property so as to make land, too, into something that individuals can own. The extension of the natural law of property to cover land is, as Rousseau attempts to show, not without a certain logic: if I used this land last season, I am entitled to use it again in the next, and when this has gone on year after year, do I not own the land itself? Yet, as I argued above, this logic is sufficiently strained to leave one wondering what justifies his remark that the mere fact of "continuous possession" (of land) "is easily transformed into property." Whatever accounts for the alleged "ease" of this transformation, it is neither, I would argue, conceptual nor causal *necessity*. Instead, to say that continuous possession easily becomes recognized property is to say that it is not difficult to understand how, without thinking much about it, humans at this level of development could slip from one practice into the other. This means that the later practice is not a rationally necessary implication of the earlier practice (or of the natural law of property itself), nor is it a causally necessary effect of it. In other words, we should understand Rousseau to be saying that private ownership of the means of production is an understandable development but that it is not legitimized or mandated by natural law, nor is it a necessary accompaniment of any real system of property whatsoever in which laborers tend to cultivate the same piece of land season after season. When Rousseau says, then, that "from the cultivation of land, its division necessarily followed," he should be taken to mean: *given the specific, primitive conditions hypothesized here* – including humans' sometimes unsatisfied desire for superior standing (see below), as well as their inability to foresee the consequences of their innovation[35] – the private ownership of land is a more or less unavoidable consequence of its cultivation but not for that reason a rationally justified consequence; nor is it a causally necessary consequence of the cultivation of land under all conditions whatsoever.

In my view, Rousseau's claim that the continuous possession of land "is easily transformed" into property in land – understood as a claim about what is likely to happen, not about what is right – becomes genuinely compelling only on the further assumption that some motivation is at work in this transformation beyond *amour de soi-même*'s concerns for survival, comfort, and efficiency. Such a motivation could indeed be found in the passion inspired by *amour propre*, already in play at this stage of the narrative, to distinguish

---

[35] The inability of undeveloped beings to foresee the pernicious consequences of their own choices is a repeated though often overlooked theme of the Second Discourse, which at various points appeals to their lack of knowledge (*DI*, 164/*OC* III, 168), false beliefs (*DI*, 173/ *OC* III, 177), simplicity (or naïveté) (*DI*, 161/*OC* III, 164), and blindness (*DI*, 197/*OC* III, 202) in explaining how the evils of civilization can be the (unintended) consequences of their own actions. Thus, Rousseau's account retains a crucial (and in substance progressive) element of the Christian version of the Fall – humans themselves are the source of evil – while at the same time completely changing its (repressive) moral and spiritual implications (since those fateful choices are no longer ascribed to an evil and irremediable human nature).

oneself in a publicly visible manner as a being of value. It is difficult to imagine that the significance of the etymological and conceptual connection between *amour propre* and *propriété* – that which is proper to, or belongs to, oneself – would have eluded Rousseau's attention, and thinking of the two phenomena as mutually reinforcing is consistent with the general contours of the story the Second Discourse tells as well as with the fundamental role it ascribes to both in explaining social inequality and the other ills of developed society. (Indeed, Rousseau explicitly acknowledges this connection when, in surveying the results of all these developments just prior to the state of war, he says: "each man's rank and lot [were] established . . . by the quantity of his goods" (*DI*, 170/*OC* III, 174).) In other words, the first man who encloses a piece of land and exclaims "this is mine!" (*ceci est à moi!*) is to be understood as also, and most fundamentally, pointing to this piece of land before others and proclaiming to them "this is me!" That private property of every conceivable type can serve as an external marker of one's standing for, and in relation to, others surely accounts for a large part of the mania with which individuals, both in Rousseau's narrative and in our own society, scramble to acquire ever more, ever better, and ever more conspicuous piles of what their neighbors and associates are constrained to recognize as "their own," which is to say, as material extensions of themselves and reflections of their standing in relation to others.

It is already possible to anticipate the significance of the distinction on which my reading is based – between property that is sanctioned by natural law and property that is based on artificial conventions (or on interpretive extensions of that law) – for Rousseau's ultimate position regarding the legitimacy of the private ownership of land: because this species of property belongs to the domain of the artificial, its legitimacy cannot be settled by natural law alone. Instead, as with all artificial institutions, its legitimacy will have to be judged by those principles – formulated first in *The Social Contract* but implicitly at work already in the Second Discourse – that define justice, or right, within human society, principles whose justification derives ultimately from their being the answer to the question: which principles could all members of society rationally consent to be ruled by, if each were concerned only with satisfying his or her fundamental interests as human beings? (I return to Rousseau's principles of right within society and point out their presence already in the Second Discourse in Chapter 4.)

It is tempting to conclude from the opening scene of Part II that Rousseau will categorically deny legitimacy to the private ownership of land – as the source of so many human ills, how could it be consistent with the fundamental interests of all? – but in fact, as the paragraph immediately following the discussion of the natural law of property reveals, this conclusion would be overly hasty. For Rousseau asserts in the later paragraph that under the right conditions the private ownership of land need not have negative consequences for society (*DI*, 169–70/*OC* III, 174). The key point here is expressed in the phrase "things in this state could have remained equal." In other words, the exploitation and loss of freedom that Rousseau goes on to describe in the Second Discourse could have been avoided, even assuming the private ownership of land, if this ownership had been conjoined with a condition of basic material equality among social members. In such a condition – where dependence existed without significant inequality – the private ownership of land would exist without prejudicing the fundamental interests of any individual, and in that case (and only then) it might well form part of a legitimate system of property relations. Thus, rather than taking an a priori position on the justice or injustice of any species of artificial social arrangement, including private ownership of the means of production, Rousseau is committed to postponing judgment as to the legitimacy of any specific set of institutions until an assessment of its consequences for the fundamental interests of all has been made. If a given system of property relations, when realized under certain specific social conditions, can be shown not to prejudice the fundamental interests of any its members, then under those conditions it counts for Rousseau as a legitimate and therefore permissible social arrangement, regardless of its relation to whatever natural laws originally govern the legitimate acquisition of property. (This methodological procedure marks the most fundamental difference between the views of Locke and Rousseau [and those of their respective followers] on property. It is no accident that John Rawls, an extraordinarily perceptive reader of *The Social Contract* and the Second Discourse, pursues a strategy very similar to Rousseau's in determining the legitimacy of social inequalities and in addressing the question as to whether capitalist or socialist property relations are sanctioned by the principles of justice. I return to this issue in Chapter 5.)

What, then, does this complicated account of the origin of property imply for Rousseau's position concerning how fundamental private property is to human society in general and whether it represents a permanent or instead an in principle eliminable feature of the social landscape? Given his thesis that there exists a *natural* law governing the acquisition of property, it seems likely that Rousseau takes private property in some form to be fundamental to human society in general and therefore a more or less necessary feature of any real society. This fundamental status of property is bound up with the Second Discourse's claim that in its most primitive form property depends only on, and is the virtually necessary consequence of, a very limited number of conditions that are themselves very basic conditions of civilization. Rousseau's implicit claim is that private property, at least in the limited form sanctioned by the natural law of property, follows more or less necessarily once minimal levels of leisure, luxury, and individual differentiation have been attained and (if my argument above is correct) once *amour propre* is sufficiently active to recommend the acquisition of property to individuals as a partial means to achieving a recognized standing for others. More specific systems of private ownership, in contrast – including property in the means of production – presuppose more complex and increasingly contingent social circumstances (including a more specialized division of labor than the simplest forms of property presuppose), and for this reason it seems unlikely that Rousseau would regard them as necessary features of any human society whatsoever. Evidence for this claim can be found in the great importance Rousseau attaches to the invention of metallurgy and agriculture for the division of labor and the development of economic inequality, conjoined with the difficulty he has, and admits to having, in explaining the necessity, even the likelihood of the discovery of these two arts "that civilized men and ruined the human species" (*DI*, 168/*OC* III, 171–2).

Still, even if private property in general is a less contingent feature of human society than private ownership of the means of production, Rousseau is far from regarding the latter as an anomalous or merely accidental phenomenon. For, as I noted above, when he says in the paragraph on property and its relation to natural law that "from the cultivation of land, its division necessarily followed" (*DI*, 169/*OC* III, 173), he is clearly claiming that, given the conditions in place, the (artificial and not logically necessary) extension of the natural law of property to the ownership of land is more than a mere possibility. (Recall that I interpreted this statement as claiming that, assuming the basic conditions of leisure, luxury, individual differentiation, and a sufficiently specialized division of labor, together with both the inability of primitive humans to foresee the undesirable consequences of what they are about to do and their awakened but not always satisfied desire to be esteemed in some way as better than others, it is hard to see how the private ownership of land, offering vast new possibilities to an aroused *amour propre*, would not follow more or less directly once the cultivation of land had become an established practice.) The important point here is the following: from the circumstance that under primitive conditions the private ownership of the means of production may be a practically unavoidable development, it does not follow that this type of property is unavoidable *for us* as well, nor that it is (in either case) permissible from the standpoint of justice. This much, I believe, is implicit already in the Second Discourse. It is only in *The Social Contract* that it becomes clear, in Rousseau's rejection of nature as the basis of right within human society (*SC*, I.1.ii), that these two questions cannot be decided a priori but only through further reflection – undertaken by us, as historically situated beings – aimed at figuring out what is (now, for us) practically achievable and which specific possible schemes of property are compatible with the basic requirement of justice, namely, that the fundamental human interests of all participants in such schemes are given their due.

In drawing a very close connection between the private ownership of land and political society (the state) – "the first person who ... enclosed a piece of land ... was the true founder of civil society" (*DI*, 161/*OC* III, 164) – Rousseau is in one respect merely following Locke, who famously located the purpose of political society in the protection of individual property and explicitly included the private ownership of land, even when distributed unequally, among the kinds of property the state is designed to protect.[36] But while Rousseau agrees that the

---

[36] John Locke, *The Second Treatise of Government*, Chapter IX, §124.

primary purpose of most existing states is the protection of private property, including in the means of production, he regards this (when differences in the ownership of such property are substantial) not as a hallmark of those states' legitimacy, as did Locke, but as an indictment of the major role they play in institutionalizing and perpetuating social inequalities, and not merely differences in wealth but a host of further inequalities as well – in prestige and social power, for example – that follow more or less directly from economic inequality. Here, too, it is easy to see why the state of the sort recommended by Locke[37] – in "fixing forever the law of property and of inequality" (*DI*, 173/*OC* III, 178) – plays a prominent role in Rousseau's account of the sources of social inequality. It is equally clear in what order of explanatory primacy the (Lockean) state stands to the other non-psychological elements of that account: it presupposes all of the other five conditions, and as soon as private property, especially in land, assumes the role of representing individuals and their standing to others, this condition is sufficient to explain the need for political society. (Political association is said also to presuppose enduring and pervasive conflict among social members – a state of war – but the state of war is itself merely a consequence of the same five conditions that make political society necessary. The intervention of the state of war in Rousseau's narrative has the interesting consequence that the purpose of the political association he considers here is not only to maintain existing property relations but also to protect the

---

[37] The agreement to found political society depicted in Part II of the Second Discourse (*DI*, 172–3/*OC* III, 176–8) – which "gives new fetters to the weak and new powers to the rich" – can be understood as a critique of Locke's version of the social contract. Even though the contract Rousseau describes here is a response to a state of war – and hence not to the state of nature as Locke understands it – the agreement itself is Lockean in the sense that its sole purpose is the protection of private property, where the latter is taken to include highly unequal amounts of property, even in land, that have been amassed in a pre-political state of nature. Rousseau's aim here is to argue that a Lockean contract is illegitimate because it merely sets in stone the inequalities (and most of the other ills) that precede it and make it necessary. More precisely, Rousseau's claim is that a *Lockean* contract is an illegitimate response to a *Hobbesian* state of war. For the Second Discourse can be read as a defense of Hobbes's account of the state of war as the pre-political condition that defines the problem the legitimate state must resolve (and at the same time, of course, as a critique of Hobbes's claim that the state of war follows from conditions imposed on human beings by *nature*). The task of *The Social Contract*, then, is to set out the principles of political association that eliminate the state of war by imposing an order within which the fundamental interests of all individuals can be satisfied.

endangered lives of individuals.[38] Because of this the Lockean state can be said to serve legitimate human interests at the same time as it perpetuates the very social conditions that make its imposition of law and order necessary in the first place. This implies in turn that it is not *merely* false consciousness that drives those who consent to the Lockean state depicted in Part II to embrace their own chains (*DI*, 173/*OC* III, 177).)

Let us now attempt to summarize the account given in this chapter by citing and then supplementing Rousseau's own summary on the last page of the Second Discourse of his answer to the question of where inequality comes from: "It follows from this account that inequality, being almost nonexistent in the state of nature, owes its force and growth to the development of our faculties and the progress of the human mind, and finally becomes stable and legitimate through the establishment of property and laws" (*DI*, 188/*OC* III, 193). This brief recap of the Second Discourse's genealogy of inequality touches on three of the four main points elaborated in this chapter: first, although some aspects of existing social inequalities can be traced back to purely natural differences among humans, these natural inequalities account for only a negligible part of the inequality found in actual societies; thus, the overwhelmingly major part of the latter is artificial, coming from us rather than from nature. Second, the principal force that drives humans to invent artificial systems of inequality is psychological. Its source is *amour propre*, the passion to achieve comparative standing in the eyes of others, which, when configured – as it very often but not always is – as a desire for superiority, motivates humans to create new forms of inequality for the sole purpose of finding public recognition of the superior standing they desire. (Moreover, this passion itself depends on the development of certain basic cognitive capacities – for comparison and self-consciousness, for example – that humans possess by virtue of their nature.) Third (and omitted in Rousseau's summary), *amour propre's* capacity to produce significant inequalities depends on a number of non-psychological enabling conditions, which include leisure, luxury, artificial individual differentiation, and some degree of the division of

---

[38] Locke, of course, understood property in its widest sense to include one's life (*The Second Treatise of Government*, Chapter VII, §87).

labor. Finally, social inequalities become truly entrenched, pervasive, and dangerous only with the development of explicitly codified practices of private ownership, which make it possible for things to serve as public representations of persons and their status, thereby opening up an entirely new, nearly infinite domain within which inequalities motivated by *amour propre* can be striven for and established. When this new domain of inequality expands, especially when it comes to include private, unequal ownership of the means of production, states are created, which not only enforce these inequalities by the threat of force but, even more important, give them the false appearance of legitimacy via political philosophy that presents the state and its laws as institutions that promote the interests of all social members and to which, for that reason, each could consent (or has actually consented).

All of the non-psychological conditions mentioned in Rousseau's genealogy of inequality play a role in generating new possibilities for inequalities of various kinds to arise and take root in society. In the absence of *amour propre*, however, those possibilities would remain largely unrealized. When they do result in new forms of inequality, it is because an awakened *amour propre*, with an indeterminate longing to do better than others, is able to latch on to them and use them to further its aim of achieving standing in the eyes of others. *Amour propre* does not by itself generate the practices and institutions that allow for all sorts of artificial inequalities to enter the world, but once those possibilities are there, it takes full advantage of them, furnishing the fuel for the inexorable growth of inequality that results finally in the various evils – enslavement, conflict, vice, misery, alienation – whose existence the Second Discourse aims to explain. It is for this reason that Rousseau singles out *amour propre* as the "origin" of social inequality, even if its capacity to originate inequality also depends on other, non-psychological conditions.

Finally, we should ask whether this account succeeds in showing that social inequality does *not* have its source in nature. Of course, the answer depends, as always, on how nature is defined. When construed in the special sense that Rousseau often gives to the term, his account does indeed avoid locating the source of social inequality in nature: because *amour propre* cannot operate independently of human consciousness and will, it and its products are never, strictly speaking, effects of nature. If this were all there were to Rousseau's position, however, his victory over philosophies that see familiar forms of inequality as necessary consequences of human nature would remain quite hollow. To the extent that he is committed to the view that *amour propre* is a fundamental component of human psychology – an element of human nature in the expanded sense – and that even desires for superior standing of some sort belong permanently to our motivational makeup, it looks like social inequality, too, must be an ineradicable feature of human existence. (And Rousseau would agree with this conclusion when formulated this simply.) The key to seeing how Rousseau's position differs from those he means to reject lies in recalling the connection he draws between human freedom and the "could have been different" nature of its products or, in what amounts to the same thing, his emphasis on the nearly infinite malleability of *amour propre* and its products. This thesis applies both to the specific forms that *amour propre* assumes at any particular time and place and to the non-psychological social conditions that play a role in his genealogy. To paraphrase a claim made above: even if desires for superior standing and the inequalities they inevitably produce are, very generally, necessary consequences of human nature in the expanded sense, there is a huge range of possible forms they can take on, and precisely how they manifest themselves is to some significant extent up to us. The important question, then, is not whether social inequalities in general should or must exist but whether those that do produce the pernicious consequences that make artificial inequality detrimental to human flourishing and therefore morally objectionable.

In Rousseau's view, his account of the source of social inequality exonerates human nature by showing that the circumstances that generate the pernicious consequences of social inequalities are not necessary consequences of human nature (not even of human nature in the expanded sense) but, at least in part, the effects of free human action that might have had, and could in the future have, different results. (Strictly speaking, Rousseau's exoneration of human nature is not complete until he writes *Emile* and *The Social Contract*, which together are meant to demonstrate the real possibility – that is, subject to the constraints of nature, both human and otherwise – of a human existence without enslavement, misery, and alienation and in which artificial inequalities, though very limited, are not completely eradicated.) Yet even if Rousseau's complex account of the source of inequality exonerates human nature in the specified sense, it does not translate into an optimistic view of human existence. For the number and complexity of the conditions that tend to produce dangerous forms of inequality imply that unless human beings can hit on just the right combination of responses to those conditions, enslavement, conflict, vice, misery, and alienation are destined to be their lot. Even though Rousseau insists that the Second Discourse has a purely diagnostic aim, offering no remedies for the ills it diagnoses, its account of the sources of those ills provides at least an orientation for thinking about those remedies that guides his positive theory of legitimate political institutions, especially as outlined in *The Social Contract*: such a theory must find a way, within the constraints imposed by nature, of restructuring social institutions and practices that allows for the satisfaction of *amour propre*, limited inequalities, forms of private property, a developed division of labor – and above all, for the various kinds of dependence fundamental to human existence – while minimizing their tendency to produce the all too familiar ills of civilization depicted in the Second Discourse. As Rousseau recognizes, this is a very tall order, given the complexity of his account of where social inequalities come from and why they are so pervasive in the societies we know.

CHAPTER 3

The normative resources of nature

The first two chapters of this book attempted to reconstruct Rousseau's answer to the first of the two main questions addressed by the Second Discourse: where does human inequality come from? Chapters 3 and 4 address the Second Discourse's normative question: is human inequality authorized by natural law? To use the terms that Rousseau himself employs in the Second Discourse's title, the first question concerns the *origin* of inequality, the second its *foundations* (*fondements*). The present chapter first briefly examines Rousseau's answer to the question of the extent to which natural law authorizes social inequalities. After doing so, it turns to the more important part of Rousseau's view concerning the extent to which nature understood more generally supplies us with the normative resources we need to give a more complete answer to the question concerning the legitimacy or permissibility of social inequalities than natural law itself is able to provide. As we shall see, the part of Rousseau's account of nature that provides these more extensive resources for judging the legitimacy of inequality is his normative conception of human nature. Here, too, we will need to distinguish *original* human nature, and the normative picture associated with it, from normative human nature *in the expanded sense*. Both normative visions of human nature provide accounts of the goods essential to human flourishing, with the only difference being that the weaker of the two (the one associated with original human nature) abstracts from the social character of humans, whereas the more robust (normative human nature in the expanded sense) includes one inherently social good – esteem, or the good opinion of others – among its list of essential human goods. It will help to recall from the previous chapter that the explanatory conception of human nature in the expanded sense merely adds *amour propre* to the elements of original human nature; in the case of the normative conceptions of human nature, it is the good associated with *amour propre*, social esteem or respect, that is added to the picture.[1]

IS SOCIAL INEQUALITY AUTHORIZED BY NATURAL LAW?

If we bear in mind Rousseau's distinction between natural and moral (or social) inequalities, the explicit answer he gives, at the very end of the Second Discourse, to the question concerning whether natural law authorizes inequality is easily summarized: "moral inequality ... is contrary to natural right[2] whenever it is not directly proportional to physical [or natural][3] inequality" (*DI*, 188/*OC* III, 193–4). It is worth noting that this claim differs from an even more austere claim the Second Discourse might be thought to be making, namely, that only natural inequalities are authorized by natural law, whereas social inequalities never are, implying that even differences in power or wealth directly grounded in natural inequalities would be illegitimate. Yet it is significant that Rousseau never says that natural inequalities themselves are authorized by natural law, presumably because those inequalities, as the products of nature, simply *are*, and therefore need no justification, whereas social inequalities alone, created and sustained by us, are subject to moral evaluation. This explains why he calls these inequalities *moral* and why only they are the subject of the Second Discourse's final statement on the conditions under which equality in general is authorized; in the case of

---

[1] One could also say that the expanded picture of the human good includes the actual development of the latent capacities that make up perfectibility. I abstract from this point here and focus exclusively on *amour propre* and its good, social recognition.

[2] In this quote Rousseau replaces the Academy's term, "natural law" (*la loi naturelle*), with "natural right" (*le droit naturel*). Since in the very next sentence he reverts to *la loi de nature*, I assume that, here at least, he is using all three expressions interchangeably. When in *The Social Contract* Rousseau refers to right (*droit*) in the state of nature ("an unlimited right to everything that tempts [one]"), however, he understands it essentially as Hobbes does: as generating moral permissions – to do whatever I deem to be in my interest – that impose no corresponding obligations on those around me (*SC*, I.8.ii). The right of nature in this sense must be distinguished from natural law as it is understood in the Second Discourse and other texts (where natural law implies genuine obligations outside political society and where the rights generated by natural law imply corresponding duties on the part of others to respect them). I am indebted to John Scott for an illuminating discussion of this issue.

[3] Recall that Rousseau equates natural and physical inequalities (*DI*, 131/*OC* III, 131).

natural inequality, in contrast, the question of authorization does not arise.

Even so, the Second Discourse's concluding answer to its normative question still looks to be (and is) implausibly simple: the only justified inequalities in wealth, honor, and social power are those directly grounded in natural differences, such as when – to use Rousseau's examples – the wise command the foolish and the young obey the old (*DI*, 188/*OC* III, 193–4) or, in a more interesting example, when parents command their children (*DI*, 177/*OC* III, 182). In other words, *from the perspective of natural law alone* all differences in wealth, honor, and social power must directly reflect natural differences in traits such as maturity, wisdom, skill, and strength; the wealthy, for example, must be in some relevant sense genuinely better than the poor, and the difference in wealth between rich and poor must match up with the extent to which the former are naturally superior to the latter.[4] As Rousseau recognizes, very few – perhaps none – of the social inequalities we are familiar with in the modern world would meet this standard;[5] a society grounded in natural law alone would permit very few social inequalities, and the disparities it did allow would be much more modest than those of existing societies. More important, it seems highly likely – and Rousseau appears to have understood this, too – that any society in which all social inequalities directly tracked natural inequalities would necessarily be extremely primitive, a society perhaps in which individuals were happy and free (in the simplest of ways) but where most of their human capacities and potentials, their perfectibility, remained undeveloped.

Rousseau's occasional talk of a right of property that follows from natural law (*DI*, 169/*OC* III, 173–4) introduces a slight complication into this otherwise simple picture, raising the possibility that he believes there to be a source of legitimacy in natural law for a certain kind of social inequality – inequality in wealth – that goes beyond the simple requirement that all social inequalities directly reflect natural ones. Rousseau's

---

[4] A brief description of such a society is given at *DI*, 181/*OC* III, 186–7.

[5] "It makes no sense to ask [regarding existing societies] . . . whether those who command are necessarily better than those who obey, and whether strength of body or of mind, wisdom or virtue, are always found . . . in proportion to power or wealth: a question that may be good for slaves to debate within hearing of their masters but not one appropriate to men . . . who seek the truth" (*DI*, 131/*OC* III, 131–2).

remarks in the Second Discourse about natural law in general, especially his critique of that notion (*DI*, 125–8/*OC* III, 124–6), are rather confusing, but if we restrict our attention to what he says about the extent to which private property has a basis in natural law, it is possible to find a reasonably coherent position to attribute to him. As I noted in the previous chapter, his view in the Second Discourse appears to be that manual labor alone renders private property legitimate (*DI*, 169/*OC* III, 173). In taking this position he presumably means to embrace some version of the doctrine, most famously endorsed by Locke, that "mixing one's labor"[6] with the resources furnished by nature makes the products of that labor – nature transformed by human activity – into one's legitimate property, imposing on others a natural obligation to respect those products as properly belonging to the person who produced them.[7]

Compared to Locke, however, Rousseau has a much stricter reading of what the natural law governing private property authorizes: he is much more cautious than Locke with respect to whether laboring on land makes it one's own,[8] and he insists that it is only one's own labor – and not "the turfs my servant has cut," as Locke allows[9] – that can generate legitimate property for me. The latter restriction means that any naturally authorized inequalities in wealth can be due only to differences in the amount, skill, or efficiency of the labor that the individual owners of property have themselves performed. Hence, the natural law of private property might end up legitimizing some degree of inequality in wealth, but any such inequalities would remain

---

[6] John Locke, *The Second Treatise of Government*, Chapter V, §27.

[7] Other statements, however, make it difficult to know if this is indeed Rousseau's view, for example, his claim later in the Second Discourse that "the right of property exists only by convention and human institution" (*DI*, 179/*OC* III, 184). This is one point where Rousseau's position on whether there is a natural law governing private property becomes difficult to determine for certain, since in other places (cited in this paragraph) he appears to claim that there is. The same lack of clarity plagues many of his remarks on natural law more generally, an issue to which I return briefly below. But since, as I interpret it, natural law ultimately plays an almost negligible role in Rousseau's critique of inequality, this apparent confusion is not very damaging to his overall position.

[8] As I suggested in Chapter 2, Rousseau's remarks on this topic are obscure – he appears to limit rights to the land one has labored on "until the harvest" – but he clearly does not believe that natural law legitimizes a more enduring "division of land" (*DI*, 169/*OC* III, 173–4). See *SC*, I.9, for more (and equally confusing) remarks on the law of nature governing private property, especially in land.

[9] Locke, *The Second Treatise of Government*, Chapter V, §28.

infinitesimally small compared to those that characterize even the most egalitarian of modern societies. Moreover, those inequalities would retain a close tie to natural inequalities, at least insofar as differences in labor performed reflect differences in natural talents. It is unlikely, however, that all such differences in labor would reflect purely natural differences, and for this reason the natural law governing private property goes a bit beyond the simple principle that only social inequalities that directly reflect natural inequalities are legitimate. Because labor is a human activity, it also depends on the free choices of laborers, and once freedom has entered the picture, we are no longer dealing with purely natural phenomena and hence no longer with purely natural differences. Insofar as the natural law governing private property legitimizes inequalities that go beyond those with a strictly natural basis, Rousseau's thought must be that it is natural (appropriate or suitable given the nature of the thing) that those who freely expend more effort than others be entitled to enjoy the fruits of that extra effort. This (quite small) part of Rousseau's account of the sources of legitimate social inequality in natural law might be understood, then, as invoking a very modest principle of moral desert – those who do the work deserve to enjoy the fruits of their work – but even this minor emendation of his original principle (that legitimate social inequalities must be directly based in natural ones) ends up legitimizing only miniscule disparities in wealth. His position remains: natural law provides no justification of the vast majority of social inequalities that mark the societies we are familiar with.

Yet, even with this qualification added, the simplicity of Rousseau's answer to the Second Discourse's question concerning the extent to which inequality is authorized by natural law obscures the complexity of his overall position on the justifiability of social inequality, or so I argue here. One sign of this complexity can be found in the important but barely noticeable fact that when Rousseau speaks about the normative task of the Second Discourse in his own voice, as opposed to that of the Academy of Dijon, he tends not to speak of the *authorization* (by natural law) of inequality but to ask instead after the ("true") *foundations* (*fondements*) of the phenomenon in question (*DI*, 127, 128, 131, 179/*OC* III, 126, 127, 131, 184). The import of this, even if the Second Discourse fails to say so explicitly, is that the specific question posed by the Academy – "whether inequality among men . . . is authorized by natural law" (*DI*, 130/*OC* III, 129) – counts for Rousseau as only one small part of the more comprehensive normative question that political philosophy ultimately seeks to answer with regard to inequality. This is because, as Rousseau makes clear later in the Second Discourse, there is a "foundation" of political legitimacy beyond the kind of authorization provided by natural law, namely, that provided by a "true contract," which depends on individuals "having, in regard to social relations, united all their wills into a single one" (*DI*, 180/*OC* III, 184–5). Later, in *The Social Contract*, Rousseau will give a detailed account of this additional foundation of right in terms of a *convention*, or a "coming together" of human wills in the form of a social contract (*SC*, I.1.ii, I.4.i). In doing so, Rousseau names contract (or convention or compact) as the foundation of right *within society*, and because it has its source in human will, he contrasts it with the natural authorization of right in laws of nature. I will discuss Rousseau's vision of the foundations of right within society at greater length in the following chapter, but for now it is sufficient to note that the distinction between natural right (or law) and right within society makes it at least conceptually possible that some social inequalities not authorized by natural law might nevertheless be legitimate; indeed, Rousseau explicitly acknowledges this possibility in the Second Discourse when he includes "instituted [or artificial] inequality" among the issues that "the rights of society" pronounce on (*DI*, 179/*OC* III, 184).

Although the conception of a kind of legitimacy that has its foundations in human consent or agreement is much more prominent in *The Social Contract* than in the Second Discourse, it is clearly present in the latter text as well (*DI*, 179–80/*OC* III, 184–5), where, I will argue, it plays an important if largely implicit role in Rousseau's critique of inequality. Revealing how the argument of the Second Discourse implicitly relies on and is related to the same concept of legitimacy at work in *The Social Contract* is an important aim of both this chapter and the next.[10] I aim to show that a careful reading of the Second Discourse

---

[10] That the project of the Second Discourse is relevant to the conception of legitimacy articulated in *The Social Contract* is made plain at *DI*, 128/*OC* III, 126: "This study of original man . . . is also the only good means . . . for resolving the host of difficulties concerning . . . the true foundations (*fondements*) of the body politic."

provides the resources for reconstructing a compelling position on social inequality, according to which some social inequalities not authorized by natural law are nevertheless morally permissible because they have their foundations in an alternative source of political legitimacy: convention, or the social contract (or, equivalently, what *The Social Contract* will call the general will). Since doing so will involve articulating a criterion of right other than natural law that distinguishes legitimate from illegitimate – permissible from impermissible – social inequalities, Rousseau's most fundamental normative question in the Second Discourse is best formulated not in the words of the Academy – is human inequality authorized by natural law? – but, more comprehensively, as: to what extent, and for what reasons, are social inequalities legitimate? Or, since the Second Discourse is primarily a critique of modern society rather than a positive account of what legitimate social and political institutions must look like (*DI*, 187–8, 201/*OC* III, 193, 205), it is probably more accurate to formulate its fundamental normative question negatively: when and for what reasons are social inequalities *il*legitimate?

It is worth pausing here to say a word about the concept of legitimacy as I am using it here. In the paragraph above I used "legitimate," when talking about social inequalities, to mean *morally acceptable* or *permissible*. Rousseau himself sometimes uses the term in this way, but there is a slightly different sense of legitimacy that is more prominent in Rousseau's texts (and in social contract theory more generally). In the latter usage it is primarily laws (*DI*, 180/*OC* III, 185) and political institutions (*DI*, 179, 180, 183/*OC* III, 184, 185, 188) that are said to be legitimate, where this implies an *obligation* on the part of citizens *to obey* the laws and the ground rules of institutions that qualify as such (*DI*, 180/*OC* III, 185). When Rousseau says that certain inequalities are legitimate (*DI*, 188/*OC* III, 193), he means that they are morally permissible, but this is also related to the more familiar notion of legitimacy (of laws and institutions whose dictates we are obligated to obey): legitimate inequalities are not mandated or directly created by laws or institutions; rather, they arise on their own, within the context of legitimate laws and institutions and, in most cases, without institutions or individuals within them intending to create them. (And, as we will see in the following chapter, one of the tasks of legitimate laws and institutions is to place limits on the amounts and kinds of inequalities that can arise within a society.) To say that inequalities are legitimate is to say, first and foremost, that citizens have no moral grounds on which to object to them. This may also generate obligations to act in certain ways that acknowledge the legitimacy of those inequalities, for example, to respect the property rights of other individuals when the economic inequalities among them meet the criteria for legitimacy. There will be other cases, however, where the legitimacy of a social inequality does not impose on those they affect any obligation to act or to refrain from acting in some particular manner: differentials in public prestige, for example, can be legitimate (permissible) without them imposing any obligation on individuals to treat those involved in any specific way. In such cases, "legitimate" means primarily "morally permissible" and implies that those involved in legitimate conditions of inequality have no moral grounds on which to object to them.

In reconstructing the Second Discourse's (mostly implicit) answer to the question "To what extent and for what reasons are social inequalities illegitimate?" the remainder of this chapter inquires into the normative resources, beyond those provided by natural law, that the Second Discourse has at its disposal for devising an answer to this question and for criticizing illegitimate forms of social inequality. Its principal focus is what I have called Rousseau's normative conception of human nature, as can be read off his account of the state of nature in Part I of the Second Discourse (and then, as explained below, supplemented by considerations regarding the basic conditions of social existence to yield a normative vision of human nature in the expanded sense). The relevance of this normative conception of human nature (or of the "human essence") for the Second Discourse's critical project is that it yields an account of the essential constituents of the human good that Rousseau appeals to in explaining the dangers and ultimately the illegitimacy of many forms of social inequality. In Chapter 4 I consider how this normative picture of human nature is used by Rousseau to generate general criteria for judging the legitimacy of laws, institutions, and social phenomena more broadly that ground his critique of social inequality.

THE NORMATIVE CONCEPTION OF HUMAN NATURE

As I claimed in Chapter 1, the original state of nature depicted in Book I of the Second Discourse has both a normative and an explanatory function. That is, it is intended not only to explain where the pervasive inequalities of human societies come from but also to help us evaluate and criticize them. Moreover, to each of these roles played by the state of nature there is a corresponding conception of *human* nature – one explanatory, one normative – the first of which could be called "original human nature" (the basic capacities and dispositions all humans are born with), the second "true human nature" (the basic components of the human good, grounded in a view of humans' distinctive and highest ends). The latter conception has "true" human nature as its object in the sense that it captures what other thinkers have called the human essence, a conception of the basic qualities or goods that define the kind of existence humans ought to have, regardless of the fact that they often fail to do so – in which case they could be said to have failed to realize their "true essence." Even though the term "human essence" appears neither in the Second Discourse nor, as far as I know, in Rousseau's other texts, there is undeniably a version of the idea of the human essence at work in his thought, as can be seen, for example, by his characterization of life and freedom as "essential gifts of nature" (*DI*, 179/*OC* III, 184). This normative conception of human nature – of the essential goods humans should strive to attain – also finds expression in the Second Discourse's depiction, in the original state of nature but also in the Golden Age, of humans who "live well in accordance with nature" (*DI*, 113/*OC* III, 109), or who enjoy "the way of life prescribed to [them] by nature" (*DI*, 138/*OC* III, 138). To say that humans realize their true nature is to say that they have achieved the most important goods available to them, or that they live lives that are uncorrupted or good or appropriate, given the kind of beings they are (*DI*, 157/*OC* III, 160).

One complicating implication of Rousseau's invocation of true human nature is the following: to the extent that his critique of inequality ultimately relies on an objective conception of the human good in order to formulate the criteria of legitimacy governing artificial social phenomena, there is a sense in which the normative standards that inform his critique of inequality *do* have their source in nature – in his conception of true human nature – even though there is also a sense in which these criteria extend beyond nature and partake of the artificial, that is, the realm of human will. Even more confusing: as I explain below, Rousseau regards the normative conception of human nature, or of the human essence, as deriving in some sense from the non-normative conception of human nature discussed in chapters 1 and 2. These are very tortured aspects of Rousseau's position – complications in his appeal to nature more generally – that I will attempt to clarify below and in Chapter 4, when examining his account of the criteria social inequalities must meet in order to count as legitimate.

It is important that contemporary readers not be prematurely put off by the talk of true human nature, or the human essence. It has become fashionable to dismiss such talk as "essentialistic," either because, according to the critics, human nature is infinitely malleable and historically conditioned or because the "fact of pluralism" and the great diversity of human goods make it impossible to specify any subset of such goods as essential to human flourishing.[11] In my view, much of the noise directed today against "essentialistic" conceptions of human nature is precisely that: facile rejections of views that their critics have failed (or not attempted) to understand. I do not mean that we should not in general be wary of philosophical claims that invoke substantive conceptions of the human essence or of true human nature. My claim, rather, is that when we encounter such language in a philosopher's texts, especially in those of one who belongs to a different historical era from ours, we should first attempt to understand what he means by such talk and why he takes himself to be justified in asserting it, rather than dismissing it out of hand as obviously benighted. If we adopt this more cautious approach in relation to Rousseau, we will see that he operates with a very sparing conception of true human nature and that the way he employs it makes it difficult to distinguish his views from those of many political philosophers who claim to make no use of the idea.

In the first place, Rousseau does not need to learn from us that human nature is highly malleable and historically conditioned; it would be closer to the truth to say that we learned it from him. That human beings vary greatly in different societies and in different epochs – that they are capable of undergoing developments of such magnitude that it is sometimes difficult to recognize them as members of the same species – is obviously a central claim of the Second

---

[11] On the "fact of pluralism" see Rawls, *PL*, 36. (For the conventions used in citing John Rawls's works see the List of Abbreviations.)

Discourse. It is highlighted on the Second Discourse's very first page in Rousseau's use of the image of "the statue of Glaucus, which time, sea, and storms had so disfigured that it less resembled a god than a ferocious beast" as a symbol for "the human soul altered in the lap of society by a thousand ... causes" (*DI*, 124/*OC* III, 122), and it is expressed even more spectacularly in his well-known suggestion, made more than once, that orangutans and humans might belong to the same species (*DI*, 205–8, 227/*OC* III, 208–11, 234). Notice, however, that the doctrine of human malleability has to do with the questions at issue in his (descriptive or explanatory) conception of original human nature – what are the basic capacities and dispositions that all humans are born with and that explain both the limits and possibilities of human variability? – rather than those addressed by his normative picture of human nature: what are the most basic components of the human good, valid (in some form) at all times and places? Notice, too, that Rousseau's non-normative conception of human nature is exceedingly modest. As we know from chapters 1 and 2, it ascribes to all human beings only a very small number of sentiments and passions: pity and *amour de soi-même* – and if one considers not merely original human nature but human nature in the expanded sense, *amour propre* – along with free will and perfectibility, the latter of which is a set of latent capacities that, rather than representing a fixed feature of human nature, is a source of great malleability among civilized humans. With respect to all these components of human nature, and especially in the case of *amour propre*, Rousseau emphasizes their fundamental malleability, their capacity to assume highly different forms under different circumstances, rather than their fixed, eternal character. Rousseau does operate, then, with some conception of a "fixed" human nature, but what is unalterable in that nature is very small indeed, translating into a set of very limited and only broadly determinable constraints on what he takes to be the nearly infinite possibilities of human existence.

Second, Rousseau's normative conception of human nature is nearly as sparing as his conception of human nature in the explanatory sense. It entails a small number of claims that are relatively uncontroversial or at least widely accepted, for example, that freedom and self-preservation are "nature's essential gifts" (*DI*, 179/*OC* III, 184) – that is, the most important human goods, which individuals may not legitimately surrender and which therefore, as we will see in the following chapter, a legitimate state must ensure for all.[12] (I argue below that Rousseau also counts well-being more generally, including happiness, among the basic goods that humans must achieve if they are to realize their true nature.) His normative conception of human nature also entails, first, that one of these goods, freedom, is the *distinctively* human good:[13] a good that, in most of its forms at least, can be achieved by humans but not by other animals;[14] second, that

[12] It is a bit odd to speak of freedom as a gift of nature if it is bound up with the very property that lifts humans above mere nature; (but see note 14). But since metaphysical freedom – the will's not being determined by natural causal laws – is not something humans *can* surrender, Rousseau must be speaking here of freedom in some normative sense as a gift of nature: the absence of domination (or, perhaps, the absence of all *obligation* to obey a foreign will). This makes some sense if we understand him to mean that in the original state of nature the conditions for the possibility of domination (as well as of any obligation to obey others) do not obtain; in that sense "nature" might be said to bestow the good of freedom on us.

[13] If social esteem (of the right sorts) and the development of latent capacities are to be included among the essential human goods – a view I endorse below – then they, too, become distinctively human goods. Although distinctively human goods, however, they are still lesser goods than freedom since they qualify neither as priceless nor as the highest human good as I define those ideas here.

[14] On this point – whether freedom is a good distinctive to humans – Rousseau appears to waver. On the one hand, he says that to renounce one's freedom is to place oneself "at the level of beasts, which are slaves of instinct" (*DI*, 179/*OC* III, 183), whereas two paragraphs earlier he ascribes a capacity and longing for a kind of freedom (being unconstrained by bits and chains) to some non-human animals, namely, "untamed steeds" and "animals born free" (*DI*, 177/*OC* III, 181). His view must be that whereas non-human animals are not metaphysically free – they do not possess freedom of the will and are therefore always slaves of their instincts – they do naturally resist being constrained to behave contrary to their inclinations and, in resisting something similar to what I describe below as domination, strive for what must be recognized as a primitive form of freedom (as non-domination). This would imply that Rousseau thinks it coherent to ascribe a striving for a *kind* of freedom to beings that are at the same time metaphysically unfree, though given how often he links the value of freedom with (exclusively) human dignity, I doubt that he has a completely consistent view on this matter. See note 30 of Chapter 1, which suggests that the good of freedom (the absence of domination) may be divorceable from a metaphysical conception of freedom.
A further question is whether the beings of the original state of nature (including non-human animals) could recognize resistance to their desires on the part of beings with wills as different in kind, and more of an evil than, resistance from purely natural phenomena (and hence whether they could be said to recognize non-*domination* as a good). See, for example, Rousseau's claim that "it would even be rather difficult [but not impossible? – F. N.] to get [savages] to understand what subjection and domination are" (*DI*, 158/*OC* III, 161). In my view, such unresolved issues arise again and again for Rousseau because, like many modern philosophers, he has not found a way to reconcile his view that freedom requires metaysical independence from laws of nature with his equally strong desire to find anticipations of all human phenomena, including our valuing of freedom, within non-human animal life. I am indebted to R. J. Leland and Robin Celikates for enlightening discussions of these points.

freedom, because it is bound up with "man's noblest faculty" (*DI*, 179/*OC* III, 184), which bestows dignity on the human species, is the *highest* human good, the renunciation of which "debases one's being" (*DI*, 179/*OC* III, 184); and, third, that (along with life) freedom is a *priceless* good that may not legitimately be traded away for any other good. The pricelessness of freedom implies – and the same holds for life – that to exchange it "at any price" is "an offense against both nature and reason" (*DI*, 179/*OC* III, 184) and that no legitimate contract (one that generates a genuine obligation to comply with its terms) can be based on its surrender. This conception of the normative status of freedom is equivalent to the hardly extravagant view that to strip human beings of their freedom – to enslave them – is to treat them as less than human and to rob them of the dignity they possess by virtue of being human beings.[15] While I do not mean to deny that invoking the idea of a true human nature (or essence) in even this relatively modest sense raises legitimate philosophical questions about its justification, I want to emphasize the spareness of Rousseau's assumptions, as well as to point out that most contemporary liberal political theories are committed to some version of these assumptions – even if they are not cloaked in the language of the human essence – insofar as they recognize a set of fundamental human interests that a legitimate state must promote or insofar as they make freedom in some guise an absolute, non-fungible good that in a just state must be respected or secured for each citizen.

Specifying the content of true human nature understood as a normative ideal is easiest if we focus first on how Rousseau makes use of the idea in Part I of the Second Discourse. For there he says fairly clearly what living in accordance with nature consists in: the inhabitant of the original state of nature is "a free being whose heart is at peace and whose body is healthy" (*DI*, 150/*OC* III, 152). Later, in Part II, the inhabitants of the Golden Age are depicted as living in accordance with nature because "they lived as free, healthy, good, and happy as their nature allowed them to be" (*DI*, 167/*OC* III, 171).

---

[15] One finds the same view in *The Social Contract* (and, in essence, in any version of liberal social contract theory): "To renounce one's freedom is to renounce one's quality as a man. . . . There can be no possible compensation for someone who renounces everything. Such a renunciation is incompatible with the nature of man" (*SC*, I.4.vi).

It is perhaps more accurate to define the ideals that characterize the original state of nature in terms of the *absence* of the many evils civilization is shown to bring with it in Part II: war, domination, vice, unsatisfied desires and needs, and alienation. In other words – to focus on only two of the most important elements of the normative conception of human nature – the *freedom* enjoyed by those primitive beings is nothing but the absence of subjection to the wills of others (or the absence of domination), and their *well-being* consists in the absence of pain, frustrated desires, and unmet needs.

In the following two sections I will examine the relevant conceptions of freedom and well-being in considerable detail. Before turning to that task, however, I want to say a few words about the status of the other major good that makes up the ideal expressed in Rousseau's normative conception of human nature: life or self-preservation. I assume that it is not necessary to consider here what staying alive consists in but only how that good stacks up, normatively speaking, to freedom and well-being. Because both life and self-preservation, in contrast with freedom, are "natural" (or naturalistic) goods bound up with the conditions of animal life – goods that can unambiguously be attributed also to non-human animals – it might be tempting simply to include self-preservation within the category of well-being, but since Rousseau does not do this, I will follow his lead on this matter. Since freedom on his view is not a natural good in this sense (I return to this below), it is not difficult to see why he regards it as a fundamentally different type of good from self-preservation. Presumably, though, it also makes sense to distinguish the order of value that self-preservation has from that of mere well-being, since remaining alive is the most basic condition of the very possibility of being well or badly off at all (just as it is the most basic condition of the possibility of being free). If a person is badly off but alive, there remains a possibility that his situation could improve and that at some future time he might enjoy both goods together, whereas the opposite combination, being dead but free of suffering, excludes that future possibility. Because of this asymmetry between life and well-being, the former occupies a higher-order position in the hierarchy of human goods. (Of course, Rousseau is sensible enough to realize that certain extremes of suffering, coupled with the assurance that future well-being is not a possibility, can justify a distressed individual's choosing the absence of pain over life; as I explain below, however, it is not the moral questions that individuals might face in specific circumstances that concern him here.)

The higher-order position of life in relation to well-being is reflected in Rousseau's claim, cited above, that both self-preservation and freedom (but not well-being) count as "nature's essential gifts," implying that, as in the case of freedom, renouncing life "at any price" is "an offense against both nature and reason" (*DI*, 179/*OC* III, 184). It is important to be clear that Rousseau is not claiming that it is morally impermissible for an individual to sacrifice her life in the name of freedom if she finds herself in circumstances where it is necessary to choose one or the other, for this is not the question he means to be addressing. (His view on this question, I believe, is that if forced to choose between life and freedom, it is morally permissible to choose either. Choosing life over freedom is permissible [*SC*, I.4.ii], even though doing so "debases one's being"; choosing freedom over life is not only permissible but also honorable, but it comes at the unrecompensably high cost of "annihilating" one's being [*DI*, 179/*OC* III, 184]. In other words, when faced with a choice between debasing or annihilating one's being, moral principles cannot decide the issue.) Instead, Rousseau's claim is that an individual's life has no *price*.[16] This means that, as the most fundamental condition of any goods an individual might enjoy, life, like freedom (*DI*, 176/*OC* III, 181), is a non-fungible good, one that may not be traded away for any amount of any other "temporal" (natural) good. (Freedom, because related to a "metaphysical" property of humans [see below], is not a natural good in the relevant sense.)[17] It is important to see that the claim that an individual's life has no price is not intended as a contribution to casuistry – to the task of figuring out how moral principles ought to be applied by individuals in difficult circumstances. To say that life has no price, rather, is to say that it may not be legitimately *bargained away*, which is to say that any agreement to exchange one's life (or one's freedom) for any other good cannot be regarded as a legitimate contract, one that

---

[16] Kant famously takes over from Rousseau this contrast between price and dignity; Immanuel Kant, *Groundwork of the Metaphysics of Morals*, ed. Mary Gregor (Cambridge University Press, 1998), 4: 434–5.

[17] But see note 14.

imposes genuine rights and obligations on those who enter into it. It may be morally permissible, under certain conditions, for me to save the lives of my family members by uttering the words, "I give you my life in exchange for preserving my spouse and children." If my words succeed in saving the lives of my loved ones, so much the better. The point, however, is that because my life has no price, I cannot be bound by the words I have spoken; if I find a way of avoiding death after my family has been spared, I have in no way wronged you. Clearly, this doctrine will have important implications for Rousseau's account of the "true" social contract and hence for his full account of the legitimacy of social inequalities to be considered in Chapter 4. Let us now turn to examining in greater detail how freedom and well-being are to be understood in the present context.

FREEDOM AS THE ABSENCE OF DOMINATION

Because freedom is crucial to Rousseau's vision of human flourishing and his indictment of modern society, it is important to get clear on what it means in this context. When Rousseau calls the beings of the original state of nature free, he is not merely reasserting his earlier claim that they possess free wills (that they have a capacity to choose spontaneously, undetermined by nature). Freedom here is not a "metaphysical" (*DI*, 140/*OC* III, 141) but a social phenomenon, the essence of which is the absence of subjugation to foreign wills – or, as I will refer to it here, the absence of domination. As Rousseau puts the point, there is no "subjection and domination" in the original state of nature, which is simply to say that no one can "succeed in getting himself obeyed by [another]" (*DI*, 158/*OC* III, 161). In short, the inhabitants of that state are free because in satisfying their needs and desires, they are not compelled to obey any will other than their own. Freedom on this conception is social in the specific sense that its very definition makes reference to the wills of others. Even though a completely isolated Robinson Crusoe would, strictly speaking, satisfy the definition of freedom as the absence of domination, it would be saying very little to point out that he was free in this sense. Literally, of course, that would be true, but being free in this way is meaningful only in a world where there are other wills whose commands one could in principle be subject to. At the same time, it does not follow from this definition alone that freedom is social in a more robust sense of the term, one that would make freedom depend on or even consist in having positive ties to others, such as bonds of affection or identification. The "moral freedom" that Rousseau ascribes to self-legislating citizens in *The Social Contract* is social in this more robust sense, but in principle individuals can be free in the sense relevant here by relating only "negatively" to the wills of others. Not losing sight of the distinction between the metaphysical and the social concepts of freedom – between free will and freedom as the absence of domination – is important to disentangling the two senses of human nature in Rousseau's thought. Free will, part of original human nature, is something humans never exist without, and so lamenting its loss or exhorting us to achieve it makes no sense. Domination, in contrast, is a common though not necessary feature of human society, and pointing out its manifestations and causes and thinking about how to prevent it are central concerns of Rousseau's social and political philosophy.

It is important to see that Rousseau has something specific in mind when he speaks of the loss of freedom in the Second Discourse. As we know, several conceptions of freedom play a role in Rousseau's thought as a whole,[18] but the one at issue here is what I will call the absence of *domination* (or of servitude, oppression, or subjection, all of which mark the same phenomenon for Rousseau). The essential characteristic of freedom in *all* its forms is "obeying only oneself" (*SC*, I.6.iv),[19] as opposed to obeying the wills of others, and in other texts Rousseau characterizes the essence of freedom similarly, as "not being subjected to the will of others" (*LWM*, 260/*OC* III, 841) and as "never

---

[18] Apart from metaphysical freedom (freedom of the will), *The Social Contract* also mentions natural, civil, and moral freedom (*SC*, I.8.i–iii). For definitions of these, see Frederick Neuhouser, *Foundations of Hegel's Social Theory: Actualizing Freedom* (Cambridge, Mass.: Harvard University Press, 2000), 56–8, 78–81, 186–9.

[19] In other words, what *The Social Contract* calls natural, civil, and moral freedom (*SC*, I.8.i–iii) – as well as freedom as the absence of domination – are different ways in which a person obeys only himself. Obeying a law one has prescribed to oneself (moral freedom) is still a form of obeying only oneself, just as freedom negatively defined – for example, as being unconstrained by others in doing what one wants – is a form of obeying only oneself. (See also note 35.) That freedom has a single essence that can be realized in a number of concrete ways is an idea Hegel takes over from Rousseau and makes central to his "dialectical" development of the concept of freedom in his social and political thought. I explain this in detail in Neuhouser, *Foundations of Hegel's Social Theory*, Chapter 1.

doing what [one] does not want to do" (*RSW*, 56/*OC* I, 1059). In emphasizing the phenomenon of domination and conceiving of freedom as the absence of domination, Rousseau is clearly following a long line of earlier republican thinkers who defined freedom in similar terms.[20] As I will argue below, however, although Rousseau nominally retains the classical republican definition of freedom, he subtly but significantly alters the conception of domination on which that definition rests.

The conception of domination developed in the Second Discourse – emphasizing *obedience* to others – is in some ways a forerunner of what Max Weber later calls *Herrschaft* (domination or rule), defined as "the likelihood of finding obedience to one's commands in others."[21] Weber's definition comes very close to how Rousseau characterizes domination in the Second Discourse, namely, as (regularly) "succeeding in getting oneself obeyed by [another]" (*DI*, 158/*OC* III, 161), where both thinkers assume that obedience is asymmetric, proceeding in one direction only. The asymmetry among individuals that is built into the definition of domination means that it itself counts for Rousseau as an instance of social inequality – it is a *privilege* "some enjoy to the prejudice of others" (*DI*, 131/*OC* III, 131) – but unlike many other social inequalities (in prestige or wealth, for example), this asymmetry of obedience, or inequality in social power, also *consists in* a loss of freedom for those who are on the disadvantaged side of this social relation (those who regularly obey their counterparts). In other words, being poorer or less esteemed than others is not itself a form of enslavement or a lack of freedom (though, as we will see in the following chapter, being poorer than others often has loss of freedom as one of its consequences), whereas regularly and unilaterally obeying a foreign will is. This means that the moral problem posed by this form of social inequality is obvious: asymmetric obedience just *is* a form of enslavement or loss of freedom.

---

[20] My characterization of the republican tradition before Rousseau is heavily indebted to Philip Pettit's account of it, *Republicanism: A Theory of Freedom and Government* (Oxford University Press, 1997), chapters 1–3. Because such indisputably republican figures as Machiavelli and Rousseau play only a small role in his account of what republicanism is, however, it is probably more accurate to say that what he calls traditional republicanism constitutes merely one important strand of the tradition as a whole.

[21] Max Weber, *Economy and Society*, ed. Guenther Roth and Claus Wittich, trans. Ephraim Fischoff et al. (Berkeley: University of California Press, 1987), vol. I, 53; translation amended.

This point brings out an important respect in which Rousseau's conception of domination differs from Weber's: whereas for Weber *Herrschaft* can be legitimate and need not represent a lamentable loss of freedom (some forms of one-sided obedience are justified),[22] domination for Rousseau always counts as an absence of freedom and warrants critique. But since Rousseau, too, believes that some forms of one-sided obedience – children obeying their parents or citizens obeying legitimate law – are compatible with freedom and therefore not instances of domination, his definition of domination merely in terms of "success in getting oneself obeyed" must be modified to reflect this fact. In other words, if we are to take seriously Rousseau's claim that "by the law of nature the father is the child's master" (*DI*, 177/ *OC* III, 182), we must be able to explain what distinguishes certain forms of one-sided obedience – parental authority,[23] as well as legitimate political authority – from those in which the individuals who obey are unfree, or dominated.

It is tempting to deal with this problem as many republican theorists do, by defining domination in a way that distinguishes the *arbitrary* wills of others from those that "track the interests and ideas" of those who obey.[24] Yet this is not how Rousseau characterizes domination, and examining why he does not reveals something important about his conception of domination and how it differs from that of much of the republican tradition before him. In contrast to Rousseau, when earlier republicans define freedom as the absence of domination, they typically do not refer to obedience at all. Instead, they tend to define domination in terms of the dominating party's ability to *interfere* arbitrarily with the choices of the dominated where "arbitrary" signifies that the interferer "is not forced to track the interests and ideas of those who suffer the interference."[25] On this view, a person or law that regularly commands or compels other persons to act in ways that in fact promote their interests – what we would call paternalism – does not qualify as a violation of the freedom

---

[22] For this reason many interpreters of Weber prefer to translate *Herrschaft* as "rule" rather than "domination."

[23] Here I depart from Rousseau by speaking of parental rather than paternal authority. It is typically only the latter that Rousseau defends when discussing power relations within the family.

[24] Pettit, *Republicanism*, 272.   [25] Pettit, *Republicanism*, 22, 272.

of those who obey because that commanding or compelling is not arbitrary. The absence of obedience from this definition – interference is a broader phenomenon than finding obedience in the wills of others – together with its emphasis on someone's being subject to arbitrary power, points to an important difference between the two conceptions of domination, as well as between their respective attitudes to paternalism: for Rousseau the core of domination resides not in being interfered with in ways that are contrary to one's own interests but in obeying a foreign will in the sense of allowing someone else's command or desire to determine what I do. This means that for him the ideal of freedom that is opposed to domination is *determining for oneself*[26] how one acts rather than, as many other republicans would have it, acting – including being compelled or commanded to act – in ways that promote my interests, regardless of whether it is I or some other agent who determines what those acts are. For Rousseau, in other words, freedom as the absence of domination is more closely connected to an ideal of free agency – determining oneself what to do, or obeying only oneself – than it is to the ideal of having one's interests promoted,[27] where the question of who determines what such promoting consists in is irrelevant. Thus, Rousseau's definition attractively places a different accent on where the wrong of domination resides: domination is a violation of a type of free agency, not a vulnerability to being interfered with by others in ways that conflict with one's interests.

Does it make no difference, then, to Rousseau's conception of domination whether the will that I obey directs me towards my own interests or whether it disregards my interests, subordinating them perhaps to those of the dominator? Is the arbitrary or non-arbitrary character of the obeyed will irrelevant to defining domination? Although Rousseau never explicitly poses this question, I believe his view is best reconstructed as follows: domination is made worse – it is

[26] The language of self-determination is not intended to suggest a positive conception of freedom; "determining for oneself" contrasts here with others deciding for one, and it is compatible with acting on desires or whims as long as they are one's own rather than someone else's. In other words, the absence of interference by others is sufficient to make one's choices and actions instances of "determining for oneself" how one acts.

[27] More precisely, the ideal is invulnerability to having one's agency interfered with in ways that disregard one's interests.

intensified *as domination* – when the will that I regularly obey commands me to act in ways that conflict with or are indifferent to my own interests. Yet – and this is the decisive point – there is still domination (assuming I am an adult) even if what that will commands me to do promotes my interests: regularly obeying a will other than my own constitutes a violation of free agency, even when the will I obey is benign. In other words, paternalism among adults *is* domination, though a less severe form of it than one that involves obeying an arbitrary will. One might explain this view by claiming, as *The Social Contract* implies, that there are two senses in which a commanding will can be foreign, or the will of another, the first of which is essential to domination, whereas the second is neither necessary nor sufficient (though its co-presence with the first increases the severity of domination). The first, more straightforward sense in which a will can be foreign to me is when the commands of that will are issued by some agent other than me. This is a question about where the commands that I follow originate: in myself or in some other individual, group, or institution (such as law)? But there is also a second sense in which a will can be foreign, namely, with respect to its content. A will that is foreign to me in this sense is one whose commands, regardless of who issues them, fail to direct me to act in ways that promote my own interests; such commands are, in the terminology used above, arbitrary. It is the converse of this thesis – a will counts as mine (in a limited respect) if it "issues from me" (*SC*, II.4.v) in the sense that it promotes my interests – that underlies *The Social Contract's* claim that the general will is *in some sense* my own will (because it promotes my interests in freedom and well-being), even when I, the citizen of a legitimate republic, do not subjectively recognize it as such.[28] And no doubt some version of this idea stands behind the claim of many earlier republicans that non-arbitrary interference is not domination and is therefore compatible with the freedom of the agent who suffers such interference.

For Rousseau, then, regular obedience of a will that is foreign in only the first of these senses qualifies as domination (and warrants

---

[28] Some version of this claim is necessary in order to make sense of Rousseau's statement that "whoever refuses to obey the general will shall be constrained to do so . . ., which means only that he will be forced to be free" (*SC*, I.7.viii). For a detailed discussion of this issue see my *Foundations of Hegel's Social Theory*, 60–3, 73, 78–9.

critique), but regularly obeying a will that is foreign in both senses will count as more intense domination than when the obeyed will fails to be foreign in the second sense. That the obeyed will is foreign in the first sense is a necessary and sufficient condition for domination, whereas its being foreign in the second sense (that it directs me in ways contrary to my interests) is neither.[29] Hence, Rousseau agrees with other republicans that being subject to others' arbitrary wills is illegitimate (*DI*, 179/*OC* III, 184) without agreeing either that it is the arbitrariness of those wills that makes that obedience domination or that domination requires arbitrariness. There is an important respect, then, in which Rousseau's conception of domination is more demanding than that of the part of the republican tradition to which I am contrasting him: by not making the arbitrary character of the will I obey a necessary condition of domination, it includes much the same phenomena the contrasting definition does while, in addition, objecting to someone's regularly obeying another will even when that will tracks his interests.

It might be objected that focusing on obedience and de-emphasizing arbitrariness runs the risk of confusing domination with the less objectionable phenomenon of paternalism. In fact, Rousseau's position enables us to define paternalism – regular, one-sided obedience of a will that is foreign in the first sense but not in the second – in a way that differentiates it from obedience to a will that is foreign in both senses and explains why the latter is more objectionable than the former (it involves obeying a will that is foreign in two senses rather than merely one). Rousseau's definition does not indeed *distinguish* paternalism (among adults) from domination, but this is one of its virtues. Paternalism among adults *is* a form of domination, and without resorting to an ad hoc strategy of invoking some other conception of freedom, much of traditional republicanism lacks the resources to criticize it as such.[30]

[29] To elaborate: if I decide on my own to act in ways contrary to my interests, the will I follow is foreign in the second but not the first sense. This is clearly not domination, although one might want to think of it as a kind of self-tyranny and perhaps even as the loss of a certain kind of freedom. Rousseau is neither blind to nor uncritical of this phenomenon (*DI*, 141/*OC* III, 142), but it is not domination.

[30] Pettit, for example, embraces this counterintuitive implication: "intentional interferences that are non-arbitrary are similar to natural obstacles in ... not compromising freedom" (Pettit, *Republicanism*, 77).

Does this imply that parents dominate their children when they command them to do what is good for them? Clearly not. Paternalism is precisely the form that legitimate authority takes within the family, and this is because in that sphere asymmetric patterns of obedience are justified by naturally, though only temporarily, unequal capacities: those who obey (children) are for natural, developmental reasons not yet in a position to be their own masters. Parental authority, then, is an instance of a legitimate social inequality that is grounded in natural inequality (and, so, "authorized" by natural law). As soon as that natural inequality ceases to exist, however, the moral basis of one-sided obedience also dissolves: children who have reached the age of maturity and have therefore become the natural equals of their parents are no longer obligated to obey them (*DI*, 177/*OC* III, 182).[31] *In relations involving only adults*, then, regularly obeying a will that is foreign in only the first sense distinguished above counts as domination, but future agents who have not reached the age of competency are not yet sovereign wills and therefore not yet possible victims of domination, though they can, of course, be oppressed, wronged, or mistreated when the adult wills they obey fail to track their own interests, including their interests as future sovereign agents.

What about obedience to legitimate political authority? The question here is whether individuals who are compelled to obey genuinely legitimate laws – where legitimacy implies an *obligation* to obey (*DI*, 180/*OC* III, 185) – but do not recognize those laws as legitimate, or do not see them as expressions of their own will, suffer domination in obeying. This case is more complicated than that of parental authority. One reason is that readers of the Second Discourse might be led to conclude that in that text at least Rousseau accords no space for the idea of legitimate political authority, since the origin of the state as he describes it there, grounded in the "specious" social contract depicted in Part II, fails to result in a political order that promotes the freedom (and other interests) of all citizens but is destined instead to give "new fetters to the weak and new forces to the rich" and to "subject the whole of humankind to ... servitude" (*DI*, 173/*OC* III, 178). Such a conclusion, however, would be mistaken. That Rousseau recognizes

---

[31] More precisely, Rousseau says that a child is obligated to obey his parents only "as long as [the child] needs [the father's] assistance" (*DI*, 177/*OC* III, 182).

the possibility of legitimate political authority even in the Second Discourse, before he has written *The Social Contract*, is made clear by his brief sketch, after an account of the events that resulted in the specious, illegitimate social contract, of what a "true" social contract would look like – one that, unlike its counterpart, satisfied the criteria for political legitimacy and generated genuine obligation (*DI*, 179–80/ *OC* III, 184–5).

If, then, there is such a thing as legitimate political authority even for the author of the Second Discourse, the question remains whether compliance with that authority, even compelled compliance, would count for him as one-sided obedience to a foreign will and, if not, what that implies for the conception of domination we are trying to understand. Because in *The Social Contract* Rousseau will characterize compelled obedience to legitimate law as being "forced to be free" (*SC*, I.7.viii), it seems unlikely that he would also want to regard it as domination. Since legitimate law is non-arbitrary rule, this might seem to push Rousseau right back into the camp of the republicans from whom I have been attempting to distinguish him (who take the non-arbitrary character of law as sufficient to make it non-dominating). Getting clear on why this is not the case further illuminates the differences between the two conceptions of domination, especially with respect to the importance of something many republicans do not emphasize: democratic rule. If the claim that legitimate law cannot dominate is to conform to the position I attributed to Rousseau above, we must be able to explain why it does not represent a foreign will in the first of the senses explicated here, even when citizens do not obey it willingly. Explaining this requires taking note of the role that the democratic form of lawmaking plays in Rousseau's conception of legitimate law.[32] One way of putting the point is to say that legitimate laws must "issue from me" (*SC*, II.4.v) not only with respect to their objective content – they must promote my fundamental interests – but also with respect to their subjective form: it must be I who determines which specific laws direct me in ways that satisfy my interests. The question, then, is how *I* can determine the specific laws that govern me, given that laws apply to all and hence, if

---

[32] See the following note.

they are to be compatible with *our* freedom, must issue from every citizen as much as they do from myself.

It is the fact that Rousseau takes this consideration very seriously that explains his insistence that sovereignty cannot be represented (*SC*, II.1.ii; III.15.v–xi). If laws – even good laws – are to avoid being a source of domination, they must actually be made, or at least explicitly approved,[33] by those who are subject to them. Because legislation must be a collective enterprise, I can determine the laws that govern me only by actively participating in a democratic process in which those laws are made (or ratified) by the sovereign assembly. As a citizen I determine for myself what I am to do only insofar as I am an active member of the group that actually makes (or ratifies) the laws that govern all of us. Moreover, my participation in that process must be sufficiently substantial that the claim that the laws issue from me – from an *us* that incorporates me as an active participant – is not merely a hollow slogan, even when some of the laws that emerge from that process diverge from my opinion of what our collective ideals and interests require us to do. This is why direct, or non-representative, democracy is not a peripheral feature of Rousseau's vision of the legitimate republic; it is, rather, essential to avoiding domination in such a republic, and on this issue his differences from many earlier republicans could hardly be starker. Rousseau agrees with them that "law that answers systematically to people's . . . interests . . . does not compromise people's liberty,"[34] but only on the further condition that those laws are, in a robust sense, collectively issued by the very people subject to them.[35]

---

[33] Since some interpreters deny that Rousseau intended for the sovereign assembly of all citizens actually to draft the laws they vote on, I add this qualifier, implying that what I am calling direct democracy might come down to citizens voting yes or no on laws proposed to them by their government (*SC*, II.7.vii; IV.2.viii). I believe the evidence for Rousseau's view on this issue is ambiguous, but even the weakest version of direct democracy includes popular participation sufficiently substantial that the laws that issue from it count as "coming from us" in the relevant sense.

[34] Pettit, *Republicanism*, 35.

[35] Moreover, this argument for the necessity of direct democracy sheds light on the connection for Rousseau between freedom defined negatively, as the absence of domination, and the positive conception of freedom usually associated with him, namely, "moral freedom" (or autonomy), defined as "obedience to the law one has prescribed to oneself" (*SC*, I.8.iii). One could say that the negative conception of freedom leads "dialectically" to the positive conception in the following way: realizing the negative conception of freedom for all

A related difference between Rousseau and other republicans seems to be that he regards beneficent paternalism among adults, when they are not bound by natural affection, as a much *rarer* phenomenon than do the latter. Many earlier republicans place a lot of faith in the possibility that one group in society might consistently legislate on behalf of others in ways that benefit rather than exploit them,[36] thereby avoiding domination according to their conception of freedom. Rousseau, in contrast, is rightfully suspicious of a class of individuals that makes a standing claim, without input from below, to know better than those they rule what is good for them. In other words, in most real-world situations involving adults – and especially in politics – a will's being foreign in the first sense distinguished here is sufficient to make it foreign in the second sense as well. If we assume further, as Rousseau seems to do, that in general the best judge of what is good for a person is that person himself,[37] then the same democratic political measures that ensure that laws are given by those who are subject to them will also go a long way towards eliminating the potential arbitrariness of law. This means that, although direct democracy is justified for Rousseau on independent grounds (as a necessary condition of law not being foreign in the first sense and therefore a source of domination), a further benefit of those democratic procedures is that the laws that result from them are more likely than they would otherwise be to track the interests of those subject to them and therefore more likely to satisfy the principal constraint traditional republicans place on non-dominating law (that it not be arbitrary in the specified sense).

(eliminating domination) requires laws that regulate material and other inequalities among interdependent citizens. (This claim is the subject of Chapter 4.) But if these laws are not themselves to be a source of enslavement, they must issue from, or be prescribed by, the same agents who are subject to them, including in the sense that citizens actually participate in the process of lawgiving. This implies that citizens who live under the conditions necessary for abolishing domination can be fully free – can fully avoid enslavement – only if they are also autonomous. See notes 18 and 19.

[36] Of course, not all republicans share this view.

[37] That in general a person is the best judge of what is good for him does not imply that being mistaken about one's good is impossible or rare. A large part of the Second Discourse is devoted to showing how individuals come to have false ideas of their interests and to seek precisely the opposite of what is good for them. Rousseau's remedy for this problem, however, is not to search for other, wiser persons to obey but to dissolve the corrupting social forces that distort individuals' vision of what their true good consists in.

Two further features of Rousseau's conception of domination must be noted before I move on to discuss the second component of his account of true human nature, well-being. The first is that, although domination is a way of "being subjected to the will of others" (*LWM*, 260/*OC* III, 841), subjection here consists not in being under someone else's authority – being obligated to obey another – but rather in being in a position in which one in fact regularly follows the will of another without reciprocation. Rousseau's view is that individuals in the original state of nature are free of subjection in both these senses – they have no obligations to others (and, so, enjoy what *The Social Contract* calls natural freedom [*SC*, I.8.ii]), nor are they dominated – but the sense of freedom most relevant to his critique of inequality is clearly the latter. Natural freedom, as defined in *The Social Contract*, is something individuals must surrender completely when entering even a "true" social contract but only because doing so can be made compatible with their "remaining as free as before" (*SC*, I.6. iv), insofar as the obligations that citizens incur in surrendering that freedom are self-imposed and therefore "issue [only] from them-selves." As we will see in Chapter 4, losing the other type of freedom (succumbing to domination) is not generally the result of some political event but an unintended, more or less necessary concomitant of the rudimentary advances of civilization, so that eliminating dom-ination completely – essential to rendering citizens as free as they were before – becomes a necessary aim of any legitimate state. The relevant point is that being dominated as Rousseau understands it is not primarily a matter of having a certain normative or legal *status* – that of a slave as opposed to a free citizen, for example – but is an empirically real condition constituted by *actual* (regular and one-sided) obedience, even when that pattern of obedience is not for-mally inscribed in moral, legal, or social statuses.[38] Later, in *The Social Contract*, Rousseau will argue that being a citizen in a legit-imate republic is a necessary condition of avoiding domination, but being free from domination does not *consist in* holding this legal status. One is free from domination only if in going about

---

[38] For traditional republicans, in contrast, freedom (as non-domination) is primarily a legal status, especially being a citizen as opposed to a slave (Pettit, *Republicanism*, 30–2, 36, 66).

the business of one's life one in fact avoids regular and one-sided obedience to a foreign will, regardless of the legal rights one can rightfully claim. Conversely, being dominated does not require having an officially recognized status – that of slave or serf, for example – that codifies one's dominated condition or enshrines it in law. As the Second Discourse helps us to see, the vast majority of actual domination, especially in modern societies, is not inscribed in legal statuses but is also not for that reason any less real.

Finally – and crucial to Rousseau's critique of social inequality – domination is distinct from coercion, and along two dimensions. First, whereas coercion can consist in a single act of obeying others, domination, as we have seen, is an enduring condition, a regular obeying of a foreign will. Second, and more important, what typically compels my actual obedience of another on Rousseau's view is not physical force or threatened punishments but (as we will see in Chapter 4) my needing the cooperation of someone who is in a more advantaged position than I. When I depend on others for the satisfaction of my needs, the mere prospect that they may do nothing – that they may refuse to cooperate because they need my help less urgently than I do theirs – can be sufficient to motivate me to obey their commands or cater to their desires. This suggests that the type of domination Rousseau is most interested in in the Second Discourse involves *obeying* a foreign will in a more robust sense than when one is coerced to obey by physical force or the overt threat of punishment.[39] This type of domination involves in some sense *willingly* obeying another – in the absence of force or threats – which means that actual, explicit consent does not by itself indicate the absence of domination, a point that is well brought out in Rousseau's consideration of the

---

[39] Regularly obeying another due to coercion still counts as domination, just not the sort Rousseau is most interested in. Perhaps this is because he thinks that few real-world instances of domination can be explained exclusively in this way. To be effective, standing threats of force usually must also rely on the (false) opinions of the dominated regarding the *legitimacy* of the dominator's commands. This means that apart from the type of case I emphasize in the text – where I obey in order not to lose the cooperation of a more advantaged party – domination can also have its source in *false consciousness* regarding the legitimacy or naturalness of social hierarchies. Of course, some instances of false consciousness may themselves be grounded in asymmetries of dependence, if, for example, my belief in the right of the more advantaged to command serves to rationalize my own subservience, making it more palatable to myself. In such cases domination exists without the dominated being aware of it as such.

specious social contract in Part II of the Second Discourse, where the propertyless consent to the terms of their own domination. Although this makes it sometimes difficult to determine precisely where free cooperation ends and domination begins – and the Second Discourse does not provide a definitive answer to that question – there can be no doubt that domination exists and is common in the societies we live in. It is, for example, the very phenomenon Adam Smith points to in *The Wealth of Nations* when he notes that because workers need to eat more urgently than their employers need to make a profit, wage disputes in capitalism are almost always decided in favor of the latter.[40] Even though the relation between workers and their employers – or, more revealingly, their "bosses" – is mediated by a contract and grounded in "free" consent, the workers (because of their disadvantaged position in relation to those on whom they depend) typically end up laboring under the conditions dictated by their employers, a prime example of obedience to a foreign will.

WELL-BEING AS THE ABSENCE OF PAIN, FRUSTRATED DESIRES, AND UNMET NEEDS

Let us consider now, more briefly, a second component of the human good that occupies a prominent place in Rousseau's picture of true human nature, what I will call well-being. Although Rousseau uses the term *bien-être* twice in the Second Discourse (*DI*, 127, 152/*OC* III, 126, 154), it is not easy to determine whether it is meant to have a specific meaning or, if so, what the concept would include. My account of well-being here is an attempt to give Rousseau's references to it – as well as to happiness, desires, needs, health, and "hearts that are at peace" (*DI*, 150/*OC* III, 152) – a more coherent form than they appear to have in the text. It is probably significant that the first of Rousseau's references to *bien-être* occurs in his initial definition of the aims of *amour de soi-même*, which he specifies as "our well-being and our self-preservation" (*DI*, 127/*OC* III, 126). This confirms my claim above that Rousseau tends to distinguish between self-preservation and

---

[40] Adam Smith, *The Wealth of Nations*, ed. Edwin Cannan (New York: Modern Library, 2000), 75–6.

well-being, and it raises the question of what goods are included in the latter category. Two passages already cited make clear that it includes at least health, happiness, and peace of heart (*DI*, 150, 167/*OC*, 152, 171). (It is both amusing and indicative of Rousseau's personal obsessions that he spends so much of the Second Discourse discussing health in pre-civilized beings and railing against features of modern life, including the practice of medicine, that allegedly ruin it.) Moreover, the fact that Rousseau mentions not only *amour de soi-même* but also pity when referring to *bien-être* suggests that the object of this sentiment, too – freedom from pain or suffering – is a part of human well-being. Although well-being includes what can look like heterogeneous goods, it makes sense to join them under a single rubric insofar as their being goods for us derives from our character as material creatures – as sentient rather than rational beings, as Rousseau puts it (*DI*, 128/*OC* III, 126) – that are subject to desires, needs, pleasures, and pains, as well as because (like self-preservation) these goods differ in kind from the highest and distinctively human good discussed above, freedom. Perhaps one way of articulating this distinction as Rousseau sees it is to say that whereas purely natural beings are needy, desirous, and vulnerable to pain – and, so, can be happy or well-off – only beings with a will can be free or unfree; and, as the Second Discourse makes clear early on, to have a will is to stand outside the realm of mechanically determined nature: freedom is a good for humans only because of their "metaphysical and moral side" (*DI*, 140/*OC* III, 141).[41]

As I indicated above, well-being as it appears in Part I of the Second Discourse is conceived of mostly negatively, as the absence of pain, frustrated desires, and unmet needs. It would be more precise, however, to say that well-being comprises two distinguishable goods: happiness and the satisfaction of needs. One reason for distinguishing the two is that whereas happiness is defined negatively – as the absence of pain and frustrated desires[42] – need satisfaction is not, since Rousseau specifies a certain, very small number of needs that must

---

[41] See, however, note 14.

[42] "What else is it to wish that someone not suffer than to wish that he be happy?" (*DI*, 153/*OC* III, 155).

be satisfied if humans are to be considered well off. Another difference is that, as I explain below, happiness is defined subjectively, whereas needs in this context are always "true" (genuine) needs (*DI*, 128, 157/ *OC* III, 126, 160), as opposed to needs that are merely perceived to be such,[43] the latter of which become possibilities for humans only with the development of imagination and *amour propre*. Of course, much of what is responsible for the well-being of the inhabitants of the original state of nature is that their desires and needs are extremely modest, limited more or less to what they require in order to survive as biological organisms in good health. In fact, the desires and needs of these hypothetical beings overlap more or less completely, or, as Rousseau puts it, their "desires do not exceed [their] physical needs" (*DI*, 142/*OC* III, 143), which he goes on to enumerate as food, sex, and sleep. Beyond this, the happiness of these simple creatures includes the absence of pain, and on this basis one might attribute to them one desire imposed on them by nature that, strictly speaking, extends (but only barely) beyond their survival needs: the desire to avoid pain in all its forms.[44] In any case, the well-being of these creatures hardly diverges from that of other animate creatures: good health, the absence of pain, and plenty of food, sex, and sleep. In striving for these goods and experiencing frustration or "unhappiness" when they fail to attain them, human animals do not differ much from their non-human counterparts.

Even if it is difficult to find a difference between the desires and needs of beings in the original state of nature, it is important that we distinguish them conceptually already here. This is because as soon as we deal with socialized, not merely hypothetical, human beings – characterized by imagination, *amour propre*, and other non-animal

---

[43] Rousseau uses "need" (*besoin*) inconsistently, though it is possible to reconstruct a coherent view that can plausibly be attributed to him. This involves, as a first step, distinguishing true (genuine) needs from merely perceived needs. While natural, biological needs are true needs in this sense, they do not exhaust that category. Roughly, true human needs refer to whatever humans require in order to realize their fundamental interests (in freedom, self-preservation, and well-being). For the hypothetical inhabitants of the original state of nature this includes biological needs as well as whatever they need in order to remain free from domination. For civilized humans, true needs include, in addition, what is required for them to find satisfying recognition from others (satisfaction of their *amour propre*). See Chapter 4, note 10.

[44] "Every feeling of pain is inseparable from the desire to be delivered from it" (*E*, 80/*OC* IV, 303).

longings – desires quickly tend to come apart from needs and to extend beyond them. The well-being of these more complex human beings can be threatened in *either* domain, that is, either when desires (no matter how distant from those in the original state of nature) are regularly frustrated or when needs are regularly unmet. In the case of socialized beings, moreover, it is possible for needs to extend beyond desires in the further sense that in such beings true needs sometimes fail to generate the appropriate corresponding desires: socialized humans are capable of getting so caught up in the pursuit of riches, power, or prestige that they "forget" to eat or sleep. This is merely one more of civilization's "achievements" that Rousseau delights in bringing to our attention.

An important difference in the way Rousseau treats desires as opposed to needs is that, whereas he appears to believe that it is possible to specify a circumscribed set of true needs the satisfaction of which is essential to well-being, he does not undertake to do this in the case of desires. One way of putting this point is to say that although there is some content, however modest, to his idea of the needs that we must be able to satisfy in order to be well off, his conception of happiness as it figures in the Second Discourse remains both formal and subjective. It is formal because happiness is conceived of simply as a correspondence between two variables, as an "equilibrium" of "power and desire" in which one's desires match up with one's real abilities to satisfy them, and, consistent with this, unhappiness is defined as a "disproportion between our desires and our faculties" (*E*, 80/*OC* IV, 304). Happiness, then, is simply experiencing no regular frustration of the desires one in fact has, including desires to be free of pain and to have one's basic needs satisfied. This definition is subjective because happiness depends on satisfying the felt, experienced desires one in fact has, not the desires one ought to have in accordance with some ideal conception of the human being. Having a heart that is at peace, then, amounts more or less to the same thing as happiness; both consist in the peace one finds when exempt from experiencing the pain of privation that every unsatisfied desire brings with it (*E*, 80/*OC* IV, 304).

This, however, is a tricky point that calls for careful attention. I am not claiming that it is impossible to extract from Rousseau's texts a more contentful conception of what true human happiness consists in, or of what kinds of desires humans ought to cultivate and which it would be best for them to avoid.[45] I mean only that insofar as it invokes the concept of happiness, the argument of the Second Discourse, especially its critique of inequality, relies only on the formal and subjective concept I am explicating here. When Rousseau refers later in the Second Discourse to the misery or unhappiness of civilized humans, he means primarily that they repeatedly (and non-accidentally) find their actual desires unsatisfied: they regularly experience frustration, given what they desire. Even if many of their desires are ones they would ultimately be better off not having, their constant experience of frustration – their unhappiness – is an evil. Yet, even though formal and subjective, this simple concept of happiness can be employed as a criterion for criticizing an individual's desires if it can be argued that, taken together, those desires are in principle unsatisfiable, for this shows that happiness is non-accidentally unattainable for that individual given what he currently desires. This same concept of happiness can become a tool of *social* critique – the Second Discourse's true concern – if it can be shown that society generates desires in its members that are not collectively satisfiable. The basic idea behind this critical strategy should be familiar from Chapter 2, where I suggested that social ills tend to ensue when *amour propre*'s concern for relative standing manifests itself in a plurality of individuals as a desire for superior standing, for, as we will see in the next chapter, in such circumstances social esteem becomes a scarce good that cannot be attained by all simultaneously, resulting in perpetual conflict, "keeping up with the Joneses," and other social phenomena that make happiness for all unattainable in principle. Indeed, much of Rousseau's conception of true human happiness and of which desires it is appropriate for humans to have is arrived at by thinking about which desires can meet this formal criterion of collective satisfiability; one of the most important (but implicit) claims of the Second Discourse is that manifestations of *amour propre* that are not satisfiable for all are to be regarded as

---

[45] This is a major concern of *Emile*, which investigates the conditions of "true happiness" (*E*, 80/*OC* IV, 304).

"inflamed" – a term I explain in Chapter 4 – and hence as hindrances to true human happiness.

TRUE HUMAN NATURE IN THE EXPANDED SENSE

Until now I have considered Rousseau's picture of true human nature only as it appears in Part I of the Second Discourse. This constitutes by far the largest part of the normative conception of human nature underlying his critique of inequality and the other ills of civilization. Nevertheless, there are two additional components to his normative conception of human nature – two further essential human goods – that must be mentioned in this context. Both can be said to belong to his picture of true human nature in an expanded sense for the reason that neither is a possible achievement for the unsocialized, isolated beings that inhabit the hypothetical original state of nature depicted in Part I. Despite this, I will argue, Rousseau means to include these two goods among those that real humans must achieve in order to realize their true nature. In effect, his account of true human nature in the expanded sense is a picture of what counts as the essential goods available to *socialized* human beings. But since humans never really exist in the isolated, unsocialized condition imagined in Part I (and would not be genuinely *human* beings if they did), his conception of true human nature in the expanded sense is not an alternative to the less expansive conception but a more complete specification of what the true good for real, socialized humans consists in. Admittedly, evidence for my claim that Rousseau operates in the Second Discourse with a conception of true human nature in an expanded sense is scant and largely implicit. In other texts, however, especially *The Social Contract* and *Emile*, it is clear that he does rely on such an expanded conception. When one returns to the Second Discourse after having made this discovery, it becomes easier to see that this earlier text, too, bears traces of that conception; more important, a convincing interpretation of the Second Discourse requires such a conception since at least one of its components – the satisfaction of *amour propre* – plays some role (again, implicitly) in the text's critique of inequality and of modern society more generally.

The two essential human goods at issue here are what I will call social recognition (the esteem or respect sought by *amour propre*) and the robust development of latent human capacities.[46] Since the latter requires only a brief explanation, I begin with it. That the robust development of human capacities is a leading ideal in *Emile* is obvious; it is especially prominent in that text's early discussion of happiness, parts of which I referred to above. There Rousseau considers two possibilities for achieving the equilibrium between desires and powers that defines happiness. On the one hand, Emile's happiness could be achieved by keeping his desires to a minimum. This is the easier way to make him happy because it would require of him little skill or exertion. On the other hand, one could foster the development of his faculties and then take care to ensure that his desires never outrun his powers. This is the more difficult alternative, but it is clearly the one Rousseau endorses, and for the explicitly stated reason that adopting the first course would mean that "a part of [Emile's] faculties would remain idle, and [he] would not enjoy [his] whole being" (*E*, 80/*OC* IV, 304). In other words, Emile's happiness is not to be purchased at the expense of the development of his capacities, and this constraint demonstrates that, in that text at least, the normative conception of nature – the guiding principle of Emile's education – includes ideals beyond those realized in the Second Discourse's original state of nature. But although this ideal is less visible in the Second Discourse, it is unmistakably present there as well, even if buried for the most part in Rousseau's notes to the text. It appears most forcefully in the passage where Rousseau asks whether the many ills of civilization he has just depicted should be taken to imply that we are to abandon society and "return to live in forests with the bears." His response to this rhetorical question, though often overlooked, is an unambiguous No, and the reason he gives – anticipating the point he will make later in *Emile* – is that to do so would be to "debase [the] species" by choosing innocent tranquility over the development, however tumultuous and unhappy, of the species' natural but latent

---

[46] I am tempted to speak of the *full* (rather than *robust*) development of human capacities, though Rousseau does not use this term. Still, he obviously operates with a pre-Darwinian conception of a species' natural capacities, according to which such capacities, though originally latent, are fixed in both number and character. On this conception it would seem to make sense to speak of a species' complete development, a notion that, after Darwin, is no longer tenable.

capacities (*DI*, 203/*OC* III, 207).[47] In rejecting a return to living in forests, Rousseau makes clear that going back to a less developed state is not only impossible but also undesirable. Yet, as I have been arguing here, the rejection of this alternative clearly relies on normative criteria other than those derived from the original state of nature: achieving freedom, self-preservation, and well-being under conditions approximating the original state of nature would debase the species because it would leave no place for an array of goods – the development of our faculties, but also various forms of satisfying respect and esteem – that enrich human existence and elevate it above that of the beasts.

Although the ideal of human development is clearly present in the Second Discourse, it plays little or no role in the text's critique of inequality or modern society. As Marx was to recognize even more clearly a century later, a failure to develop human productive capacities is not, at least in capitalism's early phases, one of modern society's shortcomings (even if its one-sided, disfiguring development of workers' capacities was soon to become an object of critique for thinkers after Rousseau). The same cannot be said, however, of social recognition, the end sought by *amour propre*, although here, too, its status as an essential human good is far from obvious in the Second Discourse. I mentioned in Chapter 2 that *amour propre* is a deeply ambiguous passion for Rousseau, the source of both "what is best and worst among men" (*DI*, 184/*OC* III, 189), and essential to conjugal love, one of "the sweetest sentiments known to men" (*DI*, 164/*OC* III, 168). Even these statements, however, fall short of claiming that esteem or respect from others is an essential human good – an integral part of true human nature – and that the systematic inability of individuals to find satisfaction of their *amour propre* is part of Rousseau's critique of modern society in the Second Discourse.

There is a widespread and stubbornly held conviction among readers of Rousseau that whereas the desires deriving from *amour*

---

[47] Readers have had trouble understanding Rousseau's point in this crucial note to the Second Discourse. It is clear, however, that he is identifying a return to forests – "renouncing [the species'] enlightenment in order to renounce its vices" – with a debasing of humanity. He says plainly in the third sentence of the note that this would be a shameful conclusion to draw from his arguments and that only his adversaries would think of doing so (*DI*, 203/*OC* III, 207).

propre, and the dependence they engender, play a decisive role in his diagnostic enterprise – in explaining where the evils of society come from – they play no positive role in his visions of the good society or of ideal human development. According to this interpretation, Rousseau denies that *amour propre* can be the source of true needs, regarding it instead as generating only perceived needs that humans would be better off without and that have no place in the ideal society or in the personalities of those who inhabit it. Although *Emile* is pretty clear in its rejection of this one-sided view of *amour propre*'s potential,[48] the picture of it painted in the Second Discourse is indeed overwhelmingly negative, and this, along with *The Social Contract*'s failure to mention *amour propre*, is undoubtedly one reason that many readers cling to the one-sided view. Since I have argued at length elsewhere that this represents a serious misreading of Rousseau,[49] here I will review only briefly three points that support my claim that social recognition, appropriately qualified, counts for him as an essential human good.

The first of these points is psychological: *amour propre* is a fundamental drive of human beings that cannot fail to be active whenever humans, as they always do, live or grow up within society. In other words, *amour propre* plays a fundamental role in Rousseau's account of the sources of human motivation: in socialized humans it is at least equal in force to *amour de soi-même* and much more powerful than pity. According to Rousseau's account of human psychology, then, even if it were desirable to rid humans of the passion to be esteemed by others, doing so would be impossible, or achievable only by doing violence to human nature in the expanded sense. This means that a social theory that required the eradication of *amour propre* or that had no resources to accommodate its demands should be dismissed as utopian and that any attempt to eliminate it from human personalities is destined to be futile and oppressive.[50] Regardless, then, of what

---

[48] *E*, 215, 246, 248, 252, 264, 436, 439/*OC* IV, 494, 538, 541, 547, 562, 806, 809. See also *GM*, 159/*OC* III, 288 and *PE*, 16, 20/*OC* III, 255, 260.

[49] Frederick Neuhouser, *Rousseau's Theodicy of Self-Love: Evil, Rationality, and the Drive for Recognition* (Oxford University Press, 2008), 15–18, and chapters 6–7.

[50] "I would find someone who wanted to prevent the birth of the passions almost as mad as someone who wanted to annihilate them; and those who believed that this was my project . . . would surely have understood me very badly" (*E*, 212/*OC* IV, 491).

kind of social institutions they inhabit, humans cannot help but perceive their longing for esteem from others as a need of considerable urgency.

The second point going beyond the mere fact that *amour propre* occupies a central place in human psychology, makes a positive normative claim about the object of its strivings. That some such further step is necessary is made evident by the following considera-tion: even if Rousseau's psychological theory succeeded in establishing that humans universally desire public esteem, this would not show that we ought to regard recognition as an essential human good. If, for example, a desire to inflict cruelty on others were shown to be ineradicable from human psychology, we would still want to ask whether it was good for humans to act on a universally shared desire of this kind. The first criterion that social recognition must satisfy if it is to count as a good is that it be a permissible end for humans to adopt and pursue. For Rousseau, settling this issue boils down to asking whether such an end can in principle be satisfied for all humans simultaneously without compromising the fundamental human inter-ests of anyone. In other words, what our psychological makeup leads us to seek can count as good only if achieving it for all at once is possible and if doing so is compatible with safeguarding the life, freedom, and basic well-being of everyone.[51] Although Rousseau never uses the language of permissibility, the constraint I am articulat-ing here is implicit in the normative device he appeals to in his positive account of legitimate political theory, the social contract; more to the point, a plausible reconstruction of the Second Discourse's critique of social inequality requires this idea.

The implication of this for assessing the goodness of what *amour propre* strives for is that, regardless of how urgently it is desired or how deeply the desire for it is ingrained in human nature, recognition will not count as a human good unless it satisfies the conditions of permissibility just outlined. Whereas the Second Discourse, with its

---

[51] According to this criterion, personal security is a permissible end since it can be realized simultaneously for all and poses no necessary obstacles to anyone else's life, freedom, or well-being. If, on the other hand, being a domestic servant is incompatible with remaining the master of one's own will, then a desire to surround oneself with servants is morally objec-tionable and therefore not part of a person's genuine good, no matter how widespread or "natural" it might be.

diagnostic focus, concentrates on the considerable obstacles *amour propre* poses to human freedom and well-being, a main task of his social thought more generally is to show that these obstacles are not intrinsic to *amour propre*'s strivings but are due instead to contingent and alterable features of the conditions under which individuals are constrained to seek to satisfy those strivings, above all to poorly ordered social institutions and faulty domestic education. *The Social Contract* and *Emile* elaborate his responses to those unfortunate conditions, and together they aim to demonstrate that the general desire for esteem or respect is both universally satisfiable and compatible with the freedom and basic well-being of all. The most important element of Rousseau's strategy for carrying out this task rests on the insight, alluded to in Chapter 2, that *amour propre* is a highly malleable passion that can seek satisfaction in a nearly infinite variety of concrete forms. One common mistake in thinking about the social consequences of the desire for public esteem, according to Rousseau, is defining the end of *amour propre* too narrowly, exclusively in terms of achieving a superior standing in relation to others, thereby guaranteeing that no systematic satisfaction of the passion is possible. Rousseau, in contrast, distinguishes between the generic desire to be esteemed or respected by others (which all humans have) and the specific forms this generic desire assumes in concrete social circumstances (which are contingent and subject to modification).[52] This enables him to separate the pernicious forms of *amour propre* with which we are so familiar from the benign or healthy forms it is capable of assuming, given the appropriate circumstances.

Rousseau's position on what qualifies as permissible pursuits of recognized standing turns out to be surprisingly complex.[53] It maintains, for example, that certain forms of the pursuit of superior standing are permissible and even, in some cases, unavoidable for human beings. These include the desire to be loved above everyone else by some other particular individual (such as one's lover), but also many common desires to be esteemed for one's excellence, that is, as better

[52] Joshua Cohen nicely articulates this crucial distinction (*Rousseau: A Free Community of Equals* (Oxford University Press, 2010), 101–4), which Rousseau himself expresses when he contrasts the form *amour propre* is capable of assuming in a well-educated human being with "the [perverted or inflamed] form we believe natural to it" (*E*, 215/*OC* IV, 494).

[53] I articulate some of these conditions in *Rousseau's Theodicy of Self-Love*, Chapter 3.

than most or all others in some specific field of endeavor (*E*, 339/*OC* IV, 670).[54] Although certain limited forms of striving to be seen as the best qualify for Rousseau as permissible pursuits, the most important form of recognition that individuals must learn to want is *equal* respect – that is, recognition of one's status as a human being, essentially like all others. Because what is sought here is equal respect, there is no reason it cannot be achieved by everyone, and for this reason it does not generate the destructive dynamic depicted in the Second Discourse that is a consequence of most desires for superior standing. As readers of *The Social Contract* know, equal respect takes a variety of forms in the legitimate republic, including: equality before the law; the safeguarding of the same rights to negative freedoms for everyone; equal rights to political participation; and (the most important constraint on legitimate legislation) that the fundamental interests of every individual count the same as all others' in the framing of laws. The thought here is that by being publicly accorded equal respect in these ways, citizens of the legitimate state find substantial satisfaction of their generic need to "count for others" in a way that is not merely compatible with universal freedom and well-being but positively promotes those ends. Moreover, in finding a significant part of their *amour propre* satisfied by equal respect, citizens will experience less of an urge to satisfy it in more destructive ways.

These two points, however, do not exhaust Rousseau's view of why the satisfaction of *amour propre* is an essential human good. While they show that the desire for esteem is a deep-seated, universally shared desire of humans and that, sufficiently constrained, it is permissible to seek to satisfy it, they do not yet establish that recognition is an essential human good the achievement of which social philosophy must regard as a matter of great importance. Although this part of Rousseau's view is articulated less explicitly than it should be, hints of it are scattered throughout his texts, including the Second Discourse. One reason Rousseau regards the object of *amour propre* as an essential human good is because esteem stands at the heart of a number of goods that are valuable in themselves and responsible for much of what gives human lives meaning, such as love, friendship,

---

[54] In addition, if *amour propre* is to count as non-inflamed, esteem must be valued in the right measure and for the right reasons.

and many other forms of affirmation by others. Even though he recognizes the artificiality of romantic love and the many problems it introduces into human affairs (precisely *because* it is inseparable from *amour propre*)[55] Rousseau regards it, as we have seen, as among the "sweetest" of human sentiments and as one of the principal advantages the Golden Age has over the original state of nature (*DI*, 164–5, 167/*OC* III, 168,171).[56]

A second and more important reason that Rousseau regards satisfying recognition as an essential human good is suggested in various statements that link the satisfaction of *amour propre* with achieving what he calls "the sentiment of one's own existence" (*DI*, 187/*OC* III, 193).[57] This concept – the sentiment, or feeling, of one's *existence* – suggests that what *amour propre* seeks is not merely the feeling of satisfaction that attends every satisfied desire but a feeling of satisfaction that brings with it something more substantial: a confirmation of one's *being* as a self, which, more than simply a subjective feeling, makes one into a kind of public object: a self with a determinate identity that is confirmed and given objective existence by the affirming regard of others.[58] According to the conception of selfhood at work here, to *be* someone – the ultimate aim of *amour propre* – is, in part, to *count as* someone for other subjects. This means that for Rousseau human beings constitute themselves as selves – they achieve real, publicly confirmed identities – only through relations of

[55] Sexual love is inseparable from *amour propre* because it involves an especially intense and intimate confirmation of one's value for another subject. Because it seeks confirmation of one's preeminent value from only one subject rather than from all or many, it makes the desire for a standing above others satisfiable in principle for everyone.

[56] Notice, too, that the beings of the Golden Age, said to "live as free, healthy, good, and happy as their nature allowed them to be" (*DI*, 167/*OC* III, 171), are already beings of *amour propre* who seek simple forms of esteem from their peers.

[57] See also *E*, 42, 61, 270/*OC* IV, 253, 279–80, 570–1. At *OC* I, 1801, the sentiment of existence is distinguished from the desire to be happy and identified with "all that seems to extend or shore up our existence," a description that clearly fits the recognition sought by *amour propre*, an affectively tinged perception of one's being as a self. Rousseau explicitly links the sentiment of one's own existence to (inflamed) *amour propre* in lamenting the tendency of civilized individuals to "derive the sentiment of [their] own existence solely from the judgment [of others]" (*DI*, 187/*OC* III, 193). Not all that extends or shores up our existence need come from the esteem of others, but in civilized beings a very large portion of it does (and alienation is the state in which all, or too much of it, does).

[58] N. J. H. Dent articulates this point very well in *Rousseau: An Introduction to His Psychological, Social and Political Theory* (Oxford: Blackwell, 1988), 49.

recognition to others. This, more than any other consideration, stands behind Rousseau's implicit view that esteem or respect from others is an essential human good, a central part of what it is to realize true human nature in the expanded sense.

CONNECTING THE DESCRIPTIVE AND NORMATIVE CONCEPTIONS OF HUMAN NATURE

Until now I have emphasized the opposition between the normative and non-normative senses of human nature because without this conceptual distinction Rousseau's claims fall quickly into incoherence. There is, however, more of a connection between these two aspects of his conception of human nature than I have so far acknowledged. Such a connection is asserted already in the Preface to the Second Discourse when Rousseau states that "so long as we do not know natural man, we shall in vain try to ascertain ... what best suits his constitution" (*DI*, 127/*OC* III, 125). In this remark the two senses of human nature are clearly distinguished: the "natural man" we are encouraged to know refers to human nature in the explanatory sense (the basic capacities and dispositions that characterize all human beings as such), and "what best suits [man's] constitution" is human nature understood as a normative ideal. The new claim here is that discovering what is best for us as humans depends on knowing the dispositions and capacities that are characteristic of our species.[59] Clearly, then, the Second Discourse adopts a version of the methodological principle that we learn what kind of existence is appropriate for humans by looking first at what our dispositions – those of original human nature, as well as ultimately, I will argue, *amour propre*, the characteristic disposition of socialized beings – incline us to do independently of the corruption, largely by acquired opinions or "prejudices," that Part II of the Second Discourse goes on to describe.[60]

---

[59] A similar claim is made in *Emile*, where we are instructed to observe a child's "original dispositions" and determine on that basis the goals an education in accordance with nature ought to have (*E*, 39, 41, 43/*OC* IV, 248, 251, 254).

[60] Of course, since *amour propre* cannot operate in the absence of opinions, it is impossible to say what it "naturally" inclines us to seek, apart from the very general goal of the good opinion of others in some form; see note 62.

The most prominent application of this principle is found in Part I of the Second Discourse, where Rousseau sets out what it means in the original state of nature to live in accordance with nature. His claim is that in the absence of corrupting opinions and artificial institutions that distort our natural aims and desires, individuals who follow their original dispositions – to avoid pain and seek pleasure, to satisfy their own desires rather than obey others – are led, without consciously intending it, to act in ways that promote their self-preservation, satisfy their simple needs and desires, and keep themselves free of domination by others. From this it is supposed to follow that self-preservation, well-being, and freedom are goods central to any life that is well suited to human beings, no matter what level of social development they have achieved. In deriving normative standards from his account of original human nature, Rousseau obviously presupposes some version of natural teleology: by providing animate beings with original dispositions and capacities, nature (or its creator, God) can be taken to set ends for its creatures; these ends are discovered by determining which behaviors those dispositions and capacities tend to produce when undistorted by acquired opinions and artificial social arrangements and by observing the functions those behaviors unwittingly serve; finally, these ends (or some version of them) constitute the good of those creatures not only in their natural state but even in artificial social conditions.[61]

It is no accident, then, that the very things our original dispositions push us to seek unreflectively end up on the list of essential human goods that correspond to Rousseau's conception of true human nature. *Amour de soi-même* impels individuals to avoid pain and to seek out what their survival requires, which is to say that it promotes individual self-preservation and well-being. Pity impels individuals to relieve the suffering of others, thereby promoting the preservation of the species and the well-being of others (*DI*, 154/*OC* III, 156). (And if we extend our view to human nature in the expanded sense,

---

[61] Similarly, when asked to define the goal of Emile's education, Rousseau replies, "it is the very same as that of nature" (*E*, 38/*OC* IV, 247). This does not mean that Emile is to be solitary, brutish, and void of opinions, like the beings of the original state of nature. It means, rather, that although he will be artificial in the sense that he will speak, reason, love, and live in society, he will do so in ways consistent with the natural values of self-preservation, well-being, and freedom.

something similar can be seen to hold: the disposition added to human nature here, *amour propre*, also leads us to seek an essential human good: a publicly affirmed confirmation of one's existence as a self.)[62] Of course, it is possible for the wholly natural sentiments of pity and *amour de soi-même* to move us in opposing directions if, for example, both of us have a need that due to specific circumstances can be satisfied for only one of us. Even here, however, nature provides clear guidance, pushing us in one of the two directions and in effect establishing an order of priority among the two dispositions. Because pity speaks with a gentler voice than *amour de soi-même*, we seek first to eliminate our pain and only after that to alleviate the suffering of others, and only if this can be accomplished without imposing significant suffering or deprivation on ourselves. Rousseau believes, then, that the natural constitution of humans – the presence and relative strength of *amour de soi-même* and pity – would impose on purely natural beings certain "principles prior to reason" that would conduce to their collective good, most notably the rule that such a being "will never harm another . . . except in the legitimate case when, his preservation at stake, he is obliged to give himself preference" (*DI*, 127/ *OC* III, 126). That Rousseau intends his account of original human nature to have implications for how it is fitting for humans to act, as well as for what their good consists in, is made clear by his claim to find in it the basis for a "maxim of natural goodness" (or "natural virtue") that remains at the heart of what more civilized humans will make into the dictates of laws, morals, and virtue: "*Do your good with the least possible harm to others*" (*DI*, 152, 154/ *OC* III, 154, 156).

---

[62] Even if there is a "natural" passion (in the expanded sense) that corresponds to the good of publicly confirmed selfhood (*amour propre*), its relation to this good is more complex than the relation that holds between, say, *amour de soi-même* and self-preservation. In the latter case, *amour de soi-même* can achieve its natural end in a wholly original state of nature, in the absence of all opinions on the part of the being in question. *Amour propre*, as we have seen, cannot operate without opinions on the part of both those who seek esteem and those who give it. This makes it much more vulnerable than the dispositions of original human nature to the corruption and distortions that opinions tend to bring with them. This increased vulnerability, however, does not detract from the goodness or importance of the end sought by *amour propre*, when it is achieved such that it is compatible with the other essential human goods. The point, rather, is that humans' quest to satisfy their *amour propre* will be especially fraught with dangers and pitfalls, which is another way one could describe the central claim of the Second Discourse.

Much of this natural teleology should seem familiar and relatively unproblematic to contemporary readers, insofar as the main ends Rousseau finds inscribed in our natural constitution are self-preservation (of both individuals and the species) and aspects of well-being closely tied to our biological nature. This natural teleology becomes trickier, however, when we move from biological ends to the other principal good supposedly revealed by the original state of nature, freedom. In this case there is no natural disposition in Rousseau's account of original human nature that inclines us to seek this good, and although the good of freedom can be matched up with a natural capacity (if not a natural disposition) – our capacity for free will – the stark difference in kind between freedom as the absence of domination and the metaphysical capacity for free will makes it difficult to see why a disposition to seek the former should follow from the presence of the latter: as we saw above, free will is something humans never exist without, and so positing a disposition to achieve it makes little sense. Yet despite the wide gap between these two senses of freedom, here too Rousseau seems to want to link the normative status of freedom with a claim that humans (and even other animals) in the original state of nature exhibit an unreflective disposition to resist obeying the wills of others; they possess, as Rousseau puts it, a "natural disposition ... against servitude," which, strictly speaking, cannot be traced back to *amour de soi-même*, *amour propre*, or pity: just "as an untamed steed ... struggles impetuously at the very sight of a bit, ... so barbarous man ... prefers the most tempestuous freedom to a tranquil subjection" (*DI*, 177/*OC* III, 181).[63]

Perhaps the closest one can come to making plausible the asserted connection between original human nature and a disposition to avoid domination is to posit a general inclination of natural beings to exercise, realize, or otherwise "fulfill" the faculties they are born with, in this case, freedom of the will. On this view, to have a natural capacity would be at the same time to have a natural disposition to exercise or develop that capacity. However, there are several problems with this suggestion, too. In the first place, Rousseau posits no such corresponding natural disposition in the case of perfectibility. The Second Discourse is clear that the latent capacities that make up

---

[63] Similar claims are made at *DI*, 158, 176, 177/*OC* III, 161, 180–1, 182; see note 14.

perfectibility begin to develop only when external circumstances make it difficult for humans in their undeveloped state to satisfy their needs deriving from *amour de soi-même* (*DI*, 141, 142, 161–2/*OC* III, 142, 143, 165). In the absence of such circumstances there is no push internal to perfectibility that impels the development of its innate faculties. Moreover, the passage cited above shows that Rousseau attributes to non-human animals as well as to humans a natural disposition to resist domination, even though he explicitly denies that the former possess free will; here at least a natural disposition seems to exist without there being a corresponding natural capacity. Perhaps this problem could be avoided by claiming that the relevant animal capacity in this case is desire, not a capacity to choose freely – indeterministically – among one's desires (or among possible ways of satisfying them), and that part of what it is to desire, for any animal, is to resist whatever forces impede one's motions towards satisfying it. Rousseau, however, avoids this route for reasons that sit pretty deeply within his overall view. Doing so would make freedom into a thoroughly naturalistic value and would rid him of the resources he relies on when claiming that freedom is the distinctive human good and the "noblest" of human attributes (*DI*, 178/*OC* III, 183).[64] It would also mean that non-human animals, too, could be the victims of domination, raising the (for him) disturbing possibility that their freedom might have to be accorded an exalted ethical status similar to that of the freedom of humans. (It is noteworthy, though, that at several places Rousseau comes very close to claiming some kind of ethical status for non-human animals grounded in their capacity to feel (but not to anticipate) pain. Still their lack of freedom means that they are not full-fledged ethical subjects (*DI*, 127–8/*OC* III, 126).) In the end we are forced to conclude, I believe, that the naturalistic impulses of Rousseau's account of human nature – including his urge to find prototypes of all forms of human behavior in the behavior of non-human animals – are never completely reconciled with his equally fundamental conviction that human

---

[64] Recall, however, my earlier suggestion that Rousseau's position might be both stronger and more consistent if he were to give up his "metaphysical" conception of freedom and invoke only a naturalistic conception of freedom; see Chapter 1, note 30.

beings' capacity for and interest in freedom set them radically apart from the rest of nature.

Even though Rousseau's natural teleology does not go so far as to assume that every innate capacity brings with it a corresponding drive to develop that capacity, in the case of perfectibility he does appear to take the presence of such capacities as a basis for concluding that their full development constitutes an important good for humans, a part of what it is to realize true human nature. That nature "intends" the development of these capacities, or sets it as an end, is suggested to him by their mere presence (in latent forms), and even more by the fact that nature also supplies us with the other basic capacity necessary for their development: free will. For as Rousseau describes it, it is only the ability of humans to deviate from the path prescribed by natural instinct that – when external circumstances render the usual ways of satisfying the needs of life untenable – makes the unfolding of their latent capacities possible (*DI*, 134–5, 140/*OC* III, 135, 141). If the presence of perfectibility points to a human good that makes up part of Rousseau's picture of true human nature, it is a good that carries no natural guarantee of being realized; nor does nature supply humans with an independent motivation for seeking to achieve it. The good that consists in the robust development of humans' latent capacities relies instead on a specific form of cooperation between nature and freedom: such development occurs only when external circumstances frustrate the natural strivings of *amour de soi-même* and when the human capacity to deviate spontaneously from what instinct dictates – or, more precisely, the complete absence in humans of instinct in the true sense (*DI*, 135/*OC* III, 135) – leads humans to set in motion a train of events that, unbeknownst to them, results in the development of what until that point had been merely latent capacities.

In any case, this strategy for making the development of capacities into an ideal for human beings – taking their natural presence in a latent form to indicate some purpose set by nature – assumes a version of natural teleology that goes somewhat beyond the more modest conception referred to above that limits nature's ends to self-preservation and biological well-being. It is easy, of course, to grasp the theological underpinnings of this teleological picture of nature: if the benevolent creator of nature equips its creatures with certain innate capacities, they must be intended to serve some purpose of His that promotes those creatures' good. While it is difficult to make even this thought work in the case of the connection between free will and freedom from domination (since being dominated does not, strictly speaking, abrogate one's metaphysical freedom), it can easily be applied to the capacities that make up perfectibility: if God gave humans but not other animals capacities for language and reason, for example, He must have had a purpose in doing so sufficient to make the development and exercise of those capacities partially constitutive of what is distinctively good for those parts of His creation.[65] However this may be, even if, after Darwin, we reject the idea of natural teleology – together with the thought that natural creatures possess a fixed set of original capacities with determinate destinies – it is not difficult to endorse the substance of the normative point Rousseau means to derive from the doctrine of perfectibility. In other words, it is still possible for us today, in what would constitute only a slight deviation from Rousseau's position, to appreciate the value of extensively developed capacities – to recognize such development as an ideal – independently of the no longer tenable belief that nature intends it or sets it as an end.[66]

The most interesting implication of Rousseau's inclusion of the development of innate capacities within his picture of true human nature – a consideration that explains why such development cannot be part of the happy existence enjoyed in the original state of nature – is that the conditions necessary for realizing this ideal stand in some tension with the conditions that enable the ideals of freedom, well-being, and self-preservation to be realized in that original state. There are probably many sources of the tension among these ideals, but the easiest to see is that development in general brings with it the birth and refinement of cognitive faculties – reason and imagination, for example – that enable humans both to distance themselves from their purely natural and salutary impulses and to inflate their desires

---

[65] As the examples of Aristotle and the Stoics demonstrate, however, a robust natural teleology of this sort need not appeal to divine creation.

[66] This is essentially the route Rawls takes when he includes "the Aristotelian Principle" in his account of the good: "human beings enjoy the exercise of their realized capacities . . ., and this enjoyment increases the more the capacity is realized, or the greater its complexity" (Rawls, *TJ*, 426).

well beyond their true needs. Indeed, the Second Discourse can be read, as it was by Kant,[67] as an extended argument for the claim that culture (including the development of human capacities), though not strictly incompatible with human freedom and happiness, poses nearly insurmountable barriers to their realization. If we take this part of Rousseau's view seriously, we are forced to conclude that the true but mostly hidden content of his natural teleology is the distinctly non-teleological doctrine that, in the sole case of human beings, nature (or God) sets *conflicting* ends for its creatures. One place this doctrine finds expression, if only obliquely, is in the Second Discourse's opening pages when Rousseau wonders aloud, as it were, whether nature "destined us to be healthy" or intended for us to reflect (*DI*, 138/*OC* III, 138), implying that, in many circumstances at least, our health is in conflict with our being reflective.

It is not that nature's ends for humans are conceptually incompatible nor even that they are non-compossible in the sense that, given the constraints of both human and non-human nature, they cannot be realized simultaneously. An all-powerful being that fashioned nature such that either of these were true would count for Rousseau as an evil demon, not a beneficent Creator. Moreover, demonstrating that the ends of true human nature in the expanded sense are really compossible is a principal aim of Rousseau's thought as a whole, especially in *Emile* and *The Social Contract*,[68] where it is not only the development of our capacities that is shown to be compatible with our freedom and well-being but also the end sought by *amour propre*, esteem or respect from others.[69] One might even locate the main

[67] "In [his Second Discourses, Rousseau] ... shows quite correctly that there is an inevitable conflict between culture and the nature of the human race as a *physical* species each of whose individual members is meant to fulfill his full destiny completely. But in his *Emile* [and] his *Social Contract* ... he attempts in turn to solve the more difficult problem of what course culture should take in order to ensure the proper development, in keeping with their destiny, of humanity's capacities as a *moral* species so that the latter will no longer conflict with its character as a natural species"; Immanuel Kant, "Conjectures on the Beginning of Human History," in *Political Writings*, ed. H. S. Reiss (Cambridge University Press, 1991), 227.

[68] It is also a central theme of Rousseau's fabulously popular novel, *Julie, or the New Heloise*. See my "Rousseau's 'Julie': Passion, Love, and the Price of Virtue," in Susan Wolf and Christopher Grau, eds., *Understanding Love through Philosophy, Film, and Literature* (Oxford University Press, 2013), 209–30.

[69] It should be noted that this is a controversial interpretation of Rousseau's thought; many interpreters read Rousseau as setting out in *Emile* and *The Social Contract* separate, not

lesson of these two works in the claim that only human intervention – only artifice of just the right kind, in both social institutions and domestic education – can bring nature's ends for the human species into harmony, making them jointly realizable. This implies that with respect to its human creatures nature requires action from outside itself – the action of free human agents – in order to achieve its purposes. For this reason, one could say, nature fails to be a teleologically self-sufficient, fully self-realizing order of being. As the Second Discourse's account of the "fall" of civilized humans makes clear, there is nothing in Rousseau's version of natural teleology that approximates either the optimistic faith in nature's ultimate goodness defended by Kant in, among other places, his "Idea for a Universal History with a Cosmopolitan Purpose" or Hegel's confidence in a dialectically guaranteed realization, within nature, of the entirety of humans' spiritual ends.[70] If nature for Rousseau is teleological in supplying ends that define the human good, it falls well short of being internally purposive in the more robust sense that, if left to itself, it would realize its ends of its own accord. In this respect Rousseau is closer to most of post-nineteenth-century thought than either Kant or Hegel.

In fact, the more one considers carefully what Rousseau says about nature in the Second Discourse and attempts to fit it into a coherent picture, the more the *limits* of his natural teleology come into view. While there can be no doubt that Rousseau regards the original state of nature as grounding his fundamental normative claim that freedom, survival, and well-being are basic constituents of the human good that any form of life must achieve if it is to accord with true human nature, the main thrust of his position is actually to move away from pre-modern strategies of looking to a teleological conception of nature in order to find a determinate picture of the kind of life

---

compossible, solutions to the problems raised in the Second Discourse and as denying the compatibility of freedom, happiness, and the ends of *amour propre*. I have argued at length against such interpretations in *Rousseau's Theodicy of Self-Love*, especially Chapter 5. For two interpretations different from mine, see: Judith Shklar, *Men and Citizens: A Study of Rousseau's Social Theory* (Cambridge University Press, 1985), 1–21; and Tzvetan Todorov, *Frail Happiness: An Essay on Rousseau*, trans. John T. Scott and Robert Zaretsky (University Park, Penn.: Pennsylvania State University Press, 2001), 12–19.

70 For the "Idea for a Universal History with a Cosmopolitan Purpose" see Kant, *Political Writings*, 50–1.

humans ought to live. In comparison with the positions of many of his predecessors, Rousseau's normative stance belongs more to the modern philosophical trend of viewing nature as "disenchanted" than to earlier traditions for which nature furnishes a reliable blueprint for human society and individual lives.

One familiar respect in which Rousseau ascribes a lesser philosophical role to nature than much of the tradition before him can be seen in the very meagerness of his account of original human nature, something he brings to our attention more than once by emphasizing how much of what other philosophers have ascribed to human nature is in fact a product of artifice, historical accident, and contingent social arrangements (*DI*, 132, 151/*OC* III, 132, 153). One of the points of attributing much less of our present way of being to nature than most of his predecessors did is to suggest that many of the desires, dispositions, beliefs, and capacities that we take to be natural to humans, and therefore invariable characteristics of them, could in fact be other than they are, implying that what to many have appeared to be fixed features of human existence are instead susceptible in principle to modification by human agency. It is less obvious, but no less important, that shifting the explanatory responsibility for so much of how we currently are from nature to our own freedom – to the effects of our opinions and actions – also diminishes the normative significance of nature. The main respect in which this is true for Rousseau is that for all beings shaped by the artifices of culture – for all real human beings, in other words – nature alone is unable to provide specific guidelines for what society and individuals within it should be like. Since his prescription is not "Go back to living in forests with bears!" the original state of nature, though furnishing a general account of some of the goods we ought to seek in whatever social arrangements we live under, is powerless to recommend any specific civilized way of life as the one that true human nature requires. As I suggested earlier, the Second Discourse's Golden Age, citizenship in the legitimate republic, and Emile's way of participating in family and society all satisfy the general criteria for a good life implicit in Rousseau's normative conception of human nature. In other words, although nature prescribes certain general ends to humans, there is a nearly infinite variety of specific ways in which they can be realized.

Indeed, one theme that one finds everywhere in the Second Discourse once one is open to seeing it is nature's *silence* in the civilized state (*DI*, 153/*OC* III, 155–6). Nature is often silent for us not only because artificial passions can mute natural pity and divert *amour de soi-même* from its natural course, thereby stifling nature's voice (*DI*, 127/*OC* III, 126), but also because in the complex circumstances of civilized life nature by itself, in the absence of philosophical reflection, is usually unable to direct us in specific directions. The theme of nature's silence with respect to how civilized humans should live is especially visible in Rousseau's critique of natural law theory in the Second Discourse's Preface (*DI*, 125–8/*OC* III, 124–6). Unfortunately, these paragraphs are also among the most confusing of the entire Second Discourse, in part because it is not clear that their arguments succeed in hitting their intended targets (since it is not clear that any natural law theorists of import actually held the views Rousseau criticizes).[71] For this reason it is best not to spend much time trying to locate in these pages a set of cogent arguments directed against real representatives of the natural law tradition but instead to concentrate on extracting from them the points most important for understanding Rousseau's position on the extent to which nature can prescribe to civilized beings how to live and organize society.

Two such points are especially relevant. The first is the claim, widely acknowledged by Rousseau's interpreters, that moral prescriptions in the strict sense – which natural laws purport to be – could have no place in a wholly natural condition of the sort the original state of nature is supposed to be. As we have seen, in such a state nature would indeed impel human creatures unreflectively to follow their *amour de soi-même* and pity and to accord preference to the former in cases where the two conflict. Moreover, following these inclinations in such a state would result in behavior that conduced to the good of both individuals and the species as a whole. Yet nature's "pushing" us to behave in ways that promote our good is not the same as its issuing moral prescriptions that obligate us, or tell us how we

---

[71] Rousseau seems not to want to reject natural law theory in all its possible guises but only specific versions of that theory endorsed by his predecessors and contemporaries. He appears to maintain that there are true "rules of natural right" and that the moral rules that obligate civilized beings are in some sense based upon them (*DI*, 127/*OC* III, 126), but the precise details of these theses remain, at least to me, obscure.

ought to act. The "maxim of natural goodness" that follows from the original configuration of our dispositions might describe or predict the behavior of purely natural beings, but it cannot dictate how they ought to act for the simple reason that, in the absence of the civilizing processes that first make it possible for there to be a gap between natural inclinations and actual behavior, such beings are not tempted to disobey nature's maxim by, for example, refusing to heed pity's natural call. (One source of this gap is that in more developed social conditions enduring conflicts of interest virtually ensure that self-interest and pity will frequently clash, creating for the first time a standing incentive – and therefore the real possibility – for humans to choose to act contrary to the maxim of natural goodness.) A maxim of *natural* goodness can articulate how it is fitting or good for creatures to act, given the kinds of beings they by nature are, but it falls short of being a moral prescription in the true sense. Only in more complex social circumstances, when compliance with the purely natural laws of animal behavior is no longer guaranteed, is it meaningful to speak of "oughts" and moral prescriptions. This is why Rousseau is careful to ascribe merely "natural virtue" (*DI*, 152/*OC* III, 154) to the hypothetical inhabitants of the original state of nature and why he denies that they would be capable of good or evil, of virtue or vice, in the true sense of those terms. Indeed, bearing this in mind – that such beings lack all "moral relations" and "known duties" (*DI*, 150/*OC* III, 152) – is essential to understanding the true content of Rousseau's frequently repeated claim that "man is naturally good" (*DI*, 197/*OC* III, 202).[72] In the end, though, this point about the inapplicability of moral concepts in the original state of nature has a relatively modest reach. Contrary to what Rousseau sometimes seems to insinuate, it does not establish, for example, that the very idea of natural law – of nature being the source of morally obligatory prescriptions for humans – is incoherent in all possible senses of the term.[73] At most it raises two

---

[72] One could think of Chapter 1 of this book as explicating Rousseau's thesis that humans are naturally good; but see also Victor Gourevitch's interpretation at *DI*, xx–xxi, and John T. Scott, "The Theodicy of the Second Discourse: The 'Pure State of Nature' and Rousseau's Political Thought," *American Political Science Review* 86 (September 1992), 704–5. For a more detailed elaboration of the thesis see Cohen, *Rousseau*, 110–13.

[73] And if note 71 is correct, this could not have been Rousseau's intention since he appears to want to retain some place for natural laws that are valid.

difficult questions that proponents of natural law must answer (versions of which will be considered further in the following chapter): how and in what sense of the term can *nature* be the source of genuinely moral prescriptions? and: if some sense can be made of this idea, how do such prescriptions compare with those that derive from the other source of right, "the true foundations of the body politic" (*DI*, 128/*OC* III, 126), which Rousseau identifies with the "coming together," or agreement, of human wills (*SC*, I.1.ii, I.4.i)?

The second, more important point to be extracted from Rousseau's discussion of natural law is that whatever normative resources can be derived from a conception of true human nature, they do not extend so far as to yield genuine laws – determinate, or specific, binding prescriptions – for real (socialized) beings who have advanced beyond their primitive state and for whom deviating from nature's original call is a standing possibility. This second point concerns not the morally binding status of nature's normative standards but the indeterminacy of their content once what is at issue is how beings in specific social circumstances should live their lives or organize their society. In Rousseau's critique of natural law theory this point is expressed in his remark that in the civilized condition genuine laws can no longer "speak immediately with the voice of nature" (*DI*, 127/*OC* III, 125). One thing this means is that in circumstances more complex than those of the original state of nature, reasoning of a certain sort (*DI*, 127, 150/*OC* III, 126, 152) is required in order for us to know what we ought to do. (The nature of this reasoning – crucial to the distinction between right in society and natural law – will be elaborated in the following chapter.) In such a condition knowing what we ought to do – knowing what conduces to our genuine collective good – requires a level of enlightenment that goes beyond the direct and unreflective intending of the good that characterizes the inhabitants of the original state of nature. This is because, even if nature continues to move socialized beings to seek their survival, well-being, and freedom, it is no easy matter, once private property, class distinctions, and inflamed *amour propre* have arisen, to know which specific actions or laws will promote those ends of nature, whether for the individual or for the species as a whole. A further difficulty – and another sense in which nature in the civilized state no longer speaks to us immediately – is that once the principles that conduce to our good cannot be simply felt or intuited, we may also need an artificial incentive in order to follow them. This is precisely why *The Social Contract* will insist that outside the state of nature, in a legitimate republic, human beings must be de-natured (*SC*, II.7.iii) – molded by artificial educative processes – if they are to know, and to be motivated to do, what achieving their good within society requires of them.

This concludes my reconstruction of the Second Discourse's normative conception of human nature. It is not difficult to recognize that its account of the essential constituents of the human good plays an important role in the Second Discourse's critique of social inequality, which relentlessly depicts ways in which inequalities are bound up in social dynamics that generate the antitheses of those goods: unhappiness, unmet needs, conflict, enslavement, alienation, and the absence of satisfying recognition. What is less clear, however, is how precisely Rousseau's catalog of the essential goods translates into principles for assessing the legitimacy of social practices, including what he calls moral inequalities. Effecting this translation and applying its results to moral (or social) inequalities, especially economic inequality, constitute the main tasks of Chapter 4.

CHAPTER 4

Judging the legitimacy of social inequalities

Chapter 3 inquired into the normative resources that Rousseau thinks nature provides us with – through both natural law and a normative conception of human nature – in order to determine the rightfulness of inequality. It considered Rousseau's answer to the specific normative question set for him by the Academy of Dijon: is inequality among humans authorized by natural law? The present chapter, in contrast, explores the resources offered by the Second Discourse for answering the broader and more interesting question: to what extent, and for what reasons, are social inequalities legitimate when judged by the normative standards that ground right within society? This chapter, in other words, aims to elaborate the more comprehensive normative criteria implicit in the Second Discourse's critique of social inequality – criteria that, once reconstructed, reveal the legitimacy, or permissibility, of certain forms of social inequality not specifically sanctioned by natural law. Accomplishing this task requires, first, investigating the causal connections between social inequalities in general and the goods that make up Rousseau's normative vision of true human nature and, second, translating this picture of the essential human goods into principles of legitimacy – principles not of natural right but of right within the social order – that determine whether laws, institutions, and social practices more generally are morally permissible or unobjectionable (and, in the case of laws, whether they obligate us to obey them). Finally, I examine what these principles imply more concretely for social critique by applying them to one particular kind of social inequality that is especially prominent in modern societies, inequality in wealth.

JUDGING INEQUALITY BY ITS CONSEQUENCES

At the end of the previous chapter I noted that social inequalities clearly play a role in the Second Discourse's critique of modern society insofar as they are part of a complex social dynamic the results of which – unhappiness, unmet needs, conflict, enslavement, wickedness, failures of recognition, alienation – are taken by Rousseau as moral indictments of the societies that generate them. In Chapter 2 we examined one aspect of this dynamic, namely, ways in which social processes, when fueled by *amour propre*, give rise to social inequalities and become the principal, "artificial" source of human inequality in general. While this thesis belongs to the project of determining the origin of inequality, the concern of this chapter is the Second Discourse's critical (and therefore normative) project, which examines the same social dynamic with an eye to determining how social inequalities help to give rise to the evils that inspire Rousseau's critique of modern society. That social inequalities are somehow implicated in this critique is obvious; our present task is to articulate precisely what role they play in it.

The first step in reconstructing Rousseau's position involves explaining why social inequality is ethically problematic – why, when viewed from the perspective of what is good for human beings generally (or from the perspective of human nature in the normative sense) – inequality should concern us. Explaining this is one of the Second Discourse's main tasks, and it provides relatively clear indications as to how, in general outline at least, it intends to answer this question. Consider, for example, Rousseau's remark immediately after he has traced human development up to roughly its present state: as soon as "equality disappeared . . . work became necessary . . . the vast forests changed into smiling fields that had to be watered with the sweat of men, and . . . slavery and misery were soon seen to sprout and grow" (*DI*, 167/*OC* III, 171). The consequences of social inequality are described in even greater detail in a well-known passage several pages later:

man, who had previously been free and independent, is now . . . subjugated by a multitude of new needs . . . especially to those of his kind, whose slave he . . . becomes even by becoming their master . . . He must therefore constantly try to interest them in his fate and to make them really or apparently find their own profit in working for his . . . Finally, consuming ambition, the ardent desire to raise one's relative fortune less out of genuine need than in order to place oneself above others, instills in all men a black inclination to harm one another . . . In a word, competition and rivalry on the one hand, conflict of interests on the other, and always the hidden desire to profit at another's expense; all these evils are . . . the inseparable consequences of nascent inequality. (*DI*, 170–1/*OC* III, 174–5)

In reconstructing Rousseau's critique of inequality I want to take seriously two aspects of the claims cited above, especially of the first passage's claim that "slavery and misery" are the principal effects of social inequality.[1] The first point is that Rousseau's critique of inequality, above all of economic inequality, focuses on its pernicious *consequences* for human beings. Inequalities in wealth, for Rousseau, are wrong not in themselves but only because of the consequences they have, and the same holds for the most part for other forms of social inequality as well.[2] There is, one might say, a significant *consequentialist* – or, more accurately perhaps, *instrumentalist* – strand in Rousseau's position.[3] The suggestion that social inequality is objectionable primarily because of its ethically objectionable consequences rather than because it is somehow wrong in itself is borne out by the well-known statement in *The Social Contract* that the general will has two principal objects or aims – freedom and equality – and that equality in wealth and power is such an aim because "freedom cannot subsist without it" (*SC*, II.11.i.). This is as clear a statement as one

---

[1] "Misery" does not mean simply poverty; it is essentially the opposite of happiness or well-being. Rousseau defines misery elsewhere as "a painful privation and suffering of body or soul" (*DI*, 150/*OC* III, 152). It is also worth noting that the inequality at issue in the passage cited is economic inequality.

[2] I make the qualification *for the most part* because for Rousseau some kinds of social inequality are wrong in themselves. A society that fails to recognize the moral equality of its members by, for example, denying them equal rights (both positive and negative), equality before the law, and equal consideration in the framing of laws commits a wrong the wrongness of which does not reside merely in its consequences. Inequalities in treatment of this (formal) nature are wrong in themselves because they violate the fundamental equality of status that, as Rousseau believes, all human beings, insofar as they are citizens, deserve as such. Moreover domination itself qualifies as a form of social inequality that, because it involves the loss of freedom, is bad in itself; see both Chapter 3's discussion of freedom as the absence of domination and note 13 below.

[3] As I make clear below, Rousseau's normative position is not consequentialist in the more robust sense that it aims to *maximize* the sum total of the goods it recognizes as important for human beings.

could hope for to the effect that the principal reason we should care about social inequality lies in the threats its consequences pose to, in this case, the freedom of social members.

The second point I want to take seriously is Rousseau's statement that slavery and misery are the most salient consequences of social inequality. These alleged consequences of inequality (combined with other factors) correspond nicely to the features of the Golden Age that, as we saw in the previous chapter, Rousseau points to when explaining why that condition is good: in it individuals "lived as free, healthy, good, and happy as their nature allowed them to be" (*DI*, 167/*OC* III, 171). What these and other passages suggest is that social inequality is ethically problematic primarily because of its tendency to hinder the achievement of two essential human goods, well-being – including happiness and the satisfaction of true needs – and freedom, understood as the absence of domination. Of course, as the longer passage above, read together with others,[4] makes clear, social inequality is also implicated in the production of other ills prominent in the Second Discourse, such as conflict, vice ("black" inclinations), and what we might call alienation (living "always outside oneself" or "only in the opinions of others" [*DI*, 187/*OC* III, 193]). These ills also play a role in Rousseau's overall critique of modern inequality, but since (with the possible exception of alienation) they can easily be subsumed under the rubric of deficiencies in well-being, I will structure my account here by focusing on the two main categories of ills produced by social inequality: diminished well-being and the loss of freedom.[5] Although *amour propre* plays a significant role in explaining both of these ills, Rousseau's account of the deficiencies in well-being caused by social inequality relies especially heavily on his view of the

---

[4] That what I am calling *alienation* is an effect of social inequality is made clear at *DI*, 184, 187/*OC* III, 189, 193.

[5] To be more precise: I will overlook most of Rousseau's claims about the relation between inequality and *vice*. That inequality leads to *conflict* is an important part of Rousseau's view, but it can easily be accommodated in a discussion of the threats inequality poses to well-being since permanent social conflict obviously impinges on the happiness of the individuals who must endure it. In discussing how inequality affects the well-being of social members I will include a brief discussion of *alienation*, even though it should probably be separated from the category of well-being since it concerns the most fundamental relation a subject has to itself and so does not easily fit together with any of the factors that constitute well-being: happiness, need satisfaction, and the absence of pain.

havoc that "inflamed" – perverted and socially destructive – manifestations of *amour propre* can wreak on society and on the well-being of its members;[6] the principal focus of this part of his critique, in other words, is how "feverish" dynamics of misrecognition have pernicious consequences for the happiness of individuals, as well as for their legitimate, or true, need to acquire a recognized standing in the eyes of others.[7] In my view it cannot be emphasized too much how important a role *amour propre* plays for Rousseau in explaining the ills associated with social inequality. Quotations such as the following are to be found throughout the Second Discourse and express, I would argue, its fundamental philosophical claim:

[the] universal desire for reputation, honors, and preferment that consumes us all . . . excites and multiplies the passions, . . . making all men competitors, rivals or rather enemies . . . [I]t is to this ardor to be talked about, to this frenzy to achieve distinction, which almost always keeps us outside ourselves, that we owe what is best and what is worst among men. (*DI*, 184/*OC* III, 189)

SOCIAL INEQUALITY AND FREEDOM (AS THE ABSENCE
OF DOMINATION)

Let us begin with the connection between inequality and freedom, which is both the more important connection and the easier to understand. There are two parts to Rousseau's claim that social inequality endangers freedom, both of which are prominent themes in the Second Discourse. The first concerns the freedom-endangering character of human dependence in general, where dependence – the opposite of self-sufficiency – refers to a condition in which one relies on the cooperation of others in order to get one's needs, or what one takes to be one's needs, satisfied. Rousseau gives expression to this part of his view when he says that "since ties of servitude [*servitude*] are formed solely by the mutual dependence of men and the reciprocal

---

[6] N. J. H. Dent was the first to establish the term "inflamed" in the secondary literature and to place the distinction between inflamed and non-inflamed manifestations of *amour propre* at the center of Rousseau's thought (*Rousseau: An Introduction to His Psychological, Social and Political Theory* (Oxford: Blackwell, 1988), 52, 256).

[7] Axel Honneth has insightfully appropriated this Rousseauian idea and, with resources borrowed from Hegel, constructed a comprehensive social philosophy around it; see especially his *Freedom's Right: The Social Foundations of Democratic Life*, trans. Joseph Ganahl (New York: Columbia University Press, 2014).

needs that unite them, it is impossible to subjugate [*asservir*] a man without first having placed him in the position of being unable to do without another" (*DI*, 159/*OC* III, 162).[8] The thought behind this claim is relatively simple: one of the fundamental ideas of the Second Discourse is that every form of human dependence carries with it the danger that dependent individuals will have to compromise their freedom in order to satisfy the needs that impel them to cooperate with others. If freedom consists in "obeying only oneself" (*SC*, I.6.iv), then dependence of any kind poses a standing threat to being free, since it opens up the possibility that in order to get what I need (or think I need), I may have little choice but to tailor my actions to conform to the wills of those on whose cooperation I rely. When regularly faced with a choice between getting what I need and following my own will, it will be no surprise if satisfying my needs often wins out over remaining free. One prominent example of this in the Second Discourse is the role Rousseau ascribes to the division of labor – especially when this involves completely independent branches of production such as metallurgy and agriculture – in explaining the ubiquity of domination (and misery) in the civilized state. It is primarily because an extensive division of labor substantially increases material dependence among individuals, ultimately endangering their freedom, that Rousseau says, with a tinge of irony, that "it is iron and wheat that civilized men and ruined humankind" (*DI*, 168/*OC* III, 171).

There are two subjective qualities of needs that explain the freedom-endangering consequences of dependence: their power and their constancy. First, needs are powerful motivators of behavior, and getting them satisfied is an important component of psychological well-being, or happiness. The feeling of lack that accompanies an unfulfilled need possesses an urgency that is not easily ignored or endured. An unsatisfied hunger or desire to be loved has the power to drive individuals to desperate action, and it is this power that explains the nearly irresistible hold that relations of dependence have over individuals once they become entangled in them; it is what explains why individuals can be motivated to sacrifice something as valuable as their freedom if doing so secures the cooperation of others that is

---

[8] *Servitude* and *asservir* are synonyms for "domination" and "dominate" (*domination* and *dominer*) (*DI*, 158/*OC* III, 161).

required to still their perceptions of urgent lack. Second, needs possess a constancy that mere inclinations do not. In contrast to whims or fleeting desires, needs constitute a relatively enduring part of the subject's appetitive makeup: when needs go unsatisfied, the urges associated with them continue to make themselves felt. Moreover, satisfying a need once does not extinguish it; rather, needs give rise to recurrent feelings of lack, which demand that the behavior leading to satisfaction be repeated. This feature of needs is important, because it makes dependence an enduring rather than a merely momentary state, and this, as we will see, is what makes ongoing relations of domination possible, as opposed to isolated, relatively inconsequential instances of obeying another's will.

It is important to note that the needs at issue here and the dependence that flows from them are not purely, or even primarily, biological in character – that is, things human organisms require in order to survive and maintain themselves in a physically healthy state. While it would be a mistake to underestimate the importance of material needs for Rousseau's critique of inequality, especially insofar as they make economic inequality possible – in the end what keeps most of us showing up for work each day is the recurring need to eat, clothe ourselves, and pay rent and doctor bills[9] – it is also true that a large part of human dependence, indeed the largest part of it, according to Rousseau, has its source in needs that go beyond the purely biological. Some of these non-biological needs are "true needs" (things we need in order to be free and genuinely well off) – including, for example, needs that have their source in legitimate aspirations, grounded in non-inflamed *amour propre*, to achieve a recognized standing for others.[10] But the Second Discourse also makes clear

---

[9] As these examples make clear, even "material" needs are not determined by a fixed, strictly biological quantity (the minimum required for survival and reproduction). Rather, our conception of the necessities of life develops historically and is informed by a conception of a minimal standard of living that is consistent with a decent human existence. To fail to achieve this minimal standard is to lead, and to be seen as leading, a less than human existence, a circumstance that is incompatible with the recognized standing sought by *amour propre*. Thus, *amour propre* is implicated even in what we often regard as biological or material needs.

[10] Rousseau uses the term "true needs" (*vrais besoins*) in the Second Discourse, though he does so inconsistently. Sometimes it means, as we saw in Chapter 2, merely perceived needs (*DI*, 164/*OC* III, 168), and sometimes it refers exclusively to the natural, or physical, needs that humans have in the original state of nature (*DI*, 157/*OC* III, 160). The sense in which I use

that, once human civilization has advanced beyond its most primitive beginnings, humans use their new-found leisure to create conveniences and luxuries that quickly come to be experienced by them as needs – as things they cannot, without significant discomfort, do without. More important, the Second Discourse also makes clear that (inflamed) *amour propre* plays a major role in increasing our needs – and, consequently, our dependence – insofar as (to focus only on the need to acquire wealth) owning things and parading them before others can easily take on the significance of publicly demonstrating our superior worth in relation to others. (This is why, as we will see below, limiting inequality in wealth, thereby restraining its capacity both to generate inflamed *amour propre* and to serve its ends, is important for Rousseau in order not only to secure freedom but also to satisfy citizens' legitimate desires for esteem from others and thereby promote their genuine happiness and well-being.)

At the same time, not all needs that motivate socialized beings to seek cooperation have material things as their objects. Since it is first and foremost the good *opinion* of others that *amour propre* seeks, there are many ways of satisfying the needs it generates that do not involve things such as material wealth. The search for love, approval, applause, honor, or fame may incorporate the acquisition of wealth into its strategy for achieving its ends, but there is no reason that it must do so, and even when it does, wealth assumes a purely instrumental significance, valued only to the extent that it helps one secure the esteem or respect from others that is *amour propre*'s ultimate aim. In any case, it is important to bear in mind that the aspects of human dependence that have their source in *amour propre*, even when they do not involve the possession of material things, also play a significant role in making us dependent on others and in endangering our freedom. (If, for example, I take myself to need your good opinion of me, I can easily be tempted to act in ways that you but not I want me to

---

"true needs" here – to refer to what we need in order to be alive, free, and genuinely well off – is closest to Rousseau's use of the term in *Emile*, where true needs are regularly opposed to whims or caprice (*E*, 84, 86/*OC* IV, 309–10, 312). This is perhaps also the sense in which he uses the term in the Second Discourse's Preface when he says that the "study of original man" is a study of "his true needs" and that determining what these are is crucial to understanding "the true foundations of the body politic [and] the reciprocal rights of its members" (*DI*, 128/*OC* III, 126). See also Chapter 3, note 43.

behave, and falling prey to this temptation counts as obeying your will rather than mine.)

As my remarks above suggest, it is impossible to reconstruct Rousseau's critique of inequality without appealing to some distinction between true and false (or illusory) needs, that is, between what we need in order to be free and genuinely well off, on the one hand, and what we experience as needs even though satisfying them does not contribute to our freedom or well-being, on the other. The latter are needs we would be better off not having since they increase our dependence, and therefore our chances of being unfree, without contributing to our well-being or freedom. As I suggested in earlier chapters, Rousseau has the resources for distinguishing between true and false needs (even if he does not in fact do so very carefully), but the needs that figure into his explanation of our dependence and the threat it poses to our freedom include whatever, for better or for worse, we take ourselves to be unable to do without. In other words, the needs invoked by Rousseau's account of the dangers of dependence are *perceived* needs, whether true or false (although one should not forget that his comprehensive remedy for those dangers will rely not only on reducing inequality but also on promoting subjective transformations in individuals that bring their perceived needs more closely in line with their true needs). What is important for understanding the conflict between dependence and freedom is not some objective quality of needs, such as whether they are in fact essential to one's well-being, but their subjective character – how they are experienced by and influence the behavior of the subjects to which they belong. All perceived needs, whether true or false, have the potential to produce dependence, as long as they are experienced as needs by the subjects that have them.

Rousseau's position is made considerably more complex by the fact that the distinction he relies on between true and false needs is not equivalent to the distinction he sometimes invokes between natural and artificial needs – needs acquired "only by habit" (*DI*, 212/*OC* III, 214) – where "artificial" implies that they depend on beliefs, or opinions, rather than on nature alone. For, as I implied above, some artificial needs – those arising from non-inflamed *amour propre*, for example – contribute positively to our genuine well-being and, even more basically, to securing the foundations of our selfhood. (This is simply one more illustration of the fact that "artificial" functions as a morally neutral term for Rousseau.) Although it is common to read Rousseau as equating artificial with false or illusory needs, this is a serious mistake, for it would imply that all needs generated by *amour propre* – all needs for esteem or respect of whatever kind – were false needs we would be better off without. While it is true that human existence would be less fraught with danger without the needs deriving from *amour propre*, Rousseau's conception of true human nature in the expanded sense makes clear that our existence would also be unimaginably impoverished without them altogether.[11]

It is worth pausing for a moment to get clear on why Rousseau ascribes far more importance to *amour propre* than to biological needs in explaining the freedom-endangering consequences of dependence. There is probably a variety of reasons for this, but most can be traced back to the fact that opinions, both one's own and others', play an essential role in *amour propre*'s strivings. In the first place, as we saw in Chapter 2, the good that *amour propre* seeks *consists in* the opinions – the favorable opinions – of others. To desire esteem just is to desire that others regard one as a being of value. Because it is impossible in principle for *amour propre* to be satisfied without the participation of others – without, indeed, relying on their *freedom*[12] – there is a necessary and direct connection between *amour propre* and dependence, whereas in the case of *amour de soi-même* this connection is indirect and contingent (since its needs, as Part I of the Second Discourse claims to show, can in principle be satisfied for solitary beings). As long as *amour propre* is present in the world, dependence will be a permanent characteristic of human relations.

Second, as we also saw in Chapter 2, opinions – in this case, others' as well as one's own – play a large role in determining where and how one seeks to satisfy one's *amour propre*. One consequence of this is that *amour propre* is able to infect nearly all of life's activities, including

---

[11] To summarize, my discussion of needs has appealed to *four* distinctions, between: (1) biological and psychological (or spiritual) needs; (2) true and false needs; (3) natural and artificial needs; and (4) perceived and unperceived needs. Although I have not mentioned this in the text, it is possible for a true need, whether biological or psychological, whether natural or artificial, to go unperceived – not experienced as such – by the subject whose need it is. Indeed, this seems to be a common occurrence in Rousseau's description of civilized beings.

[12] Recall from Chapter 1 that having an opinion or belief involves the exercise of freedom.

those originally motivated by *amour de soi-même*, investing them with its significance and commandeering them in the service of its ends. For beings affected by *amour propre* virtually no aspect of existence remains untouched by their concern for how they measure up in relation to others. This means that in the presence of *amour propre* even needs deriving from our biological nature often take on a significance bound up with the need to be recognized, and the capacity of this passion to insinuate itself into almost every aspect of what we do is crucial to Rousseau's account of its potential to wreak havoc in human affairs. As I suggested in Chapter 2, this point is essential to the Second Discourse's account of how private property originates and why it causes so much mischief once it is there: as soon as it becomes common to see one's value for others reflected in the things one possesses, even the commodities of life cease to be valued primarily as means to comfort or survival; they become, instead, objects to be owned, accumulated, and paraded before the eyes of others. When opinion plays a role in constituting the needs we take ourselves to have, our needs cease to be limited by nature and acquire the potential to be multiplied nearly endlessly, with respect to both kind and quantity.

So much for the first part of Rousseau's claim that social inequality endangers freedom (concerning the freedom-endangering character of human dependence in general). The threat that dependence poses to freedom is greatly exacerbated when the second element of Rousseau's account, social inequality, is introduced into the picture. Here, too, the idea is relatively simple: it is much less likely that dependence will translate into an enduring loss of freedom for some if interdependent beings encounter one another on an equal footing than if, from the start, one side is better positioned than the other with respect to riches, power, or some other form of social advantage. As we will explore in more detail below, this is the basis for Rousseau's advice in *The Social Contract* regarding the limits of permissible inequalities that "as for wealth, no citizen should be so rich that he can buy another, and none so poor that he is compelled to sell himself" (*SC*, II.11.ii). It is instructive here to return to the point of Smith's mentioned in the previous chapter: it is precisely *because* workers need to eat more urgently than their employers need to make a profit – precisely because the former occupy a disadvantaged position within relations of dependence – that they nearly always end up submitting to their employers' wills when disputes arise about the conditions under which their labor is to take place. Social inequality becomes dangerous, in other words, when it threatens the ability of some – the less advantaged – to follow their own wills instead of those of the better off. Although it is easy to slip into thinking that the Second Discourse's critique of inequality is directed exclusively against economic inequality, we should not lose sight of the fact that it depicts other forms of social inequality as dangerous, too. This is consistent with how Rousseau initially defines moral inequality, including within that category a range of "different privileges ... such as being more wealthy, more honored, more powerful, or even getting themselves obeyed" (*DI*, 131/*OC* III, 131). Alongside inequalities in wealth, then, differences in honor, social power, and the ability to command others' obedience (domination)[13] constitute the object of the Second Discourse's critique, and they do so because all are capable of endangering the freedom (and, as we will see below, the well-being) of those subject to them. In other words, it is not only the wealthy who can successfully command others; celebrities, too, often succeed in getting their wills obeyed, as long as there are less highly regarded individuals who believe they can enhance their own standing in the eyes of others by attaching themselves to the famous as their subordinates.

Finally, distinguishing the two elements of the Second Discourse's account of how social life can endanger our freedom – seeing that both dependence and inequality are necessary to explaining the danger – enables us to see more clearly the strategy of Rousseau's response to the problem. Since dependence in general is fundamental to human existence, and since abolishing it would do away with almost everything that makes our lives recognizably human, a good society – if such a thing is possible – must seek not to eliminate dependence but to restructure it via laws and social institutions. This means placing limits on what *can* be reduced without harming essential human interests, namely, substantial disparities in wealth, honor, and power.

---

[13] Of course, unlike the others, this type of social inequality is to be avoided not because it *brings about* enslavement; rather, domination *just is* the lack of (a certain kind of) freedom.

I turn now to a second reason the Second Discourse provides for worrying about social inequality, namely, the threat it poses to the well-being, broadly construed, of those involved in socially unequal relationships. The connection Rousseau draws between inequality and well-being is more complex than the corresponding point regarding freedom. This is mainly because well-being – the absence of pain, frustrated desires, and unmet needs – is a more heterogeneous good than freedom and is therefore susceptible to having a correspondingly larger number of causal relations to the various forms of social inequality. The complexity of this topic is further increased by the fact that it seems natural to distinguish between two main classes of inequality – inequality in material wealth and inequalities in honor or esteem (inequalities of recognition) – and to expect that each has different effects on the well-being of social members. Even if in most societies inequality in wealth also translates directly into inequality in status or esteem – wealth typically confers prestige, just as the lack of it signals low social standing – the distinction seems worth making because, first, there are many types of inequality of esteem that are independent of inequality in wealth and, second, wealth is more directly related to non-relative aspects of well-being deriving from *amour de soi-même*, especially to vital, material needs, than are schemes of social recognition not grounded in economic standing. Because of the special connection material wealth has to vital needs – in contrast to the "moral" need for recognized standing that inequalities in honor seem most relevant to – it seems plausible that the two types of inequality might have very different effects on the well-being of individuals.

In fact, however, the main connection that Rousseau asserts between social inequality and the diminished well-being of social members does not rely much on distinguishing the effects of economic inequality, on the one hand, from those of inequalities in honor or esteem, on the other. Getting clear on why this is so is crucial to understanding what precisely is at issue in Rousseau's critique of inequality. It is important to see that when dealing with economic inequality the relevant claim is not that *poverty*, measured by some absolute standard, diminishes well-being for the reason that being poor implies that many of one's needs and desires will go unsatisfied. This is certainly true, and Rousseau's theory recognizes that poverty is a grave evil (*DI*, 188/*OC* III, 194). The main object of the Second Discourse's critique, however, is not poverty (measured absolutely) but inequality, and we must keep the two ideas separate by bearing in mind that it is possible to be on the lower end of an unequal distribution of wealth without being poor in the sense of having one's basic material needs unmet. Poverty, in other words – in at least one sense we often give to the term – is defined in terms of absolute deprivation, whereas inequality is an inherently relative phenomenon.[14] If it is inequality that the Second Discourse means to criticize, then when addressing economic inequality it must ask whether disparities in wealth themselves pose dangers to the well-being (or freedom) of social members even when everyone's basic material needs are met.

Rousseau's claim is that substantial disparities in wealth, even when no one is poor, are detrimental to the well-being of social members, and not only to that of those who are worst off.[15] If, by hypothesis, no one is (absolutely) poor in a given society but substantial inequalities of wealth exist nonetheless, the problem Rousseau is interested in cannot reside in a failure of social members to satisfy the basic needs of *amour de soi-même*; it must instead be located in a failure to satisfy

---

[14] I do not mean to take a position here as to whether poverty is best defined absolutely – by some non-relative measure of deprivation – or relatively. (One widely used measure of poverty, for example, that of the Organization for Economic Co-operation and Development (OECD), defines the poor in relative terms, as those whose income falls below 60 percent of their society's median income. My guess is that Rousseau would agree that for most purposes the most meaningful way of defining poverty would incorporate relative standards.) I mean only to make clear that the question in Rousseau's critique of inequality is whether *disparities* in wealth matter even when absolute deprivation is not an issue. Someone who endorses defining poverty in relative terms in effect agrees with Rousseau's fundamental point, namely, that inequality, and not merely absolute levels of deprivation, adversely affects the well-being of the worst off.

[15] Empirical support for this claim drawn from contemporary societies can be found in Richard G. Wilkinson, *Unhealthy Societies: The Afflictions of Inequality* (London: Routledge, 1996), especially Chapter 5. His claim is that societies with great income inequality tend to have lower levels of health (in a straightforward medical sense), primarily but not exclusively among the less well off, than do more egalitarian societies: "In the developed world, it is not the richest countries which have the best health, but the most egalitarian" (3). See also Kate Pickett and Richard Wilkinson, *The Spirit Level: Why Greater Equality Makes Societies Stronger* (London: Bloomsbury Press, 2011).

other needs and desires, and it will by now come as no surprise that the main problem even here concerns the relative needs and desires informed by *amour propre*, especially in its inflamed manifestations. Rousseau's principal claim with respect to the adverse consequences that economic inequality has on well-being, then, is that substantial inequality in wealth makes it difficult for social members to satisfy their desires (and need) to achieve a recognized standing for others, an end that plays a major constitutive role in human well-being. In this respect the main effects that economic inequality has on well-being do not differ much from those of inequalities in forms of public esteem that are independent of material wealth.

When we focus on disparities in honor or esteem, including those that immediately track differences in wealth, it is easy to see how inequality produces frustrated desires and unmet needs (stemming from *amour propre*), thereby diminishing the well-being of social members. Since *amour propre* is relative – because comparison with how others fare is built into the end it seeks – inequalities in honor or esteem have a much more direct connection to the unhappiness and unmet needs of the disadvantaged than is the case when inequalities involve access to the non-relative goods sought by *amour de soi-même*, such as survival, health, and the absence of pain. For in the former case someone's being better off than I (more highly esteemed) *immediately* translates into my being less well off (less highly esteemed), as long as I measure the esteem I seek for myself in terms of my standing in relation to you. If my aim, for example, is to be regarded as the neighborhood's best gardener and you outshine me in this respect, the resulting inequality in esteem *just is* a frustration of my desire, whereas how much food or drink you have at your disposal has no necessary implications for how well I succeed in meeting my own nutritional needs. The same holds for disparities in wealth in societies, such as our own, that regard wealth as an indicator of status or worth: being at the bottom of the economic scale is typically experienced as humiliating (and regarded as such by those who are not at the bottom), making it impossible for the desires for public esteem of the worse off to be satisfied. Even if we grant the argument of anti-egalitarians that in the societies we know the largest part of what is humiliating in such situations is being poor – being unable to lead a decent life in which one's basic needs are met – rather than being worse off than others,[16] it seems clear that even when no one is poor, substantial inequalities in wealth tend to translate into corresponding inequalities in social esteem that make it difficult for the less well off to satisfy their legitimate desires for recognized standing and therefore pose a general threat to the well-being of social members.

However, the most interesting way in which Rousseau takes social inequality in general to threaten our ability to satisfy the needs and desires of *amour propre*, and hence to threaten our well-being, is more complex than this simple correspondence between disadvantage (in wealth or status) and frustrated desires (for esteem or respect). The Second Discourse's most important claim in this regard, rather, is that societies with substantial social inequality tend to produce in their members what I have been calling inflamed desires for public esteem, desires that, when widely shared by individuals, make a general satisfaction of *amour propre* impossible and so necessarily generate frustration, conflict, and unmet needs. His most interesting point, in other words, is that substantial social inequalities have destructive *formative* effects on the subjectivities of social members, at all levels of society, that pose serious obstacles to their happiness, to the satisfaction of their legitimate, or true, needs for esteem or respect (and, as he also suggests, to their ability to avoid alienation).

Although Rousseau does not use the term "inflamed" in the Second Discourse,[17] he does speak of "frenzied," "unbridled," and "violent" desires, terms he uses liberally when describing the social ills depicted in Part II (*DI*, 171, 184, 199, 203/*OC* III, 176, 189, 203, 207). In using such terms, Rousseau is no doubt thinking of Plato's *Republic*, which begins its discussion of justice with a contrast between a healthy and a "fevered" polis.[18] Similarly to Rousseau, Plato locates the source of society's fever in the feverish desires of social members that go beyond the rudimentary needs of humans – for food, clothing, and shelter – to desires for comforts and luxuries, including a desire for "the unlimited acquisition of wealth," which presumably depends on the desires for comfort and luxury themselves having become unlimited and hence

---

[16] The most compelling case for this is made by Harry Frankfurt in *The Importance of What We Care About* (Cambridge University Press, 1988), 134–7, 149–56.

[17] He uses the term in *Emile* (*E*, 247/*OC* IV, 540).

[18] Plato, *Republic*, trans. G. M. A. Grube and C. D. C. Reeve (Indianapolis: Hackett, 1992), 369a–374e.

unsatisfiable.[19] For both Plato and Rousseau, one could say, society's fever draws on the feverish desires of its members. When Rousseau speaks of feverish desires (*E*, 211/*OC* IV, 489–90), he has in mind desires that generate unhealthy amounts of heat and agitation – they are "frenzied" – and desires that are limitless and prone to increase beyond control, and are therefore "unbridled." As I have suggested, a principal claim of the Second Discourse is that all feverish (or inflamed) desires have their source in one human passion, *amour propre* (*DI*, 184/*OC* III, 189) – or, more precisely, in the inflamed forms it so readily assumes under most social conditions.

Rousseau's understanding of what counts as inflamed *amour propre* is very intricate,[20] and there are many different respects in which the desire to be thought well of by others can become socially destructive and hence inflamed. One can, for example, desire the approval of others too intensely, so that one is willing to do almost anything, even to sacrifice one's freedom or happiness, in order to obtain it. Alternatively, one can care so much about what others think of oneself that one takes *appearing* to be worthy of approval to be just as desirable as actually possessing the qualities that make one genuinely worthy of that approval. Another possibility is that the desires of *amour propre* can come to infect *all* of life's activities, turning literally everything one does – eating, working, playing, even making love – into a search for others' esteem rather than activities one can enjoy for their own sake and for the non-relative pleasures they afford. (As Rousseau puts it, *amour propre* can "consume" us (*DI*, 184/*OC* III, 189).) Finally, one's self-esteem – one's ability to be happy with who one is, or to enjoy a "sentiment of one's own existence" – can depend too much on the good opinions of others and hence be unable to persist for even short periods of time when the approving eyes of other subjects are temporarily absent. (This is the state I refer to below as alienation.) For present purposes, however – because it is above all the problem of inequality that concerns us – it is sufficient to focus on the

---

[19] Plato, *Republic*, 372d–373e. In contrast to Rousseau, Plato does not seem to regard the loss of self-sufficiency, either of the state or of the individuals within it, as posing a danger to society. Both a division of labor requiring specialization and dependence on foreign trade are unproblematically compatible with a healthy polis (370a–e).

[20] I discuss this at length in *Rousseau's Theodicy of Self-Love: Evil, Rationality, and the Drive for Recognition* (Oxford University Press, 2008), Chapter 3.

manifestation of inflamed *amour propre* that is by far the most prominent in the Second Discourse, the desire to be recognized as superior to others.[21]

The thought that the widespread existence of desires for superior standing within a society is an important source of social ills certainly does not originate with the Second Discourse (it is already prominent, for example, in Hobbes's understanding of the state of nature as a state of war),[22] but Rousseau offers a much more comprehensive and nuanced account of this problem than any philosopher before him. One obvious problem generated by shared desires for superiority is that when success is defined as achieving superior standing, the universal satisfaction of *amour propre* becomes impossible: when everyone seeks superior status, esteem becomes a scarce good, and rather than being available to all it becomes the object of unceasing competition, conflict, and frustrated desires – a source, in other words, of enduring unhappiness. A further difficulty is the familiar dynamic of "keeping up with the Joneses." This problem is explained by the fact that superior standing, once attained, tends to be insecure as long as it is achieved in relation to others who desire the same. In order to outdo the competitor who has just surpassed me, or to maintain the advantage I now enjoy, I must constantly be engaged in enhancing my own standing. In such a situation individuals acquire a limitless need to better their own positions in response to, or in anticipation of, their rivals' advances, resulting in an endless game of one-upmanship. This explains why competition and conflict are so pervasive in feverish societies – it is why Rousseau says that the "desire for reputation . . . makes all men competitors, rivals, or . . . enemies" (*DI*, 184/*OC* III, 189) – but it also has pernicious consequences for individuals' abilities to enjoy the good things they already possess. For one thing, the only satisfaction *amour propre* can find will be temporary and insecure, but it is also the case that once we are caught up in such a dynamic, our desires for the possessions and personal qualities that we hope will attract the good opinion of others become boundless

---

[21] It should be remembered from Chapter 2 that not all versions of the desire for superior standing need be inflamed, or destructive. This complication in Rousseau's view must be bracketed here.

[22] Thomas Hobbes, *Leviathan* (Oxford University Press, 1998), Chapter 13.

in a way that is inimical to our happiness. This is because such constantly expanding desires lead those who have them to spend vast amounts of energy in pursuit of goods and honors that promise to satisfy their drive for superiority, with the result that the labor invested in achieving those goods nearly always outweighs the satisfaction they actually bring.

Desires for superior standing can engender not only conflict, unhappiness, and unmet needs but also vice, including dishonesty, hypocrisy, deceit, and dissimulation (*DI*, 171/*OC* III, 175). The two vices most relevant to the general well-being of social members are the inclinations to harm and to dominate others, both of which can be explained, according to Rousseau, only by the inflamed desire to achieve superior standing in relation to those one wishes to harm or dominate. In the absence of such a desire, natural pity would normally hold us back from harming or dominating our fellow beings, but, alas – as Rousseau notes more than once – the force of natural pity is relatively weak and easily overridden when inflamed *amour propre* pushes us in opposite directions. The will to harm can, of course, seek to impose physical suffering on others, but in "civilized" society it more often takes the form of wanting to inflict psychological or moral suffering through scorn or contempt aimed at humiliating, or "bringing down," those one seeks to appear superior to. In both cases the result of the will to harm is increased pain and suffering (and therefore diminished happiness) among social members. The main point here is that, whether we are talking about physical or psychological harm, the capacity of civilized beings to will to impose harm on others depends on the comparative nature of *amour propre* and on the fact that it can easily take the form of desiring superiority: if I define doing well for myself in terms of doing better than you, then I can further my good either by improving my own situation or, what is often easier to do, by worsening yours. This is the basis for Rousseau's claim that "the fervor to raise one's relative fortune, less out of true need than in order to place oneself above others, inspires in all men a base inclination to harm one another" (*DI*, 171/*OC* III, 175), and with this view he takes himself to have discovered an artificial source of human suffering far more consequential for our happiness than the misfortunes imposed on us by nature.

The will to dominate others can be explained in a similar way. Rather than regarding it as a fundamental urge of human nature,

Rousseau explains the inclination to dominate as a commonly occurring but by no means necessary deformation of *amour propre*. This is possible because he regards that inclination as at root a desire for recognition of a kind of superior standing: being the master of others' wills is one way to find confirmation of one's higher status in the eyes of both those who are dominated and those who see that domination: when I publicly succeed in getting you to do my bidding, both you and those around us are witnesses of my superior standing in relation to you. Once again Rousseau should be understood as responding to a central thesis of Hobbes's, namely, that it is the natural condition of humans to be moved by "a perpetual and restless desire of power after power that ceaseth only in death" and that includes power over other humans.[23] Here, too, Rousseau sees himself as having discovered the artificial source, in *amour propre*, for what many philosophers have taken to be a fixed feature of human nature (*DI*, 132/*OC* III, 132).[24] While Rousseau may ultimately be mistaken in supposing that all instances in humans of the will to dominate others can be traced back to *amour propre*'s desire for public esteem, one advantage of his view is that he is able to explain why it often seems that humans seek power over others as an end in itself rather than merely as an all-purpose means that puts us in a position to be able to satisfy our other, non-relative needs and desires (as Hobbes tends to view the matter).[25] On Rousseau's view, the primary reason humans often seek to dominate others is not because doing so helps them to satisfy other desires, such as those deriving from *amour de soi-même*. The much more common reason, rather, is that for humans, dominating others can easily take on the significance of being recognized as superior to them. In such cases domination is desired not because it is useful for bringing about some other state but because achieving it *just is* achieving (a kind of) recognized status, something that, as beings of *amour propre*, we seek for its own sake. In contrast to the vice that consists in the will to harm others (and leads to a diminishment of their well-being), the will to

---

[23] Hobbes, *Leviathan*, Chapter 11, §2.

[24] Great care must be taken in interpreting and evaluating this claim. As we know, "natural" has various meanings for Rousseau, and the sense in which it is used here – as the opposite of "artificial" – is surely not the sense in which Hobbes uses it when speaking of the state of nature.

[25] Hobbes, *Leviathan*, Chapter 10, §§1–2; Chapter 11, §§1–2.

dominate others should be seen as a major – again, artificial – source of the ill discussed in the previous section, domination. Indeed, this part of Rousseau's view of the potential consequences of inflamed *amour propre* may be seen as supplying the psychological underpinnings of his account of how dependence mixed with social inequality tends to endanger freedom, for it explains why individuals in such relations might come to *want* to dominate others when their circumstances allow for it.

Before moving on to consider how social inequalities can be a cause of the inflamed desires for superior standing that pose the various threats to human well-being I have just discussed, it is worth pausing to mention a further ill that is important to Rousseau's critique of modern society but does not fit neatly into either of the two categories of ills I have emphasized thus far, domination and diminished well-being. The ill in question is what I have been calling alienation, though Rousseau never uses this word to describe it. As I noted above, Rousseau characterizes alienation in terms of individuals living "always outside" themselves, or "only in the opinions of others," a consequence of which is that they "know how to be … content with themselves [only] on the testimony of others rather than on their own" (*DI*, 187/*OC* III, 193). These formulations denote a condition in which persons lack all internal resources for self-affirmation and so are unable to enjoy a "sentiment of their own existence" unless they are unceasingly the object of the approving gaze of others. Such individuals suffer from an extraordinarily fragile sense of their own worth that makes them desperate to please, to be approved of, to be noticed, or to think the same thoughts and espouse the same values as "everyone else." This condition – describable even as a lack of *ontological* self-sufficiency, a state in which "the grounds of one's being" exist entirely outside oneself – might be regarded as a kind of enslavement (and hence as fitting better within the discussion of freedom above) or, alternatively, as a source of suffering that diminishes a person's well-being. Yet neither of these descriptions is exactly right. Alienation might be seen as a respect in which persons can fail to be free, but if so, it represents a species of enslavement quite different from domination by others. This can be seen in the fact that since the latter consists in a relation to others and the former a relation to oneself, it is possible in principle to be dominated but free of alienation, just as it is possible (though less so) to be free from domination while alienated. Moreover, even if alienation brings with it a certain kind of psychic pain, being a partial source of one's own (moral) being seems too fundamental a condition of selfhood to consider its absence as on par with an unsatisfied desire or unmet need. Perhaps another reason that alienation does not fit neatly into the interpretive scheme I have been using is that it is more difficult to locate its precise causes than is the case for domination or diminished well-being. It is not easy, for example, to trace the tendency towards alienation back to a single cause – an inflamed desire for superior standing, say, does not by itself explain it – or to identify a feature of the social world that, if changed, would eliminate the phenomenon. Nevertheless, Rousseau – rightly, in my view – regards alienation as a grave and frequent pathology in modern societies, one that is unmistakably bound up with the complex dynamic of quests for recognition gone awry that we have just been discussing. To the extent that social inequalities are implicated in this general dynamic, they no doubt also increase the likelihood of alienation, even if the connection here is less transparent than the other consequences of inequality I have been considering.

It is not difficult to see how the effects of inflamed *amour propre* – an artificially produced scarcity of esteem, incessant conflict, dynamics of competition, boundless desires, and inclinations to harm and dominate – negatively affect the well-being of social members. Now, however, it is time to consider Rousseau's main claim in this part of his critique of inequality, namely, that social inequalities in both wealth and non-economic status help to bring about those ills insofar as they have destructive formative effects on individuals, generating in them the very inflamed manifestations of *amour propre* that give rise to and then continue to fuel the ills in question. The suggestion that enables us to understand this aspect of Rousseau's position lies buried in a passage in Part II of the Second Discourse located immediately before the longer description of the feverish society cited above in which Rousseau describes "the inseparable consequences of nascent inequality":

Here, then, are all our faculties developed, ... *amour propre* interested, reason become active, and the mind almost at the limit of the perfection of which it is capable. Here are all our natural qualities set in action, every man's rank and fate set, not only as to the amount of goods and power . . . but also as to mind, beauty, strength, or skill, as to merits or talents, and since these are the only qualities that could attract consideration, one soon had to have or to affect them. (*DI*, 170/*OC* III, 174)

The key to understanding Rousseau's thesis that social inequality generates inflamed *amour propre* and leads to conditions of diminished well-being is to be found in the phrase "since these are the only qualities that could attract consideration." This qualification suggests that the power of *amour propre* to produce the ills described here depends on a certain background condition obtaining, namely, an *absence* of established ways of achieving forms of recognized standing less destructive than those available in the corrupted society of the Second Discourse. The suggestion, in other words, is that the nature of a given society affects the consequences *amour propre* will have in it by structuring the field of possibilities within which various forms of social esteem can be pursued. The problem with the society described in the Second Discourse is that it offers no practices or institutions within which its members can acquire a standing for others that does not require them constantly to seek to outdo their fellow social members. Moreover, among the ways of "standing out" that society allows for, those that bring the most prestige are superficial and invidious forms of superiority, such as opulence and domination. To repeat: how individuals seek to satisfy their *amour propre* depends on the kinds of opportunities for recognized standing their society encourages and permits, and the various schemes of inequality within that society play a major role in defining these opportunities. A society that limits disparities in wealth, for example, generates different recognitive aspirations in its members from one whose economic system feeds on and celebrates the desire to be "filthy rich"; a social order based on inherited class privileges encourages individuals to find the sentiment of their own existence differently from one that recognizes each person as entitled to the same basic rights as all others. Social institutions have, in other words, educative, or formative, effects on their members, and this explains why social inequalities of all types can be said to play a major role in producing the ills engendered by inflamed *amour propre*.

It is possible to illustrate this claim by thinking briefly about one aspect of the political measures that Rousseau will propose for solving the problems occasioned by social inequalities. The claim that individuals' feverish desires for public esteem are caused in part by social conditions, including social inequalities of various kinds, implies that any comprehensive remedy for the ills they produce must include the creation of institutions that regulate and constrain those inequalities and make stable, satisfying, and benign forms of recognized standing available to all. Indeed, this can be seen as a central task of *The Social Contract*, even if that text never explicitly claims to be seeking a solution to the problems caused by *amour propre*. This means that a well-ordered society can go a long way towards satisfying its members' need for recognized standing by structuring institutions such that all social members are guaranteed a substantial measure of equal respect, which in turn affects the self-conceptions of those who grow up within such a society, including the ways in which they seek to satisfy their generic need to be thought highly of by others. In other words, feverish desires for public esteem can be made significantly less feverish by institutions that channel our longing to have a standing for others in appropriate ways and then satisfy that longing in its benign, or non-inflamed, manifestations. This thought makes it easy to see how *The Social Contract* responds to the problems generated by *amour propre*. For the core ideal behind Rousseau's conception of the general will is the moral equality of all individuals, an ideal the legitimate republic seeks to realize by ensuring equality before the law as well as the same basic rights for all, and by requiring that all laws accord equal importance to the fundamental interests of every citizen.

It remains, however, an important question whether these political measures by themselves constitute a sufficient solution to the entire range of problems generated by social inequalities and inflamed *amour propre*. The answer to this question turns in part on whether winning *equal* respect in the political sphere is sufficient to satisfy completely the longings of even non-inflamed *amour propre*. There is plenty of evidence in the Second Discourse to suggest that this is not the case. One consideration is that *amour propre* is frequently described in ways that seem to imply that some form of superior standing is an ineliminable part of its goal (even if it can also find some, even substantial, satisfaction in equal political respect), such as when Rousseau refers to *amour propre* as a "universal desire for . . . preferment" and a "frenzy to achieve distinction" (*DI*, 184/*OC* III, 189). If we are tempted to conclude that these are merely descriptions of inflamed longings for esteem, it is worth remembering that already with the very first appearance of *amour propre* in the Second Discourse, before it could have been perverted by the corrupting developments related in Part II, individuals who "want to be looked at" are said to have desired to be regarded as "the one who sang or danced the best, the handsomest, . . . [or] the most eloquent" (*DI*, 166/*OC* III, 169). It is only in the following paragraph that individuals are also described as seeking what appears to be a type of equal respect, defined by "duties of civility," which establish how, in general, individuals are to be treated if they are to receive the respectful treatment that all persons as such deserve and claim a right to.[26] It is not difficult to surmise why forms of equal treatment cannot by themselves satisfy humans' longing for recognized standing: equal respect, whether in the form of duties of civility or the state's equal treatment of citizens, recognizes individuals not for any of their particular qualities – such as singing, dancing, or speaking particularly well – but only on the basis of abstract, universal identities (as persons, human beings, or citizens) that they share with all or many of their fellow beings and that for that reason fail to pick them out as particular individuals. It seems safe to assume, as Rousseau apparently does, that human individuals also long for confirmation from others of their value as the particular beings they are, that is, on the basis of their distinctive accomplishments and even for their natural endowments and properties that set them apart from others. If this is correct, then finding equal respect alone is unlikely to be psychologically satisfying for humans, even when their *amour propre* is not inflamed. This means, however, that Rousseau's political response to the dangers of inflamed *amour propre* and social inequality needs to be supplemented by measures that allow individuals to satisfy their need to be affirmed as the particular beings they are in ways that do not result in the social evils depicted as the consequences

---

[26] Admittedly, it is not unambiguously clear that "duties of civility" refers to the respectful treatment that all persons as such deserve (equally). The claim that "everyone claimed a right to" this species of consideration suggests to me, however, that this is the best way to interpret such duties. Victor Gourevitch appears to agree: "'civility' consists in acting in conformity with natural right towards fellow-citizens" (*DI*, li). Ultimately, the most convincing evidence for the view that *amour propre* can take an egalitarian form comes from Book IV of *Emile*.

of inflamed *amour propre*. There are reasons to think that Rousseau means to address this problem in *Emile*, where he reflects on how the right kind of domestic education can accommodate certain desires to "stand out" from others without them becoming inflamed manifestations of *amour propre*, but another possibility would be to think about how non-political social institutions might be structured such that they afford individuals the opportunity to be recognized for their particular excellences without generating undue competition, rivalry, or boundless, unsatisfiable desires for public esteem. (This is precisely one task Hegel undertakes in his *Philosophy of Right*, where he shows how two social spheres – the family and a market-governed civil society – can afford particular forms of recognition to their members that do not generate the social ills that Rousseau worries about.)[27]

THE CRITERION OF RIGHT IN SOCIETY

We have just seen how social inequality tends to produce serious threats to the freedom and well-being of those subject to inequality, and this constitutes the main idea behind Rousseau's critique of it in the Second Discourse: social inequality is deserving of moral critique because it leads to domination, unhappiness, conflict, alienation, and feverish, unsatisfying dynamics of recognition; in other words, social inequality threatens humans' ability to attain the essential goods that characterize their "true nature." Rousseau's assessment of the considerable dangers of social inequality demonstrates compellingly why social and political theory must take inequality very seriously and reflect on how it can be reduced, but it does not yet answer the more specific question of whether and when social inequalities, beyond the extremely limited ones sanctioned by natural law, might be permissible according to the standards of right that hold in society. This is an important question because, as I have suggested, advances

---

[27] G. W. F. Hegel, *Elements of the Philosophy of Right*, ed. Allen W. Wood, trans. H. B. Nisbet (Cambridge University Press, 1991), §§158, 253–4. Perhaps one can find moves in this direction in Rousseau's own texts: many of his writings emphasize, for example, that distinguishing oneself as a brave and virtuous citizen offers individuals an opportunity to win public esteem, even "glory," for particular qualities and achievements that promote the collective good (*DSA*, 23–4/*OC* III, 26; *PE*, 14–16, 21–2/*OC* III, 253–5, 261).

in civilization seem "naturally" – in the absence of human intervention and regulation – to bring both more and larger inequalities along
with them. If, as the arguments above suggest, such advances also
create conditions that corrupt human existence, then there exists a
fundamental tension between the development of human capacities
of all sorts, on the one hand, and the attainment of freedom and
human well-being, on the other. This means that if social inequalities
beyond those sanctioned by natural law are never legitimate, then
civilization's "progress" is always lamentable (which, of course, is
precisely how many readers of the Second Discourse have interpreted
its message). Based on what we have learned so far, the logical response
to the question raised above would seem to be: social inequality is
permissible when, and only when, it does not result in any of the social
ills described above. Indeed, this is the core of Rousseau's answer to
the question, but the Second Discourse suggests – and *The Social
Contract* elaborates – a more precise standard for judging the legitimacy of "instituted inequality" (*DI*, 179/*OC* III, 184) based on a
conception of what grounds right in society as opposed to in the
state of nature, a standard that determines when laws, institutions,
and social practices are morally unobjectionable. My task now is to
articulate this standard.

As I suggested above, already in the Second Discourse Rousseau
points to the basic idea that undergirds his account of "the foundation
for the rights of society," namely, that of a "true contract," in which
individuals have, "in regard to social relations, united all their wills
into a single one" (*DI*, 179–80/*OC* III, 184–5). According to this
suggestion, it is the concept of a unity or agreement among wills
that grounds right within society. The crucial idea is that human will
can serve as a non-natural source of legitimacy in the sense that
principles governing social cooperation that are unanimously agreed
to by those subject to them impose obligations of obedience on all the
consenting parties and at the same time implicitly designate other
actions or states of affairs following from them as permissible, that is,
as actions or states of affairs to which no one can legitimately object.
Yet great caution must be taken here. Rousseau's account of the
specious and therefore illegitimate social contract in Part II of the
Second Discourse (*DI*, 172–4/*OC* III, 176–9) is proof that he does not
take just any actual agreement among individuals to be a source of

right, or of genuinely binding moral principles.[28] Again, it is the real consequences of this contract that explain its illegitimacy, despite its having garnered the actual consent of all. The important truth that actual unanimous agreement can generate illegitimate institutions is what Rousseau has in mind when he speaks of the need in moral and political philosophy to "test facts by right" (*DI*, 178/*OC* III, 182).[29] The specious contract described in the Second Discourse usurps rather than institutes right because it has the effect of codifying and reinforcing existing inequalities, especially in wealth, which in turn produces and perpetuates the various pernicious consequences for human freedom and well-being outlined above. In effect this kind of agreement among wills gives "new fetters to the weak and new forces to the rich" and "for the benefit of a few ... subjugate[s] the whole of humankind to ... servitude and misery." In this case those who consented "ran [in fact] towards their chains" even if they did so "in the belief that they were securing their freedom" (*DI*, 173/*OC* III, 177–8). It is for these reasons – because even "the voluntary establishment of tyranny" cannot be the foundation of right (*DI*, 178/*OC* III, 182) – that Rousseau explicitly denies the validity of the specious social contract.

If the real consequences of laws and institutions play such a large role in determining their legitimacy – and if actual, unanimous consent appears to count for nothing – then in what sense can will rather than nature be said to ground right within society? The full answer to this question turns out to be surprisingly complex, but a beginning can be made by examining some of the (few) things Rousseau has to say about a "true" social contract in the Second Discourse (*DI*, 180/*OC* III, 184). Perhaps his most important remarks are these: "it is the fundamental maxim of all political right that peoples [give] themselves chiefs to defend their freedom and not to be enslaved by them"; and, somewhat more informatively: why should individuals "give themselves superiors if not to defend themselves against oppression, and to protect their goods, their freedoms,

---

[28] For a comprehensive account of this specious contract, see Jean-Fabien Spitz, *La liberté politique* (Paris: Presses Universitaires de France, 1995), 349–63.
[29] Here I follow Lester Crocker's translation, *The Social Contract and Discourse on the Origin of Inequality* (New York: Washington Square Press, 1967), 233.

and their lives, which are, so to speak, the constitutive elements of their being?" (*DI*, 176/*OC* III, 180–1). The idea here, confirmed and elaborated in *The Social Contract*, is that a social contract is true, or a genuine source of right and legitimacy, only if it secures and protects "the constitutive elements" of the being of every individual subject to the principles established by the contract – only, in other words, if the terms of the contract secure and protect what might be called the fundamental human interests of each associate. Not surprisingly, Rousseau's list of these fundamental interests, cited above, closely tracks those goods – "nature's essential gifts" (*DI*, 179/*OC* III, 184) – that I invoked in the previous chapter when articulating his normative conception of human nature. Any contract that violates the fundamental interests of any of its parties – including, of course, a social contract intended as a grounding for political society – is for this reason null and void and fails to generate obligations or to establish the permissibility of any individual actions or social arrangements.

One thing this basic principle of right within society makes clear is that the social contract must respect – secure and protect – the fundamental interests of every one of its parties if it is to be legitimate. In a sense this converges with one of the features of the original state of nature that, though mostly implicitly, explained the goodness of that state, namely, its being good universally, for *all* who inhabit it. What makes the original state of nature good, in other words, is not that some or most of its inhabitants are well off and free but rather that all are (or, more precisely, in principle could be). To say that this condition meets the well-being criterion for good social arrangements is to say that its basic features pose no systematic obstacles to the collective satisfaction of its members' needs and desires. This implies, for example, that individuals' desires are generally not of the type that, if widely shared, would guarantee their own or others' frustration (such as would be true, for example, of many versions of the desire for superior standing.) The same principle is evident in Rousseau's efforts to show that in the original state of nature – without private property, sophisticated needs, and inflamed *amour propre* – there can be no systematic conflict of interests. It is only because of its implications for the collective good of its members – only because "the state of nature is the state in which the care for our own preservation is least prejudicial to the self-preservation of others" – that "it follows that this state was . . . the best suited to humankind" (*DI*, 151/*OC* III, 153). A similar concern for the systematic consequences of social arrangements informs the claim that the original state of nature is a state of freedom, where, as we have seen, the general lack of dependence guarantees the absence of domination for everyone. In sum, the original state of nature is good – it accords with human nature in the normative sense – only because in it the freedom of each is compatible with the well-being, including the happiness, of all. In the fundamental principle that articulates the standards for right in society, the requirement that the basic conditions of freedom and well-being be *universally* satisfied is merely brought out more clearly than it is in Rousseau's description of the original state of nature, and it is the former's condition of unanimous consent – the requirement that every citizen, concerned only with promoting his own fundamental interests, be able to consent to the contract's terms – that makes this feature of the foundation of right explicit.

It should be clear by now that when Rousseau claims to find the source of right within society in the agreement of its members' wills, he is thinking not of their actual but their rational, or hypothetical,[30] consent. One indication of this is that, even in the Second Discourse, Rousseau consistently associates the true foundation of right in society with reason (and sometimes with "public reason"), a sure sign that reason and will are not intended as alternative sources of political legitimacy (*DI*, 127, 150, 198/*OC* III, 126, 153, 202). With this in mind, his criterion for legitimate social arrangements can be translated into the following question: Which laws and institutions could every citizen *rationally* consent to? which is to ask, Which could they agree to unanimously, if all parties were to choose only with an eye to safeguarding their fundamental interests as human beings and were fully aware of the consequences the arrangements to be decided on would have for those interests? Interpreting Rousseau in this way can easily give rise to the impression that it would be more accurate to designate reason rather than will as the source of right within society. There is some truth to this objection, which is reflected in two important considerations: first, will (or consent or agreement) really

---

[30] The term is made famous by Rawls, who argues that social contract theory is best interpreted as based on hypothetical rather than actual consent (Rawls, *LHPP*, 15; *TJ*, 12).

does mean *rational* will (or consent or agreement) in this context; and, second, reason and will have at least this much in common: both line up on the same side of the nature–artifice divide as Rousseau conceives of it. Regardless, then, of whether we think of the source of right within society as reason or will – though, we should be warned: neither alternative will be exactly right if either term is understood as excluding the other – one of Rousseau's principal claims about that source (that it is something more than nature) will still be preserved.

At the same time, there are good reasons for resisting the objection that, if agreement means rational, hypothetical consent, it is not really will at all in any straightforward sense that grounds right within society. Getting clear on these reasons will reveal that there is some role for the *actual* consent of social members to play in assessing the legitimacy of their institutions. The crucial point is that the interests appealed to by the criterion of rational consent – our interests in life, freedom, and the basic conditions of well-being – are interests that humans can easily, and generally do, recognize as of great importance. No philosopher-king, no divine intellect, no deep understanding of the universe's mysteries is required to appreciate the essential value of these basic goods.[31] This means that the fundamental rationality, or reasonableness, of legitimate laws and institutions, when defined in terms of rational consent, is in principle readily accessible to normal human beings, including those who can claim no special knowledge of metaphysical principles or privileged access to divinely revealed truths. (Indeed, Rousseau seems to believe, with some plausibility, that claims to either of the latter generally decrease rather than increase one's chances of grasping clearly what is of real value in human existence.) This in turn means that societies that (for the most part) do in fact satisfy the rational conditions of legitimacy will also tend to be recognized as doing so by most members of those societies. A society's meeting the criterion of unanimous rational consent is about as good a guarantee as one could hope for that it will also enjoy the actual consent of most of its members; actual

---

[31] A complication here is that one of the Second Discourse's critiques of modern society is that corrupt institutions can also corrupt our ability to recognize the true nature of our needs, happiness, and freedom and to value our essential goods. In such a situation the conditions that make possible the consent required to legitimize social arrangements are ultimately lacking; in such a society there can be no right and no real freedom.

consent may never reach unanimity in legitimate societies, but widespread dissent can be taken as clear empirical evidence of illegitimacy. (In addition, as *The Social Contract* makes clear, actual consent enters Rousseau's account of political legitimacy at another point, insofar as legitimate laws must result from real votes taken by an assembly of all citizens; Rousseau recognizes, of course, that here, too, actual consent will seldom be unanimous (*SC*, IV.2.i,viii).)

We are now in a position to articulate more clearly how right within society both relies on nature and at the same time goes beyond it, a point that Rousseau expresses enigmatically by saying that "it is from the cooperation of [*amour de soi-même* and pity] ... that all the rules of natural right ... flow, rules which reason is subsequently forced to reestablish on other foundations" (*DI*, 127/*OC* III, 126). As should be clear by now, Rousseau's account of the fundamental human interests that are to be respected by right within society have their source in his normative conception of our true nature, which in turn (as discussed in Chapter 3) is intimately bound up with his understanding of human nature in the descriptive or explanatory sense. Rousseau's conception of nature supplies, as it were, a general picture of the most important human goods as well as an account of the basic sentiments that, in the absence of corrupting influences, generally incline humans to seek (and attain) them. What his conception of right within society adds to this picture is the more specific idea that legitimate laws and institutions must be compatible with every individual's ability to achieve these goods. That assessing the legitimacy of social arrangements requires applying a hypothetical universalizability test of this kind is sufficient for Rousseau to bring it within the domain of reason – indeed, of *public* reason – and, by implication, to distinguish it from an immediate "sensing" of how to treat others that would be the guide of beings in an original state of nature (*DI*, 150/*OC* III, 153).[32] Once reason enters the picture, so too does artificiality, a claim that seems to me best understood as referring to what is necessarily involved both in knowing what right requires and in being motivated to do it.

---

[32] Clearly, this conception of public reason is closely related to how Kant, in appropriating Rousseau, will later characterize the core of moral ("pure practical") reason; Kant, *Groundwork of the Metaphysics of Morals*, ed. Mary Gregor (Cambridge University Press, 1998), 4: 420–1.

In the first place, in circumstances more complex than those of the original state of nature, knowing what right obligates and permits one to do requires a significant degree of non-natural "enlightenment." This is because, though nature might move us to seek our own survival, happiness, and freedom and to relieve the misery of others, it is no easy matter, once property, *amour propre*, and differences of all kinds have appeared on the scene, to know which actions or policies will actually promote those "natural" ends. An example of this can be seen in Rousseau's admission, in discussing the right of property, that changes in social circumstances – in this case, the division of land – make it necessary to institute new laws that go beyond what natural law dictates (*DI*, 169/*OC* III, 173–4). Once needs, desires, and interests acquire even a modest degree of complexity, reasoning that aspires to universality is required in order to ascertain precisely what each must do to promote the survival, well-being, and freedom of all. (The universality of reason's standpoint, together with the fact that it is best carried out collectively, in a legislative assembly of all citizens, explains why Rousseau conceives of it as public in contrast to private reason (*DI*, 198/*OC* III, 202).) One could reformulate this point by saying that in the circumstances of civilization, nature on its own, without the aid of reflection, is unable to supply us with determinate principles of right action. One might also say that in the case of *human* beings (those outside the original state of nature), nature's fundamental ends continue to have normative force but can be achieved only through will and artifice. The fact that knowing what we may and ought to do within society requires adopting so sophisticated and so "unnatural" a standpoint as that taken up by a universalizing legislator is sufficient to make such reasoning artificial – something that, as a component of perfectibility, humans have it in their nature to be able to do but that at the same time must be learned through processes of cultural formation.

It stands to reason that if knowledge of right within society requires the artificial exercise of (naturally given) cognitive faculties, then *doing* what right prescribes will depend no less on motivational resources beyond those immediately available to beings in the original state of nature. In this domain, too, Rousseau believes that nature continues to operate beyond the purely natural state, insofar as it furnishes the most basic elements from which, in civilized beings, the motivation to engage in rightful behavior can be constructed: "what are generosity, clemency, and humanity, if not pity applied to the weak, the guilty, or the species in general?" (*DI*, 153/*OC* III, 155). And, in the Second Discourse's famous footnote defining *amour propre* he expands this claim by saying that "*amour de soi-même*. . ., guided . . . by reason and modified by pity, produces humanity and virtue" (*DI*, 218/*OC* III, 219). Regardless of how precisely Rousseau envisages these two sentiments cooperating within civilized beings to motivate rightful behavior,[33] the important point is that pity needs to be *applied* to humanity in general, and *amour de soi-même* to be *guided* by reason and *modified* by pity, if humans are to acquire the motivations they need in order to follow the principles of right in society. Pity, for example, in its natural, untutored form is too imprecise with respect to the objects it fastens onto to be an accurate guide for rightful action within even a minimally complex social world, where persons' interests are intertwined in complicated ways and one's actions often affect individuals beyond the immediate circle of one's closest acquaintances. For this reason if pity is to be harnessed to serve the ends of morality, it must be transformed into something both more universal – extended to humanity itself – and more abstract; that is, one's pity must be trained to judge the urgency of others' pains independently of their proximity to oneself and to attach equal importance to the deprivations of persons without regard to whose deprivations they are. Like the fashioning of our cognitive resources discussed above, making our sentiments take on the form required of them if they are to serve moral ends can be achieved only artificially, through cultural formation, which explains why education is such a prominent theme in those works, especially *The Social Contract* (*SC*, I.7.iii) and *Emile*,[34] that are devoted to finding positive solutions to the problems set out in the Second Discourse. (It should not be forgotten that the subtitle of *Emile* is *On Education*.)

---

[33] In some places Rousseau even suggests that *amour propre* contributes to making moral motivation possible; see Neuhouser, *Rousseau's Theodicy of Self-Love*, 229–64.

[34] Book IV of *Emile* is devoted almost exclusively to the education of Emile's passions so as to make him virtuous, capable of willing and doing what morality requires.

THE CRITERION OF RIGHT IN SOCIETY APPLIED
TO ECONOMIC INEQUALITY

The fundamental implication of Rousseau's criterion of right in society for the Second Discourse's second main question, concerning the legitimacy of social inequality, is then as follows: social inequality is contrary to right whenever it is incompatible with securing the life, freedom, and the basic social conditions of the well-being of each member of society. Conversely, any inequality that does not violate the fundamental human interests of any social member qualifies as legitimate, no matter how artificial or distant from the dictates of natural law that inequality might be. An instance of social inequality that meets this criterion, although not "authorized by natural law," is nevertheless permissible, or morally unobjectionable, from the point of view of what right in society requires or allows. Perhaps the most important feature of this criterion of right is that, although it attends to the negative consequences of inequalities in assessing their legitimacy, it is not consequentialist in the stricter sense of seeking to maximize the sum total of the goods it aims to promote (freedom, self-preservation, and the social conditions of well-being) without regard for how those goods are distributed among individuals. Rousseau's view is that legitimate laws and institutions aim primarily to promote the realization of certain states of affairs in the world (the goods listed above) – and in this respect it shares something with consequentialism – yet his position fits squarely within the social contract tradition in political philosophy, for which equal distribution (realizing the fundamental interests of each) takes precedence over society-wide maximization. There is even some sense in which talk of equal distribution is misleading here, for with respect at least to the goods of self-preservation and freedom, the idea of equal amounts makes little sense. In the former case this is obvious – self-preservation is manifestly not a good one can divide up and enjoy to various degrees – but talk of equal amounts is also out of place in the case of freedom, understood as the absence of domination. Since domination is defined in terms of regular, systematic asymmetries in the ability to get oneself obeyed (rather than merely sporadic instances of the same), it is unlikely that Rousseau's theory could accept any level of domination as legitimate. As defined by the basic terms of the social contract, then, legitimate laws and institutions seek not to equalize freedom and self-preservation but rather to secure the latter good for all and to eliminate domination wherever it is found.

It must be acknowledged that the general formulation given here of the criterion of right in society leaves many questions unanswered about how it is to be applied so as to yield precise judgments about specific laws and institutions. For this reason it is important to spend some time in this concluding section considering how Rousseau's criterion for legitimacy might be applied more concretely to one especially important type of social inequality, inequality in wealth. I will do so by outlining the threats economic inequality poses to both the freedom and the well-being of social members. In the following, concluding chapter I will attempt to make Rousseau's ideas more concrete by comparing them with similarly minded approaches to economic inequality in contemporary political philosophy, especially with the most carefully elaborated of these, John Rawls's theory of justice. Part of my aim in doing so will be to determine whether Rousseau still has something distinctive to contribute to contemporary debates in political philosophy.

Let us begin with the relation between economic inequality and freedom. The basic idea, of course, has already been presented: like social inequalities in general, disparities in wealth easily lead to asymmetries among interdependent individuals that make it difficult for the disadvantaged to avoid regularly obeying the wills of those advantaged individuals on whose cooperation they rely in order to satisfy their needs.[35] Hence, one part of Rousseau's answer to the question regarding the legitimacy of economic inequality – probably the most important part, given the supreme importance of freedom – is that disparities in wealth are permissible only when they do not pose systematic obstacles to the freedom of any individual, especially to the freedom of the less well off.[36] Although *The Social Contract* makes

---

[35] "What is most needful ... is ... to protect the poor against the tyranny of the rich ... It is therefore one of the most important tasks of government to prevent extreme inequality of fortunes ... by depriving everyone of the means to accumulate treasures [and] ... by shielding citizens from becoming poor" (*PE*, 19/*OC* III, 258).

[36] Rousseau's principle converges nicely with what Elizabeth S. Anderson calls "democratic equality," which "guarantees all law-abiding citizens effective access to the social conditions of their freedom" ("What Is the Point of Equality?" *Ethics* 109 [January 1999], 289).

it clear that there are several forms of freedom a legitimate state must make available to all, the form I emphasize here – both because it is the one most relevant to his position on economic inequality and because it is most prominent in the Second Discourse – is freedom as the absence of domination. Applying the normative constraints implicit in the idea of the social contract to this conception of freedom yields the principle that economic inequality is permissible only to the extent that it is compatible with the absence of regular relations of domination among social members.

Yet, as I have also suggested, the specific implications of this general principle are far from evident. I have already noted the complication that because it is compatible with the actual consent of the dominated, domination is sometimes difficult to distinguish from genuine cooperation. But there are other problems as well: does the principle apply to all forms of domination, or are there instances of domination that, because they belong to a "private" domain more or less unaffected by social and political conditions, are not subject to the principle? And for forms of domination that are the proper object of the state's concern, how does one determine the "tipping point" at which economic inequality goes from being benign to posing substantial obstacles to the freedom of the worse off? Despite such questions concerning its application, however, Rousseau's principle provides a quite general but still helpful orientation for thinking more concretely about the limits of permissible economic inequality. More precisely, it directs us to ask: which types and degrees of economic inequality are compatible with the social conditions individuals require in order to be able to satisfy their needs while avoiding regular obedience to foreign wills?

Once again, it may be helpful to return to the form of economically based domination to which Smith draws our attention, as summed up in his claim that workers are generally compelled to obey their employers' wills because the latter's greater economic resources give them a superior bargaining position in disputes over wages and laboring conditions. In this case Rousseau's principle might be interpreted as ruling out the very divisions in economic class that Smith's example presupposes, where the freedom of some is threatened by a basic inequality grounded in the fact that some own only their own labor power, while others own the means of production, access to which everyone needs in order to live. Alternatively, the principle might serve as the basis for arguing for institutions – strong labor unions with aggressive laws protecting the bargaining rights of workers, for example – that mitigate the freedom-endangering potential of class distinctions while leaving that fundamental inequality in place. In other words, even if Rousseau's principle does not by itself yield a fully determinate picture of the laws and institutions a free society should aim at, it succeeds in defining a major problem to be addressed – a problem that, moreover, contemporary liberal positions tend to lose sight of – as well as in providing a basic orientation for thinking about the kinds and degrees of economic inequality that must be avoided if the social contract's ideal of freedom for all is to be realized.

At the same time, Rousseau's own position on this issue is probably a bit clearer than I have just implied. For much of the *tone* of the Second Discourse – for example, its pessimistic view of the "crimes, wars, murders, ... miseries, and horrors" that private property in the means of production (in this case, in land) necessarily brings in its wake (*DI*, 161/*OC* III, 164) – seems to express a general preference for the first of the two strategies for responding to the freedom-endangering potential of economic inequality alluded to above.[37] This strategy, the more radical of the two, involves reforming society from the bottom up in order to eliminate the fundamental causes of inequality (in this case, by eradicating class differences), whereas the second accepts those basic inequalities but seeks to correct for their freedom-endangering potential through measures that attempt to balance out the power disparities among the parties involved, perhaps by strengthening the ability of workers to bargain collectively or by instituting laws or constitutional provisions requiring that workers

[37] More precisely, Rousseau seems to believe that less radical strategies for reform are nearly always destined to be futile because they fail to address the root causes of the problems they aim to solve. This, however, does not make him an advocate of revolution in most real cases where states fail to meet the conditions of legitimacy, for he also believes that once political corruption has set in, it is nearly impossible to cure, even through revolution. I describe Rousseau here as advocating the more radical political alternative because his view is that *if remedies are to be found*, they require (in most cases) rebuilding society from the bottom up. In taking Rousseau's political thought as their inspiration, the protagonists of the French Revolution understood the latter point but ignored the former.

have equal say in matters that concern them.[38] (That Rousseau generally favors the former can be seen in his approving remarks concerning Lycurgus who, rather than reforming Sparta piecemeal, undertook to "set aside all the old materials" and to rebuild its political institutions from the ground up [*DI*, 175/*OC* III, 180].) Whatever the corrective measures of the second strategy consist in, however, they will likely rely on political efforts directed at mitigating the effects of underlying economic inequalities. The part of Rousseau's view that pushes him towards the first strategy – one of several respects in which his position anticipates Marx's – is a fundamental pessimism about the power of purely political measures to correct imbalances residing in a society's economic structure. The specious social contract, which institutionalizes asymmetries in social power rooted in economic inequality, seems to him a virtually unavoidable consequence of that basic inequality (*DI*, 172–3/*OC* III, 176–8). Once individuals' particular interests are as deeply opposed and entrenched as they are in societies divided into propertied and non-propertied classes, and as long as the power of money reigns supreme in such societies, the former classes will nearly always find ingenious and effective ways to circumvent whatever laws attempt to eliminate conditions of domination and reduce their power to command. As Marx was to argue much later in "On the Jewish Question,"[39] the aims of politics cannot be so out of line with the pattern of interests in the economic sphere if the former is to succeed in remedying the problems generated by the latter: a harmony of interests "at the top" (in the political sphere) requires some basis for that harmony "below" (at the level of economic interests).

Before moving on, it is worth returning briefly to an issue raised earlier in this chapter to ask whether the arguments presented here concerning the threat that economic inequality poses to freedom really tell against relative deficiencies in wealth as opposed to absolute conditions of privation. In other words, is what threatens freedom

---

[38] Philip Pettit distinguishes the same two strategies, but his version of republicanism, unlike Rousseau's, favors the second (*Republicanism: A Theory of Freedom and Government* [Oxford University Press, 1997], 67, 85).

[39] In Karl Marx and Friedrich Engels, *The Marx-Engels Reader*, 2nd edn, ed. Robert C. Tucker (New York: Norton, 1972), 33.

having less than others or merely being poor (defined in absolute terms)? The answer to this question is probably "both," since under the right circumstances each can contribute to increasing the likelihood of domination.[40] Although I will suggest below that it is sometimes helpful to make qualitative distinctions among economic inequalities – to focus on certain kinds of inequalities in wealth as more dangerous than others – inequality, and not merely absolute deprivation, remains the essential factor in understanding why freedom is under threat in such cases. It might be thought that the arguments presented above imply that being poor is the true threat to avoiding domination since the connection between inequality and the likelihood of domination relies on the claim that dependence – the lack of self-sufficiency with respect to satisfying *needs* – is a necessary condition of being motivated to obey the wills of others. If, so the objection goes, people's basic needs are met – that is, as long as they are not poor – inequalities in wealth will be unproblematic because no one will be compelled by need to obey others, and in the absence of that incentive no one, or very few, will be inclined to do so. It is not, in other words, inequality alone that produces domination but inequality conjoined with dependence and need. This would imply that if the worse off ceased to be poor (in absolute terms), their being worse off, even considerably worse off, than others would no longer pose a substantial obstacle to obeying only themselves. (Of course, even if this objection were correct, Rousseau's arguments would point out an often overlooked evil of poverty under conditions of inequality: beyond merely having one's needs unmet or falling short of the material requirements for a decent life, being poor makes one vulnerable to domination by the non-poor.)

This objection gets something right: being both poor and worse off than others poses a greater danger to one's freedom than merely having less than others, for being poor in addition to having less than others means that one experiences greater and more urgent neediness, thereby increasing the incentive one has to obey foreign

---

[40] As I explain below, Rousseau's position must be that economic inequality is a necessary condition for domination (whereas poverty without inequality does not produce it) but that once such inequality exists, being poor makes one even more vulnerable to domination than merely having less than others.

wills. Yet, even so, Rousseau's principle is justified in singling out inequality rather than poverty as the essential threat to freedom understood as the absence of domination. One reason is that absolute deprivation is not by itself, in the absence of inequality, sufficient to generate domination (whereas, as I argue below, inequality can generate domination in the absence of absolute deprivation). This is because equal absolute deprivation, though bad for other reasons, creates no basis for asymmetries in patterns of obedience to arise. To re-invoke Rousseau's initial characterization of moral inequalities: domination is a relative phenomenon – a "privilege that some enjoy to the prejudice of others" (*DI*, 131/*OC* III, 131) – and as such its source must be a relative phenomenon as well, economic inequality and not merely neediness absolutely defined.

A second reason Rousseau is correct to highlight inequality is that, as many defenders of egalitarianism have pointed out, our ideas of what our basic needs consist in, or of what is necessary to live a decent human life, are not historically fixed but change in response to social and cultural developments. If, as seems likely, these historical variables include the overall wealth of a society, as well as how well off various groups within that society are, it is doubtful that, except perhaps in very extreme cases, poverty can ever be defined wholly in absolute terms. If our conception of what it is to live a minimally decent human life depends in part on how much social wealth there is generally, or on how well off other groups in society are, then inequality, and not merely some absolutely conceived standard of poverty, is a justified target of Rousseau's principle. Another way of putting this point is to say that, except perhaps for societies with extremely primitive levels of technological development, the concept of need (and hence of poverty) is itself a relative notion, and relative not only to existing technology but also to how much wealth others in the same society have. Alternatively, using Rousseau's account of the fundamental components of human nature, one could say that considerations of *amour propre* – of what appropriately reflects the worth or dignity of human beings – and not merely those of *amour de soi-même* enter into our conception of what individuals in a given society need or must have available to them in order to live a decent human life. One implication of this view is that even when public policy declares poverty its enemy, it is often, though perhaps unwittingly, targeting inequality as well.[41] Rousseau's point, however, is not this – that reducing inequality is good because it tends to reduce poverty – but rather that we have an important reason to reduce inequality beyond our usual reason for condemning poverty (that people fail to get their needs satisfied or to meet the minimal standards for living a decent human life), namely, because inequality generates domination.

Rousseau's claim that poverty as we normally think of it is less important than inequality in generating domination is reinforced by the fact that the needs invoked in explaining the connection among dependence, inequality, and domination do not have to be "true" but only perceived needs since the latter, too, suffice to provide dependent individuals with an incentive to obey others in order to secure their cooperation: the danger of domination arises whenever the worse off perceive themselves as needing something that cooperation with the better off could give them. And since the judgments of *amour propre* – judgments of what we need in order to secure a recognized status relative to others – are by far the most important factor in turning whims or desires into perceived needs, inequalities can be expected to increase dependence (by increasing what we think we need in order to have our sense of self confirmed by others), which under the conditions of that very inequality easily translates into relations of

---

[41] Another implication of the partially relative character of poverty is that in theory it is possible to reduce poverty merely by reducing inequality without improving the absolute lot of the worst off. Even more paradoxically, it would be possible to reduce poverty by reducing inequality even if doing so made the least advantaged worse off in absolute terms than they were before those "anti-poverty" measures. Rawls's difference principle, considered in abstraction from the other principles of justice, could tolerate the first measure but not the second. In principle Rousseau's position could justify either measure, but if so, then only for the purpose of reducing domination (a consideration the difference principle by itself is insensitive to). Because Rousseau provides us with grounds for endorsing the second scenario under certain circumstances – it is permissible (even necessary) to make the worst off even worse off in absolute terms if doing so is necessary to avoid their domination – he furnishes us with a reason the difference principle cannot for sometimes preferring equality over max-imizing the position of the worst off. There being such a reason reflects the priority for him of freedom over well-being. (Presumably, a similar outcome, also grounded in a preference for freedom [of a different kind] over well-being, is open to Rawls, too, if economic inequality threatens the fair value of equal political liberties.) In assessing the difference between Rawls and Rousseau on this point of policy the key question is whether considerations in Rawls's theory beyond the difference principle – for example, guaranteeing fair equality of opportu-nity or the fair value of equal political liberties – will in the end yield similar results with respect to permissible levels of economic inequality. I consider this question in the following chapter.

domination: in order to acquire what we take ourselves to need in order to count publicly as someone, we are more likely to be tempted to follow the wills of more favorably situated individuals whose cooperation – perhaps their good opinion of us – promises to enable us to succeed in doing so.

Let us proceed now to the relation between economic inequality and well-being. Here, too, we have already encountered the core of Rousseau's claim, namely, that substantial inequalities in wealth make it difficult for social members to satisfy their desires (and need) to achieve a recognized standing for others. In arguing that disparities in wealth pose a threat not only to the freedom but also to the well-being of social members, his theory furnishes us with a second set of resources for imposing constraints on economic inequality, even if he never formulates these constraints explicitly. Expressed in the terms supplied by his general criterion of right in society, Rousseau's position is that economic inequality is impermissible to the extent that it engenders in individuals inflamed desires for a recognized standing that make the universal satisfaction of *amour propre* – a fundamental constituent of human well-being – impossible. In other words, schemes of inequality that make it impossible for each individual to satisfy the legitimate human need for recognition could not be rationally consented to by all and are therefore illegitimate.

This part of Rousseau's position no doubt seems hopelessly vague at first, but it is not contentless, and Rousseau himself fills in some of the details of how it might be applied. We have already seen that the various ways in which a legitimate republic accords equal political respect to each of its citizens are meant to go a long way towards providing all individuals with adequate sources of recognized standing. This constitutes the largest part of Rousseau's strategy for addressing individuals' legitimate needs for esteem or respect and for preventing inflamed forms of *amour propre* from arising in the first place, but, as I suggested above, equal political respect cannot remedy all the socially caused pathologies of recognition that make the universal satisfaction of *amour propre* impossible. For equal political respect might coexist with various forms of social, non-political inequalities – inequalities in wealth, for example – that continue to generate pathological dynamics of recognition that render satisfaction for all unachievable. For this reason the distribution of wealth (and of other social privileges), and not merely the political equality of citizens, must be of concern to a theory that makes the social contract as Rousseau conceives of it into the source of legitimacy in society. This implies that social and not merely political institutions come under the purview of his account of how a society must be organized if the conditions of right are to be realized within it. In fact, however, Rousseau does not himself carry this thought very far. Unlike Hegel after him, he does not develop an extensive social theory that considers in detail how non-political institutions – the family and the economy,[42] for example – need to be structured if right is to be fully realized. Most of his efforts in this direction are aimed instead at criticizing the substantial inequalities of wealth that arise "naturally" in an unregulated economy for reasons we are by now familiar with: to the extent that economic inequalities are responsible for generating inflamed desires for recognition in individuals, a political philosophy committed to securing the fundamental interests of all its members must be concerned with regulating those inequalities. The basic task of the social contract – to find a form of association that protects each associate's fundamental interests in freedom and well-being – cannot be accomplished without paying attention to the ways in which non-political social life shapes the recognitive aspirations of its participants, and it is plausible that reducing the possibilities for great inequalities in wealth could have a significant role to play in carrying out this task.

Because many of the claims made in this chapter involve arguments of considerable complexity, it may be helpful to summarize the main points of my reconstruction of Rousseau's critique of economic inequality:

1 Rousseau's critique draws our attention to one specific kind of illegitimate social power, domination (regularly obeying a foreign will), as well as to its source in economic inequality. As I will argue in the following chapter, both of these issues, though not completely

---

[42] The aim of Rousseau's *Discourse on Political Economy* is, of course, to present such a theory of the economy, but, unlike Hegel's treatment of this topic (and Rawls's more limited remarks on it), Rousseau's is not very relevant to modern, market-based economies. Nevertheless, the existence of this text shows that the subject matter of political economy – "the public good . . . based on a conception of justice" (Rawls, *TJ*, §41) – has an important place in Rousseau's overall project, even if the detail of his actual account of economic matters is barely relevant to us today.

absent in liberal political theories, tend to be overlooked or under-theorized by them.

2 Rousseau's locating the source of domination in asymmetric relations of dependence enables us to see how there can be widespread domination in the absence of coercion and even in the presence of actual consent (when the motivation for obedience is to secure the cooperation one requires in order to satisfy one's needs). Domination is a much broader phenomenon than being coerced to obey.

3 Rousseau shows us that domination often extends beyond the political realm and assumes a presence in other areas of social life as well, especially in the economy (but also, if we extrapolate from Rousseau's principles, the family). Domination is not only, or even primarily, a relation among *citizens*, where some have more effective say than others in determining laws.

4 Rousseau argues convincingly that economic inequality, especially class inequality, typically generates domination among interdependent individuals and that a just social order must be committed to eradicating the material conditions of domination, ensuring that it provides no basis for the systematic domination of any individual or group.

CODA: GENEALOGY AND CRITIQUE

In the introduction to this book I characterized the Second Discourse as a genealogy that aimed simultaneously to explain the origin and to evaluate the legitimacy of social inequality and that conceived of these tasks as crucially interlinked. Now that we have reconstructed the main argument of the Second Discourse, it is time to return briefly to the methodological question I posed at the beginning of this work: why does Rousseau proceed, similarly to Nietzsche more than a hundred years later,[43] as if there were a deep connection between the Second Discourse's explanatory inquiry – asking where social inequality comes from – and its normative task of evaluating the legitimacy of social inequality? Or, as I put the question originally: why should determining where a thing comes from be essential to

---

[43] Nietzsche, *On the Genealogy of Morals*, trans. Walter Kaufman (New York: Random House, 1967), Preface, §3.

assessing whether it is good in some way? In previous chapters I have argued that Rousseau's genealogy does not intend to answer factual, historical questions about when or why certain real events actually took place but is instead an analytic inquiry that attempts to explain complex human phenomena – various human practices that create and sustain inequality – by separating out the diverse factors that, when joined together, explain their existence. The question of inequality's origin for Rousseau is a question about which forces must generally be at work in human beings and their world for inequality to be as pervasive and enduring a feature of that world as our experience shows it to be. And, as we have seen, the Second Discourse locates the primary "origin" of social inequality in a single psychological force, *amour propre*, when it operates unconstrained within certain social conditions created by human beings themselves, who then become subject to "artificial" conditions of inequality.

Emphasizing the analytic rather than the historical character of Rousseau's genealogy does not, however, answer the methodological question posed above, for analysis of this kind still aims at explaining, not evaluating, its object. Moreover, if my reconstruction of Rousseau's critique of inequality is sound – if I am correct in my claim that it is their *consequences* that make social inequalities legitimate or illegitimate – then it is hard to see how an account of origins of the sort offered by the Second Discourse can have any evaluative function at all. If we understand Rousseau's genealogy as I have said we must – as primarily tracing social inequality back to its psychological source – then it is hard to see how pointing out where inequality comes from can play any role in his account of what is wrong with it. (On this point Rousseau's genealogy probably differs from Nietzsche's, since the critical force of the latter appears to depend, at least in part, on revealing the psychological source of morality to be *ressentiment*.)[44] Nor does locating the source of inequality in an artificial passion constitute a critique of it since, as I have argued, showing social inequality to be unnatural (in the present context) merely means that it cannot be explained on the basis of original human nature alone – or, expressed differently, that it is an inherently

---

[44] Nietzsche, *On the Genealogy of Morals*, I, §10.

social phenomenon, not a possible feature of human individuals "in themselves" (apart from all relations to others).

Still, paying attention to the implications of *amour propre*'s artificiality may help to clarify how genealogy and critique work together in the Second Discourse. Here it is important to remember the link Rousseau draws between artificiality and malleability (as well as his associating both of these with the social). From this perspective the "developments" recounted in the Second Discourse can be seen as part of an analytic exercise aimed at distinguishing what in human reality comes from our original nature (and is therefore not up to us) from what comes from our social existence (and is therefore mutable and, in some sense at least, our own doing). Locating the source of moral inequalities in *amour propre* rather than in original human nature allows us to see them as our creations rather than as necessary consequences of our nature, and this opens up the possibility that *amour propre* might be able to assume forms different from those we are most familiar with, producing very different results from the degenerate society depicted in the Second Discourse. Another way of putting this point is to say that tracing moral inequality back to an artificial passion helps us to see where contingency enters human reality. It is important to remember, though, that what is contingent is not merely the presence of *amour propre* in some guise or another but rather the particular forms it assumes in specific social circumstances. More precisely, Rousseau's genealogical claim is that even though *amour propre* appears so pervasively in our society in its inflamed forms – even though *amour propre* as we know it is the source of domination and unhappiness – this is a contingent and potentially corrigible fact, not a necessary feature of the human condition.

Moreover, inflamed *amour propre* is not the only contingency that enters Rousseau's story. As he insists again and again, many of the social developments that figure in his genealogy, including the specific rules of private property and particular forms of the division of labor, are also "fortuitous ... circumstances ... that could very well never have occurred" (*DI*, 139/*OC* III, 140). This, of course, is related to the contingency of inflamed *amour propre*, since on Rousseau's view, much of *amour propre*'s inflammation is due precisely to the influence of unfortunate social arrangements (and some of these conditions are themselves caused or influenced by inflamed *amour propre*). When

Rousseau ends the Second Discourse by saying, "it is enough for me to have proved that this is not man's original state" (*DI*, 187/*OC* III, 193), we are to understand him as asserting that the state of fallenness he has just described is not a necessary result of human social life in all its possible forms. Genealogy, then, is intimately related to critique because it serves to "de-naturalize" a host of social conditions whose legitimacy we tend to accept unreflectively precisely because we view those arrangements as "eternal givens" or "due to the nature of things." (Indeed, the strains of Rousseau's de-naturalizing project are unmistakable already in the Second Discourse's opening pages [*DI*, 124–5/*OC* III, 122–3].) Genealogy disrupts our unreflective "consent" to the inequalities of what we take to be a naturally given social order, and in doing so it undermines one of the principal conditions of their continued existence. This point also sheds light on why real history is not completely irrelevant to Rousseau's genealogy: if one of genealogy's aims is to demonstrate the contingency of our own social arrangements – if one of its goals is to show that there are alternatives to private property, the drive for wealth, and the division of labor as *we* know them – then empirical evidence illustrating the rich diversity of forms that human life has in fact taken is surely to the point. The examples of the Hottentots, who can see as far with the naked eye as the Dutch can with telescopes (*DI*, 140/*OC* III, 141), and the Caribs, who have no notion of stocking up for tomorrow (*DI*, 143/*OC* III, 144), reinforce the claim that previous philosophers attributed far too many contingent features of their own society to a statically conceived human nature (*DI*, 132/*OC* III, 132).

Although these interpretive claims about Rousseau's genealogy are, I believe, correct in substance, there is also something misleading about characterizing the developments depicted in the Second Discourse as *merely* accidental. For, as I intimated in Chapter 2, Rousseau believes that the degeneration of *amour propre* into unconstrained, socially injurious quests for superior standing, while not necessary, is the most likely outcome of the circumstances he describes, especially when there is no artificial intervention into the social world to ensure that *amour propre* assume a benign rather than a destructive form. But even if fallenness is the most likely result of social existence, there is still a point to seeing it as contingent (not necessary). The point is that what is not necessary can in principle be transformed into something different, and working out how this is possible is Rousseau's task in other parts of his philosophy. This means that genealogy is relevant not only to critique but also to social transformation. Rousseau points to this aspect of genealogy when, in a letter to Voltaire recounting the accomplishments of the Second Discourse, he says, "I showed men how they bring their miseries upon themselves and hence *how they might avoid them*" (LV, 234/*OC* III, 1061; emphasis added). If I have understood Rousseau correctly, the tools of genealogy enable us to discover how particular contingent forms of private property – the private ownership of land (or means of production), for example – create new, destructive opportunities for seeking social recognition and so exacerbate and give free rein to the harmful potential of *amour propre*. But understanding these connections is essential to systematic reflection on how the social world would have to be reconfigured if *amour propre* and the inequalities it tends to produce are to be kept within limits that make freedom and well-being possible for all without eliminating social inequality entirely. This suggests that genealogy has a further analytic function, namely, the disentangling of the various strands or elements that have come together (contingently) to form the particular complex phenomenon under investigation.[45] Genealogy asks: which in principle separable developments and events have in fact joined together to produce a given contingent phenomenon? By disentangling a complex human phenomenon into its component elements and recognizing where contingency enters into its formation, genealogy enables us to think productively about how the elements of that phenomenon might be put back together again in ways that enable us to avoid some of the dangers and disadvantages of the ones we know. This aspect of Rousseau's genealogy is also one that Nietzsche appropriated for his own;[46] like so many other features of the Second Discourse, it, too, has left an indelible mark on the trajectory Western philosophy was to take both immediately after Rousseau and up to the present.

---

[45] Rousseau uses the language of "disentangling" at *DI*, 125/*OC* III, 123.
[46] Nietzsche, *On the Genealogy of Morals*, II, §24.

CHAPTER 5

The contemporary relevance
of Rousseau's critique

As I suggested in the preceding chapter, Rousseau's position on the illegitimacy of economic inequality can be brought more sharply into focus by situating his critique in relation to similar approaches to the topic in contemporary political philosophy, above all in the version of liberalism developed by John Rawls. Although some contemporary positions may be slightly closer to Rousseau's than is Rawls's,[1] the two thinkers share one very important feature that makes a comparison of their views especially apt: in contrast to most contemporary liberal political theory, both share a general tendency to broaden the traditional concerns of liberalism to include reflections about how non-political social life must be organized if justice is to be realized.[2] This is very generally the direction Rawls takes when – much more systematically than most earlier social contract theorists – he extends the principles of justice to include the basic structure of society and argues that the realization of a political value (justice) depends on certain non-political institutions: the market economy and nuclear family. Less obviously, the similarities between Rousseau and Rawls extend beyond this shared general orientation to theorizing about social and not merely political institutions. As I demonstrate below, Rawls's complex treatment of economic inequality also incorporates, probably knowingly, many of the specific elements of Rousseau's critique. With respect to economic inequality's relation to both freedom and the basic conditions of well-being, Rawls proves to be an

---

[1] Elizabeth S. Anderson's, for example, in "What Is the Point of Equality?" *Ethics* 109 (January 1999), 287–337. Despite this I will focus primarily on Rawls since his views on economic inequality are more fully elaborated than hers.
[2] See Chapter 4, note 42.

insightful appropriator of Rousseau's views, even to such an extent that it is sometimes difficult in the end to find differences between their positions. Indeed, the extent of overlap between them is initially very surprising (at least it was to me). It becomes significantly less so, however, when one takes into account that Rawls developed his own position only after many years spent digesting, criticizing, and reconstructing the classical texts of political philosophy, among which Rousseau's count for him as especially important (although this fact is not so clear in *A Theory of Justice* itself).[3]

I begin, very briefly, with the part of Rousseau's view we examined last in Chapter 4, the idea that limiting inequalities in wealth must be part of a strategy for preventing desires for recognition generated in non-political social life from becoming inflamed in ways that guarantee frustration, conflict, and unmet needs for recognition. Nowhere is Rawls's debt to Rousseau more visible than in his claim that "the social bases of self-respect" are "perhaps the most important" of the primary goods that just institutions must distribute fairly.[4] (The very concept of a primary good also comes, at least in part, from Rousseau; it is very close to what I have been calling a fundamental interest, and Rawls sometimes uses the latter term as well.)[5] Although Rawls emphasizes primarily *self*-respect rather than esteem or respect from others, the intimate connection between the two, acknowledged by Rawls himself, makes his position on the fundamental importance of recognition nearly indistinguishable from Rousseau's: he explicitly includes "finding our person and deeds appreciated and confirmed by others" among the circumstances required for the primary good of self-respect: in achieving the latter we depend on others "to confirm the sense of our own worth."[6] Both thinkers agree, then, that securing what I have called the social conditions of satisfying recognition for all is a principal task of the just state and an important condition of legitimate social arrangements. In fact, Rawls seems to have incorporated Rousseau's reflections on the relation between economic inequality and the satisfaction of *amour propre* to such a degree that it is difficult

---

[3] Rawls's reliance on the history of political philosophy is made much clearer in Rawls, *LHPP*, 191–248.

[4] Rawls, *JF*, 60; *TJ*, 440; see also *TJ*, 546.

[5] Rawls, *JF*, 102–3, 105–7, 110, 113; *LHPP*, 219, 217–18, 225–6.   [6] Rawls, *TJ*, 440, 443.

to find a fundamental difference between them on this score. For after showing how certain basic features of a just society – private property, private associations, equal rights of citizenship and liberty[7] – help to establish the social bases of self-respect for all, Rawls goes on to allow for the possibility that applying the difference principle (see below) might require reducing the gap in wealth between society's extremes solely for the purpose of preventing the rise of inflamed passions – most prominently, envy[8] – that, when status is linked to relative wealth, generate the very pathologies of recognition that Rousseau highlights in the Second Discourse.[9] While there may be subtle differences between the two views on this issue,[10] the degree to which they overlap far outweighs their disagreement. For each the bottom line is that economic inequalities are illegitimate to the extent that they create unhealthy dynamics of recognition that makes satisfying levels of social recognition – or of the self-respect that is grounded in such recognition – unavailable to each social member. Because of this fundamental overlap in their positions on this issue, I will focus primarily on the more complicated relationship between their views on the connection between *freedom* and economic inequality and on the need to place constraints on the latter for the purpose of insuring the absence of domination for all social members.

First, however, it is worth noting that the basic idea behind Rousseau's views on the relation between freedom and economic inequality aligns well with that of contemporary *republicanism* as represented by Philip

---

[7] See, respectively, Rawls, *JF*, 114; *TJ*, 440; and *TJ*, 536.

[8] Since Rousseau believes that envy has its source in (and is a manifestation of) inflamed *amour propre*, there is considerable overlap between the two positions, even if Rousseau has a more comprehensive understanding of the dangers of inflamed social passions.

[9] Rawls includes self-respect in the set of primary goods whose distribution is to be regulated by the difference principle (*TJ*, 546, *JF*, 59). This implies – the Rousseauian point – that permissible distributions of wealth might be constrained by considerations about the effects economic inequalities have on the ability of each citizen to achieve an adequate measure of self-respect: "to some extent men's sense of their own worth may hinge upon their institutional position and their income share" (Rawls, *TJ*, 546); for further proof of this point, see Rawls, *LHPP*, 245. Elizabeth Anderson endorses a similar position: "The degree of acceptable income inequality would depend in part on how easy it was to convert income into status inequality" ("What Is the Point of Equality?" 326).

[10] They probably differ on the centrality and weight of the problems caused by inflamed *amour propre*. Rawls addresses these issues relatively late in *TJ* (§82) and regards them as "best decided from the standpoint of the legislative stage" rather than at the more fundamental levels of his theory (Rawls, *TJ*, 546).

Pettit. According to Pettit, whereas traditional republicanism[11] believed that very little could be done, practically speaking, to reduce the material bases of domination by decreasing inequalities in wealth or economic status, his own version of republicanism requires the state to undertake substantive redistributive measures when they are necessary to foster the economic independence of every citizen.[12] Such measures, as Pettit understands them, consist primarily in state-guaranteed welfare aid designed to ensure that all individuals have the basic capabilities they need in order to function "normally and properly" within society.[13] More radical transformations that address power asymmetries embedded in the economic structure of society, though not strictly ruled out, play little role in his reflections on the policy implications of republican thought, though they share with Rousseau the basic thought that economic inequality is an important obstacle to individuals' freedom. (I indicated in Chapter 4 why Rousseau thinks that mere redistributive measures, such as those advocated by Pettit, are unlikely to achieve their ends.) As we will see below, Rawls's proposals for avoiding asymmetric economic dependence are not only worked out in much greater detail than Pettit's; they also prescribe more fundamental economic changes than the latter and are therefore closer in content to Rousseau's views. For these reasons comparing Rousseau's position with Rawls's will result in a richer understanding of the former than attempting to situate him any more carefully in relation to other members of the republican tradition.[14]

Getting clear on the differences and similarities between Rawls and Rousseau on the issue of economic inequality and its relation to

---

[11] Recall that while Rousseau is generally thought to belong to this tradition as well, Pettit argues that Rousseau diverges from it in important respects. It is probably more accurate, however, to say that there is a great deal of diversity within the republican tradition and that not all of its representatives share the features that Pettit chooses to regard as central to it; see Chapter 3, note 20.

[12] Philip Pettit, *Republicanism: A Theory of Freedom and Government* (Oxford University Press, 1997), 158–63.

[13] Pettit, *Republicanism*, 158.

[14] This statement assumes that Rawls is not part of the republican tradition but is instead, to use Pettit's categories, a liberal. While there is no doubt that Rawls should be considered a liberal (in the broadest sense), it is not clear to me that, on Rawls's construal of what liberalism entails, this excludes him from the ranks of republican theorists. At the very least, there are also substantial republican elements in Rawls's thought, including his central ideal of free and equal citizenship.

freedom is no easy task. Although at first glance there seem to be clear differences with respect to both specific policy recommendations and fundamental principles – Rawls, for example, does not place material dependence and domination, or the connection between them, at the center of his theory – in fact the differences turn out to be much smaller once the entirety of Rawls's complex position is taken into account. If Rousseau's principal reason for limiting economic inequality is to eliminate domination, Rawls's principal reason seems to lie elsewhere, in a consideration that plays no, or only a very small, role for Rousseau. If we think of the difference principle as Rawls's main response to the problem of economic inequality, this contrast comes into view. For the point of the difference principle is not to eliminate the conditions of domination (or to promote freedom in any other way) but instead to ensure a *fair* distribution of the benefits of social cooperation. It is difficult to overemphasize the importance that the idea of society as a system of mutually advantageous cooperation plays in Rawls's theory of justice, and this idea is especially prominent in his justification of the difference principle: if cooperation is a win–win situation, producing greater social wealth than non-cooperating individuals would produce on their own, then the question arises as to how the advantages of cooperation are to be divided fairly among those who participate in society's cooperative scheme. (Rousseau and Rawls agree that having this distribution determined by free market mechanisms does not ensure its being just.) This means that the question addressed by the difference principle would arise for Rawls even in a society where domination (and poverty) were eliminated. The point of the principle is not to lift the poor out of poverty (defined in absolute terms) or to make them free but to ensure that the less well off, regardless of how well off they are absolutely, receive a fair share of the advantages of the cooperative scheme in which they are participants.[15]

---

[15] This point is especially complex. The purpose of the difference principle is to secure a fair share of a *certain subset* of primary goods to all citizens, who are thought of as participants in a cooperative scheme. Freedom as Rawls primarily conceives it (the "basic liberties") is not governed by the difference principle since it must be distributed equally, and before the distribution of other primary goods is determined. For those primary goods whose distribution is governed by the difference principle, fairness is defined in terms of a maximin principle, which requires selecting the scheme of cooperation that is best for those who are worst off (subject to the constraint of equal liberty for all). As I suggest above, the social bases of self-respect can be regarded as one of

Focusing on the difference principle can easily suggest that Rawls and Rousseau also disagree on the degree of economic inequality that is permissible in a just society since, as many have pointed out, the difference principle is in principle capable of justifying very large disparities in wealth, whereas Rousseau believed even modest inequalities to have the potential to produce conditions of domination. (The difference principle by itself justifies unlimited increases in the gap between the best and the worst off, as long as these increases improve the absolute condition of the latter.) This, however, is where Rawls's position becomes complex. His view is that while considerations about a fair distribution of the advantages of cooperation, taken by themselves, do not rule out large inequalities in wealth, a theory of justice has other reasons for limiting them, and once these reasons are taken into account, the range of permissible inequality is greatly reduced, perhaps even to a level that would satisfy Rousseau. This claim is confirmed by the argument Rawls develops towards the end of his career that only *alternatives* to capitalism – property-owning democracy but not welfare-state or laissez-faire capitalism – are consistent with the principles of justice.[16] Property-owning democracy is an "alternative to capitalism" because it ensures "widespread ownership of productive assets and human capital," thereby obliterating (or greatly reducing) the class distinctions – where "a small class [has] a near monopoly of the means of production" – on which capitalist production depends.[17] Whatever property-owning democracy might look like when fleshed out in more detail than Rawls provides,[18] it is surely not remote from the kind of society Rousseau, if writing in the twenty-first century, might have endorsed.

The deeper philosophical question is whether Rawls's reasons for endorsing property-owning democracy are the same as Rousseau's would be. There are grounds for thinking they are not. For the main

---

the primary goods covered by the difference principle, which implies that economic inequality can be regulated so as to improve the worst offs' chances of finding both self-respect and its precondition, social recognition. But the difference principle itself provides us with no reasons to limit economic inequality for the purpose of equalizing *freedom*, whether this is conceived of as Rawls does or as the absence of domination.

[16] Rawls, *JF*, 135–6.   [17] Rawls, *JF*, 139.

[18] For ideas concerning what such a system might look like, see the recent collection of Martin O'Neill and Thad Williamson, eds., *Property-Owning Democracy: Rawls and Beyond* (Hoboken, NJ: Wiley-Blackwell, 2012).

reason Rawls limits economic inequality beyond what the difference principle requires is to create the social conditions under which both the *fair value of equal political liberties* and *fair equality of opportunity* can be realized.[19] In neither of these arguments does the avoidance of domination appear to play a central role, but in fact the issue of domination does creep into Rawls's justification for both principles. Let me begin with fair equality of opportunity. As with the difference principle, Rawls's main reason for worrying about equality of opportunity has to do not with avoiding domination but with ensuring fairness, in this case fairness in competition for public offices and social positions. To the extent that various measures for limiting economic inequality are necessary in order to ensure that those who are "similarly motivated and endowed" have "the same prospects of . . . achievement" regardless of the social class they are born into, those measures are required by the principle of fair equality of opportunity.[20]

Fairness of opportunity is not the same thing as freedom from domination, but perhaps the two ideals are more closely linked than they first seem to be. In this regard it is noteworthy that Rawls sometimes articulates the purpose of measures dictated by the principle of fair equality of opportunity in terms of avoiding domination: in spelling out the implications of this principle, Rawls pleads for institutions that "adjust the long-term trend of economic forces so as to prevent excessive concentrations of . . . wealth, especially those likely to lead to political domination."[21] This certainly sounds like a version of Rousseau's principle – limit economic inequality to the extent necessary to avoid domination – but it is worth asking first how precisely inequality of opportunity is related to domination here. As Rawls says, it is political domination that is at issue, and his thought must be that large inequalities of wealth adversely affect the chances of the less well off to attain the public offices through which citizens make and execute the laws of the state. This counts as a form of domination in Rousseau's sense because when one group has a long-term advantage in determining the laws that another group must

---

[19] For more on how these two ideals function to limit economic inequality within a Rawlsian framework, see Erin Kelly, "Inequality, Difference, and Prospects for Democracy," in Jon Mandle and David A. Reidy, eds., *A Companion to Rawls* (Oxford: Wiley-Blackwell, 2013).
[20] Rawls, *JF*, 43–4.   [21] Rawls, *JF*, 44.

obey, the former have succeeded in getting themselves obeyed by the latter, even though this obedience takes the form of obeying laws. Yet despite the fact that part of the reason Rawls endorses fair equality of opportunity seems to be because it prevents a kind of domination, it is important to note that there is a conceptual distinction between aiming to achieve fairness (of opportunity) and aiming to eliminate domination. In other words, Rawls's reflections on fair equality of opportunity give us *two* – converging but still separate – reasons for limiting inequalities in wealth: doing so is a condition of achieving fairness in the opportunities citizens have available to them, but it also guards against a certain type of domination, where one group regularly succeeds in getting its will, expressed in laws, obeyed by others. (Fairness, of course, is defined independently of the consequences that limiting inequalities has for avoiding domination.)[22]

Does the point I am attributing to Rousseau imply, though, a substantive critique of Rawls? It seems doubtful that it does at the level of institutional arrangements. And with respect to philosophical commitments, it is implausible to claim that Rawls's emphasis on fairness means that his theory is unconcerned with the problem of domination. Given the central role the ideal of equal citizenship plays in Rawls's theory, it would be odd to regard the absence of political domination as merely a happy consequence of achieving fairness. At most, Rousseau's point invites us to reflect further than Rawls himself did on the relation between the values of fairness and freedom understood as the absence of domination. For example: is it possible for fairness and freedom (in this sense) to generate conflicting – rather than, as in this case, converging – requirements, and if so, which of the two has priority? And, even if fairness and freedom are conceptually distinct, is it the case that aiming at perfect fairness in matters concerning economic inequality automatically takes care of the problem of domination, without our needing to worry about what additional measures, beyond those required to achieve fairness, might be necessary

---

[22] This is very close to the point made by Thomas Scanlon when he distinguishes, as different reasons for pursuing equality, between ensuring the fairness of distributive processes and ensuring that some do not have "an unacceptable degree of control over the lives of others"; see his *The Difficulty of Tolerance: Essays in Political Philosophy* (Cambridge University Press, 2003), 205–6.

to ensure that social members are able to avoid the conditions of inequality that make domination virtually inescapable?

I now turn briefly to the second set of reasons Rawls has for limiting economic inequality beyond what the difference principle requires, namely, those deriving from the aim of realizing the fair value of equal political liberties. Here economic inequality is clearly brought into relation with freedom: some liberties remain "merely formal" unless a certain degree of such equality[23] provides citizens with the means they need in order to be able to exercise their rights to a more or less equal extent and thereby realize the "fair value" of those rights. The question, though, is whether this part of Rawls's view addresses the threat that Rousseau sees economic inequality as posing to freedom understood as the absence of domination. Interestingly, the answer to this question is precisely the one we encountered above in discussing fair equality of opportunity: assuring the fair value of equal political liberties – and it is only political liberties[24] whose fair value is assured – is also aimed at eliminating domination in the political sphere. As Rawls puts the point: "the fair value of the political liberties ensures that citizens ... have roughly an equal chance of influencing the government's policy and of attaining positions of authority irrespective of their economic ... class."[25] Thus, as Rawls himself admits, guaranteeing the fair value of political liberties comes down in the end to guaranteeing a specific kind of fair equality of opportunity, namely, the opportunity to attain positions of political authority and to influence legislation.[26] Both principles, then, though primarily intended to achieve a kind of fairness (of opportunity), also work to reduce the likelihood of a specific kind of domination in Rousseau's sense, namely, political domination.

The conclusion to be drawn from all of this is that, when thought through from the perspective of Rousseau's reflections on inequality and domination, Rawls's positions on fair equality of opportunity and the fair value of equal political liberties agree in giving us two reasons for limiting economic inequality – fairness (of opportunity) and the

---

[23] Notice that what is at issue here is relative and not merely absolute wealth. Exercising one's political liberties involves *competing* with others for political influence (Rawls, *JF*, 46).
[24] That is, rights to vote, participate in politics, run for political office, engage in party politics (Rawls, *JF*, 44, 148).
[25] Rawls, *JF*, 46.   [26] Rawls, *JF*, 149.

avoidance of domination – and that, even if this makes minimal difference at the level of institutional details, it urges us to reflect further on the relation between these two ideals. If there is a philosophical critique to be made of Rawls from Rousseau's perspective, it is suggested by the fact that both principles are directed against specifically political forms of domination. Political domination is a genuine concern of Rousseau's; it is criticized in his treatment of the specious social contract, and it is what he is worried about in *The Social Contract* when he disallows factions within the assembly where the opinions of one group as to what should be law consistently win out over others', resulting, in effect, in the latter having regularly to obey the will of the former (*SC*, II.3.iii). Yet political domination is by no means the only kind of domination that alarms Rousseau. This can be seen in the fact that domination arises in the Second Discourse long before political society is established (*DI*, 167/*OC* III, 171), and pointing out the threat of non-political forms of domination – where it is not law that compels us to obey another will but simply the combination of dependence and economic inequality – is surely one of that text's main goals. While Rawls is sensitive to how economic inequality can translate into political domination, the Second Discourse urges us to ask whether his theory overlooks other, nonpolitical forms of domination that a theory of justice should also be concerned to eliminate.

Perhaps one way of bringing this question into focus is to note the importance that the concept of the citizen plays in Rawls's theory of justice. Whether defining primary goods, determining basic liberties, or addressing the domination that can result from economic inequality, it is always the interests of individuals *qua* citizens that Rawls has in view. In drawing up the list of basic liberties, for example, the question he asks is: which "liberties provide the political and social conditions essential for the ... full exercise" of the moral powers "essential to us as free and equal citizens?"[27] We might think of the Second Discourse as suggesting that there are other descriptions, beyond that of citizen, under which individuals can be seen to have fundamental interests worthy of protection. Or, more precisely, we can think of the Second Discourse as pointing out that there are social

[27] Rawls, *JF*, 45.

spheres other than the political in which individuals' fundamental interests – especially their interest in remaining free of domination – are vulnerable and in need of protection by the state (where the state, for Rawls, too, not only issues laws but also shapes the basic structure of society, including that of non-political social spheres).[28] As Smith's example of asymmetric obedience points out, as long as the relationship between workers and their employers is characterized by fundamental inequality, there will be a systematic tendency, grounded in the economic structure of society, for domination to arise. But the domination Smith draws our attention to is not in the first instance political; the problem he points to is not that workers are subject to laws made only by employers and their representatives (though this, too, is likely to be the case).[29] Rather, it is that one group of individuals finds itself in a position in which, constrained by the mix of dependence and inequality, it must regularly follow the dictates of another group, with respect to wages and laboring conditions, if it is to be able to satisfy its material needs. The site of this domination is not politics but everyday, economic life, where everything from the number of bathroom breaks to policies for hiring and firing workers are dictated by those who occupy the advantaged position of the unequal relationship.[30]

Finally, it is unclear whether even this point – that a theory of justice should worry as much about domination in the economic sphere as it does about political domination – is one that Rawls completely overlooks or that his theory could not accommodate. His very sparing description of property-owning democracy – in any case, a very late addition to his theory of justice – makes it difficult to know for sure, but he does say that property-owning democracy "disperse[s] ownership of

---

[28] Samuel Scheffler emphasizes that for Rawls equality is not only a political but also a social ideal, implying that non-political forms of domination worry him as much as political forms (*Equality and Tradition* [Oxford University Press, 2010]), 191, 199, 225.

[29] Moreover, Smith probably thought, unlike Rousseau and Marx, that the problem of domination in the economic sphere could indeed be adequately addressed by political means, without fundamental changes in society's class structure.

[30] One might even extend this Rousseauian point to a social sphere where he did not envisage it being applied, the family. While it would be wrong to locate the entire source of gendered domination in the family to economic inequalities between husband and wife, it seems clear that inequalities, in control of the family's wealth but also in earning power, are part of the source of that domination and that equalizing the economic positions of women and men could help reduce it.

wealth ... to prevent a small part of society from controlling the economy" and that it aims to "put all citizens in a position to manage their own affairs on a footing of a suitable degree of social and economic equality."[31] Also relevant is his claim that "excess market power must be prevented and fair bargaining power should obtain between employers and employees."[32] At one point Rawls even seems to connect these considerations to Rousseau's claim that economic inequality is to be controlled "so as to prevent a part of society from dominating the rest."[33] Yet the scattered nature of these remarks raises the same question mentioned above concerning the relation between the values of fairness and freedom (as the absence of economic domination) and how precisely freedom in this sense fits in with the main values Rawls appeals to when defining primary goods, determining basic liberties, and arguing for the fair equality of opportunity, namely: the exercise of the moral powers essential to us as free and equal citizens. The beginning of a Rawlsian answer to this question is surely that avoiding domination in the economic sphere is essential if individuals are to be able fully to pursue their own conceptions of the good. At the very least, however, the distinction between these two types of domination – and the importance of non-political forms – is under-theorized by Rawls, even if incorporating Rousseau's insights on this topic might not in the end put much strain on the complex edifice that his theory of justice, taken in its entirety, turns out to be.

I end my account of Rousseau's critique of inequality by briefly expressing two reservations about his position. The first is that inequality alone might be too coarse a concept to pick out the specific economic features of society that produce the ills Rousseau is worried about. Questions raised earlier about the indeterminacy of Rousseau's criteria for freedom-endangering inequality[34] should lead us to wonder whether economic inequality, defined purely quantitatively, is too indefinite to distinguish economic conditions that pose substantial threats to freedom from those that are unlikely to result in domination. Indeed, Smith's example suggests that Rousseau's point about

---

[31] Rawls, *JF*, 139.   [32] Rawls, *PL*, 267.   [33] Rawls, *LHPP*, 245.

[34] Where is the "tipping point" at which economic inequality begins to pose obstacles to the freedom of the worse off? And which specific laws and institutions, among a variety of possible remedies, does Rousseau's theory recommend?

the connection between inequality and domination might be better formulated by focusing on specific types of economic inequality that track not merely quantitative differences but more consequential structural or functional features of economic life. Rousseau's understanding of the basis of this connection encourages us to ask: which *types* of inequalities tend to produce enduring, asymmetric relations of dependence with respect to needs of such urgency that the disadvantaged are likely to judge that they have no other choice but regularly to follow the wills of those they depend on in order to satisfy those needs? Smith's example, grounded in his keen sense for how capitalism relies on differences in economic class – defined not quantitatively but by the different economic functions (based on different relations to the means of production) the classes in question perform – exemplifies one powerful way of refining the concept of economic inequality so as to make it more precise and more useful for political theory, at least within the context of actually existing capitalist societies.

My second reservation also pushes Rousseau in the direction of Marx. Even if loss of freedom in the economic sphere remains a phenomenon political theory needs to address, a question arises as to whether domination, as Rousseau defines it, picks out the most important ill of modern economies that readers sympathetic to the Second Discourse should worry about. In defining domination, Rousseau focuses on the phenomenon of obeying the *wills* of others and on how this compromises the freedom of those who obey. This emphasis on obeying foreign wills is understandable if one bears in mind that Rousseau presupposes a picture of economic life different in important ways from contemporary, or even nineteenth-century, economic reality in the West. His picture of society still bears significant traces of a feudal, or at least pre-modern, world where capitalist relations, mediated by an impersonal market, have not yet fully developed.[35] For this reason Rousseau's critique runs the risk of missing instances of illegitimate asymmetries in social power that are more prominent in modern society than domination, construed strictly as he defines it.

The suggestion here is that the most prominent instances of asymmetries in social power in capitalist societies do not involve relations

[35] This can be seen in the fact that much of his critique of Parisian society, for example, is directed at remnants of an earlier, aristocracy-based social order.

among wills in the sense that one party obeys the commands of another. This is precisely the thought that leads Max Weber to distinguish domination from social power more generally or, more precisely, to regard domination as merely one form that asymmetries in social power can assume.[36] Using Weber's terminology, we can say that by far the most common way capitalists oppress or assert power over workers does not involve the latter obeying the commands of the former. With respect to determining the basic terms according to which the advantages of social cooperation are to be distributed, the free market, together with the basic inequality in the economic positions of the classes, assures that a property-owning class will be able to assert its will – to get much more of what it wants – in relation to a property-less class, without the former needing to issue commands that the latter obeys. In capitalist economies there is, as it were, a clash of wills – more precisely, a clash of interests – that is regularly decided in favor of one of the parties, without those wills ever needing to come into direct contact and without any will needing to issue commands to another. (Interestingly, though, the globalization of the world economy has produced a situation where domination in Rousseau's narrow sense is [again] a major form of oppression among countries: organizations such as the International Monetary Fund, controlled by and advancing the interests of rich nations – or, more precisely, of those within the rich nations who already own the majority of their societies' wealth – dictate in extraordinary detail the internal policies of poorer, asymmetrically dependent nations.)[37] If Rousseau's critique of economic inequality is to capture important ways that asymmetries of social power manifest themselves in the modern world, his narrow focus on relations of obedience needs to be extended to include ways in which, within the "free" market, the wills of the advantaged determine the actions of the disadvantaged without commands being issued or obeyed. In other words, Rousseau's political theory would be defective if it were taken to imply that domination were the only kind of illegitimate social power that economic inequality made possible or the only kind that political

---

[36] Weber, *Economy and Society*, ed. Guenther Roth and Claus Wittich, trans. Ephraim Fischof et al. (Berkeley: University of California Press, 1987), vol. I, 53.

[37] Joseph E. Stiglitz, *Globalization and Its Discontents* (New York: W. W. Norton, 2003), 6–8, 19, and throughout.

theory should care about. Some other forms of illegitimate social power are closely related to domination in that they involve, for example, the wills of one class regularly winning out over those of another in market competition without anyone issuing commands that are obeyed by others. Other forms of illegitimate social power that political theory should care about include: violence, marginalization, exploitation, and treating others with contempt.[38] Yet even if domination, strictly defined, plays a less important role in capitalism than in pre-modern class societies, it remains a real and important phenomenon, especially in our current globalized capitalist system.

[38] I take this list from Anderson, "What Is the Point of Equality?" 312.

Suggestions for further reading

The secondary literature on Rousseau, even on the Second Discourse specifically, is excellent and vast, and I list here only a very small part of it. In selecting which works to mention I gave priority to those that seemed to me: (1) primarily philosophical rather than philological in nature; (2) accessible to English-speakers; and (3) of value even to less advanced students of Rousseau. There are, of course, many works that meet these criteria beyond those included here, and I encourage the readers of this book to venture fearlessly beyond these few suggestions.

Brooke, Christopher, "Rousseau's Second Discourse: Between Epicureanism and Stoicism," in Christie McDonald and Stanley Hoffmann, eds., *Rousseau and Freedom* (Cambridge University Press, 2010), 44–57.

Cassirer, Ernst, *The Question of Jean-Jacques Rousseau*, trans. Peter Gay (New Haven, Conn.: Yale University Press, 1989); reprinted in Scott, ed., *Jean-Jacques Rousseau: Critical Assessments*, vol. I, 48–78.

Chitty, Andrew, "Needs in the Philosophy of History: Rousseau to Marx," PhD thesis (Oxford, 1994).

Cohen, Joshua, "The Natural Goodness of Humanity," in Andrews Reath, Barbara Herman, and Christine M. Korsgaard, eds., *Reclaiming the History of Ethics* (Cambridge University Press, 1997), 102–39.

Cooper, Laurence D., *Rousseau, Nature, and the Problem of the Good Life* (University Park: Pennsylvania State University Press, 1999).

Dent, N. J. H., *Rousseau: An Introduction to His Psychological, Social and Political Theory* (Oxford: Blackwell, 1988), chapters 1–3.

Gourevitch, Victor, "Rousseau's Pure State of Nature," *Interpretation* 16 (Fall 1988), 23–59.

Kelly, Christopher and Roger D. Masters, "Human Nature, Liberty and Progress: Rousseau's Dialogue with the Critics of the *Discours sur l'Inégalité*," in Scott, ed., *Jean-Jacques Rousseau: Critical Assessments*, vol. II, 257–71.

Lovejoy, Arthur O., "The Supposed Primitivism of Rousseau's Discourse on Inequality," in A. O. Lovejoy, *Essays in the History of Ideas* (Baltimore: Johns Hopkins Press, 1948); reprinted in Scott, ed., *Jean-Jacques Rousseau: Critical Assessments*, vol. I, 29–47.

Masters, Roger D., *The Political Philosophy of Rousseau* (Princeton University Press, 1979), chapters 3–4.

Melzer, Arthur M., *The Natural Goodness of Man* (University of Chicago Press, 1990), parts 1–2.

Neiman, Susan, "Metaphysics, Philosophy: Rousseau on the Problem of Evil," in Andrews Reath, Barbara Herman, and Christine M. Korsgaard, eds., *Reclaiming the History of Ethics* (Cambridge University Press, 1997), 140–69.

Neuhouser, Frederick, *Rousseau's Theodicy of Self-Love: Evil, Rationality, and the Drive for Recognition* (Oxford University Press, 2008), chapters 1–4.

Neuhouser, Frederick, "The Critical Function of Genealogy in the Thought of J.-J. Rousseau," *Review of Politics* 74 (2012), 371–87.

O'Hagan, Timothy, *Rousseau* (London: Routledge, 1999), Chapter 2.

O'Hagan, Timothy, "On Six Facets of *Amour-propre*," in Scott, ed., *Jean-Jacques Rousseau: Critical Assessments*, vol. II, 338–53.

Plattner, Marc F., *Rousseau's State of Nature: An Interpretation of the Discourse on Inequality* (DeKalb: Northern Illinois University Press, 1979).

Scott, John T., ed., *Jean-Jacques Rousseau: Critical Assessments*, 4 vols. (Oxford: Routledge, 2006).

Scott, John T., "The Theodicy of the Second Discourse: The 'Pure State of Nature' and Rousseau's Political Thought," *American Political Science Review* 86 (September 1992), 696–711; reprinted in Scott, ed., *Jean-Jacques Rousseau: Critical Assessments*, vol. II, 225–56.

Siep, Ludwig, "Rousseau's Normative Idea of Nature," *Finnish Yearbook of Political Thought* 4 (2000), 53–72.

Starobinski, Jean, *Jean-Jacques Rousseau: Transparency and Obstruction*, trans. Arthur Goldhammer (University of Chicago Press, 1988), chapters 2–3.

Index

Printed in Great Britain
by Amazon

13504602R00142